WITCHES

Tracy Borman studied and taught history at the University of Hull and was awarded a PhD in 1997. She went on to a successful career in heritage, and is now Chief Executive of the Heritage Education Trust and interim Chief Curator of Historic Royal Palaces.

Tracy is the author of a number of highly acclaimed books, including *Matilda: Wife of the Conqueror, First Queen of England* and *Elizabeth's Women*, which was Book of the Week on Radio 4. She regularly appears on television and radio, and is a contributor to *BBC History Magazine*. Tracy gives public talks and lectures across the country on a wide range of subjects. She lives in Surrey with her daughter.

TRACY BORMAN

Witches

James I and the English Witch Hunts

VINTAGE BOOKS

London

Published by Vintage 2014

14

Copyright © Tracy Borman 2013

Tracy Borman has asserted her right under the Copyright, Designs and Patents Act 1988 to be identified as the author of this work

First published in Great Britain in 2013 by
Jonathan Cape

Vintage
Random House, 20 Vauxhall Bridge Road,
London SW1V 2SA

www.vintage-books.co.uk

Addresses for companies within The Random House Group Limited can be found at: www.randomhouse.co.uk/offices.htm

The Random House Group Limited Reg. No. 954009

A CIP catalogue record for this book
is available from the British Library

ISBN 9780099549147

Penguin Random House is committed to a sustainable future for our business, our readers and our planet. This book is made from Forest Stewardship Council® certified paper.

MIX
Paper from
responsible sources
FSC® C018179

Typeset in Dante MT by Palimpsest Book Production Limited,
Falkirk, Stirlingshire

Printed and bound in Great Britain by Clays Ltd, Elcograf S.p.A.

In memory of Eva Reeson,
with love

Contents

List of Illustrations

The keep, Belvoir Castle. (By kind permission of The Duke and Duchess of Rutland, © Belvoir Castle, Leicestershire, UK/The Bridgeman Art Library)

Francis Manners, 6th Earl of Rutland. (By kind permission of The Duke and Duchess of Rutland)

The interior of St Mary's Church, Bottesford.

Detail of the tomb, showing the two Manners boys.

A seventeenth-century woodcut showing a witch kissing Satan on the buttocks. (© akg-images)

Witch riding a broomstick. (© Wellcome Library, London)

Le Départ pour le Sabbat, by David Teniers the Younger. (© Deutsches Historisches Museum, Berlin/A. Psille)

The Witches' Sabbath, by Francisco Goya. (© Museo Lazaro Galdiano, Madrid, Spain/The Bridgeman Art Library)

Woodcut from *Newes from Scotland*. (© Private Collection/The Bridgeman Art Library)

The title page of *Daemonologie*. (© The British Library Board/C.95. aa.11)

James I of England and VI of Scotland, after John De Critz the Elder. (© National Portrait Gallery, London)

George Villiers, Duke of Buckingham, and family. (© National Portrait Gallery, London)

The hanging of four witches. (© Time & Life Pictures/Getty Images)

The 'swimming' of a witch. (© Wellcome Library, London)

The title page of the contemporary pamphlet telling the story of Joan Flower and her daughters. (© The British Library Board/C.27.b.35)

Preface

Nestling in the far north-eastern corner of Leicestershire, on the edge of the Vale of Belvoir, is the magnificent church of St Mary's, Bottesford. A testament to the God-fearing and prosperous inhabitants of the nearby castle, it is one of the largest village churches in England and its lofty spire can be seen for miles around. The fame of the so-called 'Lady of the Vale' derives not from its scale and magnificence, however: it is from something altogether darker.

At the eastern end of the church lies the chancel, which houses the tombs of the lords of Belvoir Castle. In order to accommodate these cumbersome monuments, the arches and capitals were hacked into, and the roof of the chancel was pushed upwards. Even so, there was barely room to house the most unwieldy tomb of them all – a classical-style 'mass of pretentious vulgarity', flanked by pillars and crowned by an enormous canopy, on top of which a peacock crest is jammed in with its head touching the rafters.[1] This is the tomb of Francis Manners, 6th Earl of Rutland.

But the figures who immediately draw attention are the two small boys kneeling alongside, each clutching a skull. The long and 'insufferably pompous' inscription records that the earl's second wife, Lady Cecilia Hungerford, bore him these two sons, 'both who dyed in their infancy by wicked practice & sorcerye'.[2] The earl was so determined that the shocking story of his sons' demise would live on after his own death that he personally commissioned this extraordinary inscription. It is the only reference to witchcraft that can be found in an English church.

The alleged murderers of his two boys were Joan Flower and her daughters Margaret and Phillipa – the Witches of Belvoir.

Introduction

'The works of darknesse'

What is a witch? To this deceptively simple question, history provides a myriad of different answers. The late-sixteenth-century commentator George Gifford produced the following succinct definition: 'A Witch is one that woorketh by the Devill, or by some develish or curious art, either hurting or healing.'[1] His contemporary, William Perkins, agreed: 'A witch is a Magician, who either by open or secret league, wittingly and willingly, consenteth to use the aide and assistance of the Devill, in the working of wonders.'[2] The author of the pamphlet about the Belvoir witches attempted a more detailed definition, which included categorising the different types of witches. These included 'Phythonissae' (who dealt with artificial charms), 'Necromancers' (who exhumed corpses and used them to foretell the future), 'Geomantici' (who conversed with spirits and used incantations), 'Ventriloqui' (who spoke with 'hollow voyces' as if they were possessed by devils), and 'Venefici' (who used poison to either cure or kill).[3]

In a tract published during Elizabeth I's reign, William West provided no fewer than six classes of witch: magicians, soothsayers, divinators, jugglers, enchanters and witches. The latter were defined most closely.

A witch or hag is she who – deluded by a pact made with the devil through his persuasion, inspiration and juggling – thinks she can bring about all manner of evil things, either by thought or imprecation, such as to shake the air with lightnings and thunder, to cause hail and tempests, to remove green corn or trees to another place, to be carried on her familiar spirit (which has taken upon him the deceitful shape of a goat, swine, or calf, etc.) into some mountain far distant, in a wonderfully short space of time, and sometimes to fly upon a staff or fork, or some other instrument, and to spend all the night after with her sweetheart, in playing, sporting, banqueting, dancing, dalliance, and divers other develish lusts and lewd disports, and to show a thousand such monstrous mockeries.[4]

All of the authorities on the subject agreed that there were both good ('white') and bad ('black') witches. The former, often known as 'cunning folk', used their powers to provide a range of useful services to their community, such as healing the sick, finding lost or stolen goods, or predicting the future. In his *Treatise Against Witchcraft* – which was the first pamphlet on witchcraft to be published in England – Henry Holland attempted to explain the difference: 'Hereby it is manifest, that hurtfull magitians and witches which kill and hurt mens bodies and goods, are onely to be avoyded, and so they doe amongst us, but such of these practitioners, as can and will cure the sicke, finde thinges loste, have a good neere gesse in praedictions, and are not in any wise to be blamed . . . are often sought after in necessities unto this day, and they seeme to doe no man harme, but much good, and they speake the very trueth often.'[5] Not everyone took such a positive view of them. The influential pamphleteer, Richard Bernard declared: 'All Witches, in truth, are bad Witches, and none good.'[6]

The main crimes attributed to 'black' witches included the causing of death or injury to another person. They might also harm or kill farm animals, which in a primarily agricultural economy could spell disaster. A single cow could be vital to the well-being of a poor family, so it is not surprising that there was almost as much concern for the health of animals as for that of friends or family members. One Norfolk farmer lamented that thanks to the maleficium of a local woman, his boar 'could not cry or grunt as beforetime' and five of his calves 'were in such case as we could not endure to come nigh them by reason of a filthy noisome savour, their hair standing upright on their backs and they shaking in such sort as I never saw'.[7] Meanwhile, in neighbouring Suffolk a woman stood accused of committing various acts of sorcery against one Thomas Aldus, including having 'caused one of his cows to skip over a stile and burst her neck'.[8]

Witches were also accused of interfering with nature by ruining a harvest, preventing a cow from producing milk, or frustrating some other domestic operation. On the Continent, their powers were believed to extend to commanding the weather. In Wiesensteig, in south-western Germany, 63 women were executed as witches between 1562 and 1563 for causing a violent hailstorm. The trial records are also littered with accusations that suspected witches had disrupted sexual relations. Such cases were relatively rare in England, which had the highest proportion of female witches; elsewhere in Europe a significant number of men were convicted of the crime.

The word 'witch' has several possible derivations. These include the old English *wicca* (meaning sorceress) and the German *wichelen* (to bewitch or foretell). Although the words 'witchcraft' and 'sorcery' tended to be used interchangeably, they were different disciplines. Witchcraft was an innate power which might be inherited or conferred by the Devil. Sorcery, on the other hand, was the employment of destructive spells, charms and the like. Anyone could learn to be a sorcerer, but to be a witch, one had to be born to it. The methods of maleficent sorcerers were thought to vary from the straightforward uttering of curses or evil prophesies, to the use of technical aids. Among the most common of these were making a wax image of the victim and sticking pins in it; stealing their hair, fingernails or even excrement and manipulating this in some way; burying their clothing; or writing their name on a piece of paper and then burning it.

By such means, suspected witches were believed to have caused many thousands of deaths, injuries and illnesses in England alone during the sixteenth and seventeenth centuries. Little wonder that they were feared and reviled in equal measure.

One of the most famous witch hunters in history was James I, who was King of England from 1603 to 1625. His personal crusade resulted in the deaths of thousands of women in Scotland, his native land, and hundreds more south of the border. Among the latter were Joan, Margaret and Phillipa Flower, who became known as the Witches of Belvoir. Their story could have been taken from the pages of a fairy tale, albeit one with a dark and terrible twist. There is the contented, prosperous and noble couple whose carefree existence in their castle is brought to an abrupt end when malevolent witches curse their children. As in all classic fairy tales, the story concludes with good triumphing over evil when the witches are put to death. But the children of Francis and Cecilia Manners were not to enjoy the happy ending of Sleeping Beauty, Snow White and the rest. The spell was never broken; they never awoke from their entranced slumber. Instead, as their tomb bears testimony, they met the same fate as their wicked bewitchers.

Notorious in its time, the case of the Belvoir witches has since faded from memory. In the historiography of the period it is overshadowed by trials such as Pendle in 1612, or the infamous Hopkins witch hunts of the mid seventeenth century. That I knew of it was due to the fact that the women involved were tried and executed in my native city of Lincoln, but even there the story is neglected. One can search in vain for any mention of it in the guidebooks to the city, or even to the castle, where the Flower women met their grim fate.

Wicked Practise & Sorcerye, an excellent and painstakingly researched study by Michael Honeybone, an eminent local historian, has gone some way towards redressing the balance. The Belvoir witches also inspired a novel by Hilda Lewis: *The Witch and the Priest* (1967). By contrast, there is a wealth of general histories of witchcraft, most notably Keith Thomas's seminal work, *Religion and the Decline of Magic*, which first appeared in 1973 and has since been reprinted numerous times.

The popularity of books such as this proves the huge groundswell of interest in witchcraft. This is reflected by the internet. Even the most cursory of searches for the word 'witch' results in more than 6.5 million sites, and there are as many again for 'sorcery', 'dark arts', 'spells' and the like. Almost half a million websites are dedicated to the history of witchcraft, and a number of these refer to the Belvoir witches as being one of the most curious of all the cases that were brought before the courts of seventeenth-century England.

As well as being one of the most enduringly popular topics of historical research, witchcraft is also one of the most fiercely debated. Given that the contemporary sources are both startlingly vivid and frustratingly patchy, this is perhaps inevitable. Historians have long attempted to explain the reason why, between 1450 and 1750, around 100,000 people – most of them women – were tried for this crime in Europe, and a little under half put to death. What were the beliefs and fears which led to these executions? How and why did the legal systems of countries across Europe support them? And why were

scores of the most intelligent scholars so convinced of the existence
of witches that they wrote long books supporting their persecution?
For every question, there are at least a dozen answers, none of them
convincing enough on their own to lay the debate to rest.

Despite all the extraordinarily rich and vivid contemporary accounts
of witches, their victims and their fate, there are substantial gaps in
the sources – notably the complete absence of trial records in most
counties of England. Moreover, because the vast majority of the
accused were among the poorer members of society, their lives were
generally obscure until they gained notoriety as a result of their
supposed crimes. Although there are numerous contemporary
pamphlets describing particular witchcraft trials or condemning the
practice in general, the accused women's own voices are almost
entirely absent. This is perhaps not surprising, given that most were
illiterate. It is also indicative of their powerlessness in the face of their
accusers, and of the subservient position that women in general
endured at this time.

Likewise, although the scores of witchcraft pamphlets attracted a
diverse readership, the fact is that they were invariably written by the
educated elite. There is no comparable source for the uneducated,
illiterate masses who made up the vast majority of the population.
Their views can only be reconstructed from scattered shards of
evidence, rather than lengthy treatises. The latter tend to represent
ordinary people's perceptions of witchcraft as being rooted in ignorance and superstition. Glimpses of their true opinions can be gained
from the patchy records of witchcraft trials, which suggest a genuine,
deep-seated fear of the dark arts, as well as the strength of mystical
traditions. They also reveal the tensions that existed in local communities, which led to many more cynically motivated accusations being
levelled. In short, popular perceptions of witchcraft were every bit as
rich and complex as those held by the so-called elite members of
society.

The deeply held beliefs, superstitions, faith and world-view of the
people who lived through these times are, inevitably, alien to modern
readers. We can imagine, we can (to an extent) empathise, but we
cannot enter the minds of those who practised the magical arts, those
who believed they had fallen victim to such people, or those who
hunted them down. Partly as a result, the theories as to why the witch

hunts dominated European society for so long – and, equally, why they disappeared so suddenly – are many and varied. But the key to gaining a deeper understanding of the subject perhaps lies not in assessing the phenomenon as a whole, but in conducting a detailed case study of a particular trial. Such is the aim of this book.

The story of the Belvoir witches is one of the most extraordinary of all the witchcraft trials that took place in the seventeenth century. It has all the classic elements of the dark arts: spells, familiars, sexual deviancy and pacts with the Devil. And yet it is also set apart from the many other cases of witchcraft in Jacobean England because it was not merely the product of a dispute between neighbours, but involved one of the foremost aristocratic families in the country. The tendrils of this darkly fascinating tale stretch to the court itself, with James I and his closest favourite playing a significant, possibly sinister, part.

It is for this reason that the sources are richer than for many other witchcraft trials. Such was the Flower women's notoriety that court letters, diaries and state papers have all offered illuminating insights into the case, enabling me to reconstruct the witches' history and that of their 'victims' at Belvoir Castle. Principal among the contemporary records consulted, though, has been *The Wonderful Discoverie of the Witchcrafts of Margaret and Phillippa Flower, Daughters of Joan Flower, neere Bever Castle*, a salacious pamphlet published shortly after their trial in March 1619. Glorious for its sensationalist descriptions of the spells, familiars and other 'devilish arts' with which Joan Flower and her daughters were able to destroy the young scions of the noblest family in England, it is also suspiciously biased, confused and inaccurate on numerous points of detail. A true reflection of the events it described, or a cynical attempt to disguise the real culprits? The answer to this, and to the question of the Flower women's guilt, became gradually – shockingly – clear as I sifted through the shards of evidence to build the narrative. It led me to believe that theirs was not just one of the many ordinary tragic miscarriages of justice that marked the long history of the witch hunts; it had at its heart a murderous conspiracy that has remained hidden for almost 400 years.

I

'Naturally inclin'd to Superstition'

The picturesque village of Bottesford lies some 16 miles north of Melton Mowbray in the Vale of Belvoir, part of modern-day Leicestershire.[1] To the west is Nottinghamshire and to the east is Lincolnshire. The nearest urban centre is Grantham, which in the seventeenth century was a prosperous market town. Belvoir Castle dominates the skyline, built by the Normans on top of the only hill for miles around. Its residents, the Manners family, earls of Rutland, were one of the most ancient and distinguished noble dynasties in the country. As the name Belvoir suggests, the area is one of outstanding natural beauty, characterised by a gently undulating land-scape intersected by rivers and woodland.

At the centre of Bottesford is a marketplace with its cross and stocks still preserved. Nearby is the magnificent church of St Mary's, founded in the fourteenth century. One of the largest village churches in England, it boasts the highest spire in Leicestershire. An early-seventeenth-century commentator described it as 'very faire and large, with a high spire Steeple'.[2] St Mary's was the focus of community life for the residents of Bottesford. As in parishes across England, it provided the most common and well-attended meeting place, and anyone who chose not to go would have earned the censure of their neighbours. The church was often also the political centre of the village: a place where parish officers would be elected, and important deeds and other documents kept.

Villages such as Bottesford were naturally very tightly knit entities in which daily interaction between neighbours was not merely a choice but a necessity. The village economy depended upon small exchanges of goods and services; there were common fields and pasture, shared labour and many matters which required communal decisions. Great importance was placed upon harmony and conformity. The year was marked by various traditional rituals and festivities, such as Easter 'drinkings' and 'love feasts', as well as by weddings, baptisms and funerals, in which every member of the community was expected to take part. Such events reaffirmed neighbourly ties and the collective identity of a community, and were, as one contemporary put it, occasions to 'increase love among neighbours'.

A sixteenth-century account of the fetching and decoration of a maypole provides a vivid illustration of one of the most popular events in the annual calendar.

> Against May Day, Whitsunday, or other time, all the young men and maids, old men and wives, run gadding overnight to the woods, groves, hills and mountains, where they spend all the night in pleasant pastimes; and in the morning, they return, bringing with them birch and branches of trees, to deck their assemblies withal . . . But the chiefest jewel they bring from thence is their May-pole, which they bring home with great veneration, as thus. They have twenty or forty yoke of oxen, every ox having a sweet nose-gay of flowers placed on the tip of his horns, and these oxen draw home this May-pole (this stinking idol, rather), which is covered all over with flowers and herbs, bound round about with strings, from the top to the bottom, and sometime painted with variable colours, with two or three hundred men, women and children following it with great devotion. And thus being reared up, with handkerchieves and flags hovering on the top, they strew the ground round about, bind green boughs around it, set up summer halls, bowers and arbours hard by it. And then they fall to dance about it.[3]

Although some of the village events degenerated into drunken brawls, sparking new animosities between neighbours, on the whole they symbolised the desire for unity and accord. Anyone who refused to join in was immediately the subject of suspicion and hostility. No matter how joyous and light-hearted such festivities might appear on the surface, there was an elaborate code governing the interaction, whether it was the seating plan in the church or the order of procession at a dance or feast. Everything was symbolic of status and position. During the services at St Mary's, for example, the lord of Belvoir Castle and his family occupied pride of place at the front of the church.

The rest of the congregation may have stood up and bowed out of respect when they entered – a practice that was common in churches across England. Meanwhile, the Earl of Rutland's servants, tenants, yeomen and other members of the community were seated in strict order of precedence. Women were segregated from men, and young women from matrons.

As well as these major events in the life of a village community, there were numerous other occasions when its members got together. The daily round of informal recreation could include conversations at work, chance meetings when out walking in country lanes or shopping in the marketplace, convening in alehouses to drink, talk, sing or play games, or – more soberly – after church services. All of this was governed by the same strict observance of social etiquette between equals or superiors and inferiors which dictated the course of more formal gatherings. Relationships were thus established and maintained within a very local context, and there were ample opportunities to identify and gossip about anyone who did not fit in. It was a short step from not fitting in to being actively persecuted.

Those who stood out as troublemakers were swiftly punished, either by the community or the church courts. It was enough for a person to be of 'ill fame' for the latter to prosecute. Clergy were also instructed to refuse Communion to quarrelling parishioners. Meanwhile, community-led punishments included the cucking stool, putting the offender in a cage, or leading them around the streets by a metal bridle. The most frequent offenders were 'scolds', legally defined as 'a troublesome and angry woman who, by her brawling and wrangling amongst her neighbours, doth break the public peace and beget, cherish and increase public discord'.[4] That both the law and community justice were so harsh on them suggests that there was a close association between scolding and witchcraft. Reginald Scot, one of the leading authorities on the subject, claimed that the 'chief fault' of witches 'is that they are scolds'.[5]

With a desire for conformity in village communities came a distinct lack of privacy. A man's personal affairs were viewed as the legitimate concern of the entire community. It was the age of the nosy neighbour par excellence: everyone knew everyone else's business. Partly this was sparked by natural curiosity and a desire to enliven the sometimes dreary, monotonous existence of rural dwellers. But there was also an element of self-preservation, of wishing to protect oneself – and one's village – against evil. The arrival of outsiders often prompted intense speculation and suspicion, and they could expect to be the subject of scrutiny for some considerable time.

The community of Bottesford was more insular than most. The people of the 'Vale' were even more suspicious of outsiders and troublemakers than were those in many of the other 10,000 or so parishes in England. Marriages tended to be forged between local families,which made communities very static. The local records attest that families such as the Fairbairns, Stanages, Gills, Houghs and Vavasours had been part of the Bottesford community for many years, and there was very little migration between parishes, let alone counties.

Most of Bottesford's inhabitants would have been tenants or servants of the Earl of Rutland. Although they would have considered themselves as being of the 'better sort', their living conditions were extremely poor by modern standards. There were small local markets instead of shops, no public services, and the church was the only public building. There were no metalled roads, only dirt tracks, which could become virtually impassable in poor weather. Water (often stagnant) was drawn from the local well, and the privies, which were little better than holes in the ground, bred noisome smells as well as disease. Houses were damp, uncomfortable and malodorous, with most people sharing their living space with animals. The poorest dwellings were infested with vermin of all kinds.

The hard, unsanitary living conditions were fertile breeding grounds for diseases. For many sudden and virulent diseases, such as smallpox, typhus and – most terrifying of all – the bubonic plague, there was no known cure. From the beginning of the sixteenth to the middle of the seventeenth century, the latter was only absent for a dozen years. Even though it was most prevalent in larger cities and towns, ignorance about how to contain it meant that it could be rapidly spread to rural communities by tradesmen and other travellers. In the absence of any known cure, people of all classes resorted to whatever means they could to avoid infection. Sir Christopher Hatton famously sent Elizabeth I a ring to protect her from it. Meanwhile, severe outbreaks of plague during the same period created a deeply insecure and volatile society. A succession of bad harvests and near famines, such as occurred at Trier in Germany in the late sixteenth century, coincided exactly with a period of frenzied witch hunting. Likewise, an outbreak of plague in the town of Ellwangen in 1611 prompted a spate of witchcraft cases.

For centuries a staging post due to its central position in the country, Bottesford proved more resilient to the depredations of famine and floods that other, more isolated, rural communities fell prey to. Nevertheless, it suffered badly from plague in the early seventeenth century. One hundred and twenty-five people died in a single year – five times the average annual toll in the village. 'The dying poisoned many, Th'infection was so great whereat it came it scarce left any,' lamented the parish curate.[6] This might have signalled the decline of a more isolated village, but its geographical location enabled Bottesford to recover more quickly than many others, and by the end of the seventeenth century its population was higher than ever.

Nevertheless, the average life expectancy here as elsewhere was much lower in the seventeenth century than it is today. 'We shall find more who have died within thirty or thirty-five years of age than passed it,' observed one writer in 1635.[7] Infant mortality was particularly high, and even among the richer classes a third of children died before the age of five.

Many of those who did survive could look forward to a life beset by chronic pain from ailments which were either resistant to, or exacerbated by, the ministrations of doctors and cunning folk. Poor diet accounted for a high proportion of the common health complaints. The upper classes ate too much meat and scorned fresh vegetables and milk. Contemporary medical records show that they frequently sought relief from gout, bladder stones, urinary tract infections, constipation and rotten teeth. By contrast, the diet of the poorer members of society included more vegetables, but insufficient meat and dairy produce, and what little they ate had often gone bad. The widespread undernourishment among this class made them vulnerable to influenza, tuberculosis and gastric upsets, and many were also anaemic because of the lack of iron in their diet.

The sixteenth and seventeenth centuries witnessed a considerable growth in population, with England's population alone doubling from around two and a half million in 1530 to around five million in 1630.[8] This put increasing pressure on economic resources, and a flooded labour market resulted in a prolonged period of high unemployment and low wages. At the same time, a succession of poor harvests led to food shortages and even famine. What little food was available was so expensive that only the richer members of society could afford it. By 1650, the price of bread was six times what it had been in 1500. Pre-existing social divides were therefore accentuated, which led to tensions within communities.

In an increasingly unstable and volatile society, people clung ever more tightly to their deeply held superstitions – even those who claimed to have embraced the new religion. The Kingdom of Darkness was as real to them as the Kingdom of Heaven, and ordinary people everywhere believed in devils, imps, fairies, goblins and ghosts, as well as legendary creatures such as vampires, werewolves and unicorns. Everyone feared evil portents, such as a hare crossing one's path or a picture falling from the wall. A pregnant woman must avoid gazing at the moon because it would render her baby insane. In one of his tracts on witchcraft, George Gifford described a number of signs which were believed to augur evil – from salt spilt at a banquet to the sudden onset of a nosebleed: 'Heavy newes is brought unto some, that her father, or her mother, or her brother is dead: I did even looke for such a matter (saith she) for my nose this day did sodainly break forth a bleeding.'[9]

Children were frightened into obedience by their mothers or nursemaids with tales of evil witches, spirits, elves and fantastical creatures. Women were grouped together with the sick and infirm as being particularly susceptible to 'vaine dreames and continuall feare' as a result of their 'weaknesse of mind and bodie'. Even grown men were afraid of the dark, for this was when it was believed spirits most often appeared. 'Some never feare the divell, but in a darke night; and then a polled sheepe is a perillous beast, and manie times is taken for our fathers soule, speciallie in a churchyard, where a right hardie man heretofore scant durst pass by night but his haire would stand upright.'[10] One of the earliest works on witchcraft, published in 1486, claimed: 'The imagination of some men is so vivid that they think they see actual figures and appearances which are but the reflection of their thoughts, and then these are believed to be the apparitions of evil spirits or even the spectres of witches.'[11]

The greatest fear was reserved for Satan, God's chief adversary on earth. Belief in the existence of the Devil was synonymous with belief in the existence of God. 'If there be a God, as we most stead-fastly must believe,' asserted the East Anglian minister Robert Hutchinson, 'verily there is a Devil also.'[12] Satan was evil, God was good; the former dark, the latter light. Medieval preachers terrified their parishioners with tales of the Devil's wickedness, and the ease with which humans could fall prey to his temptations. He could whip up thunderstorms, cause untold pain and suffering, prompt lustful thoughts, and carry sinners off to the torments of hell. The depic-tions of Satan in medieval iconography, with his horns, tail and forked beard, have changed little over time. They inspired a host of grotesque gargoyles and wood sculptures in churches, which would peer down at a terrified congregation as they fervently muttered prayers to protect themselves from his power. But the Devil did not act alone. As well as the demons, goblins and imps of hell, he enlisted human beings as witches to carry out his evil intent. He was 'the Witches and Sorcerers great and graund Master', according to the leading pamphleteer John Cotta.[13]

Notions of magic and witchcraft infiltrated cultural as well as social and political life. The celebrated Elizabethan poet Edmund Spenser created an influential portrait of a witch, secreted away in her lonely cottage and inflicting evil upon the rest of society:

> There, in a gloomy hollow glen, she found
> A little cottage built of sticks and weeds,
> In homely wise, and walled with sods around,
> In which a witch did dwell in loathly weeds
> And wilful want, all careless of her needs;
> So choosing solitary to abide,
> Far from her neighbours, that her devilish deeds

And hellish art from people she might hide,
And hurt far off, unknown, whomever she envied.[14]

Belief in witchcraft helped to give reason to the often cruel randomness of life, as one Elizabethan sceptic, Reginald Scot, observed: 'If
any adversitie, greefe, sicknesse, losse of children, corne, cattell, or
libertie happen unto them; by & by they exclaime uppon witches.'[15]
George Gifford agreed: 'Men look no further then unto ye witch: they
fret and rage against her . . . they think if shee were not, they should
doo well enough: shee is made the cause of all plagues and mischiefes.'
He added that the opinion of the 'multitude' was that 'Witches can
worke at their pleasure, & so are the comon plague of the earth,
breedeth so innumerable sins, that it is as a monster with many
heads.'[16] Even Richard Bernard, who wrote a detailed guide for those
involved in the prosecution of witches, admitted: 'It is the generall
madnesse of people to ascribe unto Witchcraft, whatsoever falleth
out unknowne, or strange to vulgar sence.' He scoffed that: 'Feare
and imagination make many Witches among countrey people, being
superstitiously addicted, and led with foolish observations, and imagin-
arie signes of good and bad lucke', and urged his readers: 'Let such
as suspect themselves to bee bewitched, consider whether the cause
of their vexation be not naturall and enquire not of a devellish Wizard,
but of learned and judicious Physicians to know their disease.'[17]

Another branch of magic which remained enduringly popular,
despite the advent of religious and social change, was astrology. This
was most popular with the richer members of society, many of whom
retained a personal astrologer in their households. They were also to
be found in most of the royal courts of Europe. Elizabeth I famously
consulted Dr John Dee for much of her reign, but she was only
following the example of her father, Henry VIII, and many others like
him. As well as offering cures for maladies and foretelling the future,
astrologers could advise on the most propitious time for a birth, a
coronation or even a war. With the introduction of the printing press,
astrology gained much more widespread popularity. Charts and alma-
nacs that set out in great detail the various astronomical events of
the coming year, and thereby the most propitious time to make decisions or take action, could be reproduced on a much greater scale
than ever before.

Astrology had clearly taken hold in Bottesford and the surrounding area by the early seventeenth century. Ellen Green, an associate of the Flower family, confessed that her familiars came to suck her blood at certain phases of the moon.[18] Meanwhile, during her interrogation, one of her co-conspirators, Anne Baker, described her dealings with the planets at some length, declaring that they came in four colours: 'black, yellow, green and blue, and that black is always death'. She also noted that she had seen the blue planet strike one Thomas Fairebarne, a local resident.[19] The idea that planets of various colours could influence a person's health and well-being was rooted in the medical lore of the Middle Ages, and also had links to the ancient theory of the four humours.

It may seem ridiculous to modern observers that people in the past should base their lives around the movements of the stars and planets. But living conditions made everyone far more aware of the heavenly bodies than they are today. In an age before artificial lighting, ordinary people had a much greater knowledge of the stars and planets. They would tell the time by the sun, and plan their journeys to coincide with a full moon. In the sixteenth and seventeenth centuries, the working day was longer in the summer than in the winter because there was more daylight.

As a means of being able to disentangle some of the mysteries of life and provide explanations for the apparent randomness of events, astrology remained extremely popular throughout the early modern period. Little matter that many of its predictions proved inaccurate: the comfort and sense of control that its adherents drew from their consultations and charts was enough to safeguard its reputation. An allied practice was alchemy. Its central premise was a belief that base metals could be turned into gold or silver, as well as an elixir of life which conferred eternal youth and immortality. Alchemy divided up the metals between the planets, and drew upon teachings which dated back to classical times. Although viewed as a mystical art, it was the precursor of modern chemistry and medicine, and even celebrated scientists such as Sir Isaac Newton were said to be secret practitioners.

A problematic fact for the likes of Elizabeth I and James I, under whose rule healers were subjected to intense scrutiny and many prosecuted as witches, was that the belief in the magical power of the royal touch remained strong until the early eighteenth century. Monarchs had traditionally participated in ceremonies designed to relieve the suffering of epilepsy or the 'falling sickness'. Special rings known as 'cramp rings' were blessed by the king or queen and distributed to sufferers at an annual ceremony. This practice died out with the accession of Elizabeth I, but the tradition of touching for the 'King's Evil' proved much more durable.

This tradition had originated in the reign of Edward the Confessor, and the full ceremonial that accompanied it was laid down by Henry VII. The King's Evil was the name given to scrofula, or struma, an inflammation of the lymph glands or neck, but it came to encompass a variety of complaints affecting the head, neck and eyes, including sores, blisters, tumours and swellings. The unsightly and very visible nature of the condition meant that many sufferers were prepared to go to great lengths to find a cure. Parish authorities from the furthest-flung corners of the kingdom would routinely raise funds in order to send the affected persons to the royal court in London, and the efficacy of the monarch's touch was so renowned that some even came from overseas. The popularity of the practice grew rapidly. By the end of the thirteenth century, Edward I was touching 1,000 sufferers per year, whereas Charles II ministered to more than 90,000 over a 20-year period.

Special religious ceremonies were held for the purpose, to which hundreds of sufferers would flock. One by one the patients would approach the royal throne and kneel before it. Their sovereign would then touch them lightly on the face, while a chaplain read aloud the verse from St Mark: 'They shall lay hands on the sick and they recover.' The king or queen would then hang round their neck a gold coin strung from a white silk ribbon. This served as a talisman against future evil, and Mary Tudor urged her patients never to part with it – although many sufferers judged its monetary value to be even greater and sold it as soon as the ceremony was over.

The monarch's power to heal sprang in theory from their consecration with holy oil at their coronation, which emphasised their sacred status. This, together with the Biblical passages that were repeated at the ceremony, made it clear that they were God's representative on earth, and it was from Him that their power was derived. However, some monarchs did not wait to be crowned before performing the ceremony, and as far as most people were concerned, the power to heal was an innate, mystical ability bound up with royal status. As such, it carried enormous psychological weight for those who took part: if the power of a local cunning woman could be believed in, then how much more so that of their sovereign? Perhaps this was why some people swore by the healing value of the royal touch. The seventeenth-century surgeon Richard Wiseman claimed that Charles II cured more sufferers in one year 'than all the surgeons of London had done in an age'.[20] But Wiseman, like others who extolled the benefits of the practice, was a devout royalist, keen to promote the omnipotence of his sovereign. Those patients who were 'cured' by the royal touch would probably have recovered naturally anyway, for glandular disorders often recede with time. 'Physicians do attribute the cause more to the parties' imagination than to the virtue of the touch,' observed one sceptic.[21] The Venetian ambassador was similarly doubtful, and when reporting the practice to his masters, he added that 'it remains to be seen with what result'.[22]

Touching for the King's Evil was an essentially superstitious practice, and as such it was at odds with the Reformation. Subsequent monarchs (Mary Tudor excepted) thus found it somewhat difficult to reconcile with their religious beliefs. But they came to appreciate the usefulness of the ceremony as a means of reinforcing their royal power, for it was believed that only a legitimate sovereign could heal scrofula. Elizabeth I found it particularly valuable in establishing her somewhat shaky position on the English throne in the wake of Pope Pius V's Bull of Excommunication in 1570. Likewise, the future Charles II began touching for the King's Evil while still in exile, and it was no coincidence that he became one of the greatest advocates of it after the Restoration in 1660. Only after the Glorious Revolution in 1688 did the practice begin to fall out of use; the last English monarch to employ it was Queen Anne.

But there was one monarch who proved more reluctant than all of the rest to perform the ceremony, and it was only after considerable pressure from his advisers that he agreed to set aside his scruples and uphold the tradition. His reluctance was understandable, for he was deeply averse to the practice of magic and would become one of the most feared witch hunters in Europe. He was James VI of

Scotland, whose fate was about to become inextricably bound up with the inhabitants of Belvoir Castle.

The early part of the seventeenth century was a turbulent time for Bottesford, as it was for many communities across England. The first two decades saw a marked increase in enclosures in Leicestershire, by which process common land was systematically eroded and the local aristocracy and other landowners restricted it for their own use. In short, public land was increasingly appropriated for private gain. This deprived thousands of people of their livelihood and resulted in the destruction of entire villages. Little wonder that the enclosure system was one of the most unpopular innovations ever to be intro-duced into English rural society, and it soon sparked widespread unrest.

In late April 1607, the so-called Midland Revolt broke out in Northamptonshire and quickly spread to Warwickshire and Leicestershire. Led by John Reynolds, otherwise known as 'Captain Pouch', a tinker from Desborough, it attracted considerable support. Reynolds told his followers that he had authority from God and King James to destroy enclosures, and urged them to join him in the task. He also promised to protect protesters with the contents of his pouch, carried by his side, which he said would keep them from all harm.[23] Three thousand protesters gathered at Hillmorton in Warwickshire, and a further five thousand at Cotesbach in Leicestershire. Meanwhile, in Leicester itself a curfew was imposed because it was feared people would stream out of the city to join the riots. A gibbet was also erected as a warning, but was pulled down by the citizens. Matters came to a head in June, when 1,000 rioters converged upon Newton in Northamptonshire to protest against the voracious enclosures of Thomas Tresham, who hailed from a notorious family of Roman Catholic landowners, one of whom – Francis Tresham – had been involved in the Gunpowder Plot two years earlier. James I issued a proclamation, ordering his deputy lieutenants in Northamptonshire to quell the riots. A pitched battle ensued, and between 40 and 50 men were killed. The leaders of the riot – including Reynolds – were captured and executed, but the deep-seated resentment among the common people simmered on, and their relations with the local landowners – the Manners family of Belvoir Castle included – remained volatile.

The turbulence that the community of Bottesford had experienced during the late sixteenth and early seventeenth centuries was mirrored elsewhere in England and Europe. Foremost among the changes with which the population had had to come to terms was the revolution in religious practices and beliefs. And it is no coincidence that witch hunting most commonly occurred in areas that had experienced significant religious change, particularly those at the forefront of the Reformation and the Counter-Reformation. Indeed, it has been persuasively argued that witchcraft filled the void created by the demise of the 'old religion', Catholicism, in the sixteenth and seventeenth centuries.

The dividing line between Catholicism and magic had always been blurred. At the heart of Catholicism was the belief in the power of rituals and relics which were virtually indistinguishable from the spells and potions peddled by the local cunning folk or white witches. Chief among them was the ceremony of the Mass, during which it was (and is) believed that the bread and wine actually became Christ's body and blood, and thus had supernatural powers for all who consumed them.

The worship of saints and their relics was another integral part of the Catholic religion, and most churches had their own patron saints – with an accompanying collection of associated relics. The intercession of saints was regularly sought by people in need or distress, or simply to avoid ill fortune. Midwives urged pregnant women to carry holy relics to protect their unborn child, and to call upon the Virgin Mary to reduce the pain of labour, or to appeal to St Felicitas if they wished the child to be a boy. Rich and poor alike resorted to such means, and royalty believed in them as devoutly as everyone else. In preparing for the birth of one of her children, Henry VII's queen, Elizabeth of York, paid 6s.8d to a monk for a girdle belonging to the Virgin Mary. One hundred years later, an enterprising Oxford recusant named John Allyn made a small fortune from selling vials of Christ's blood at £20 a drop.[24] This was well beyond the means of ordinary folk, so most of his clients must have been drawn from aristocratic circles.

There was a raft of other methods employed by the medieval church to invoke God's power or ward off evil spirits. They included rituals for blessing people, animals, houses or objects. Holy water was routinely scattered on fields to ensure plentiful harvests, or given to the sick as a remedy. Even in the late sixteenth century, many people were still using the sign of the cross to protect themselves from Satan and his minions. The use of talismans and amulets was also common-place. 'About these Catholics' necks and hands are always hanging charms, That serve against all miseries and unhappy harms,' scoffed the sixteenth-century Protestant theologian Thomas Naogeorgus.[25] The most popular was the agnus dei, a small wax cake bearing the image of a lamb and flag, which was believed to guard its owner against the assaults of the Devil.

Medieval clergy thus had at their disposal a bewildering array of supernatural methods for protecting and improving the lives of their parishioners. There was practically no evil the church could not ward off, no desire it could not fulfil. As well as their own traditional rituals, the clergy were not averse to employing more blatantly magical practices when occasion demanded. Thus, for example, when the fourteenth-century Pope John XXII feared he was being poisoned, he procured a magic snakeskin to detect any suspicious potions in his food and drink. Some clergy – not always Catholic – practised magical healing, such as Dr Richard Napier, rector of Great Linford in Buckinghamshire. A contemporary of the Flower women, he was known as an 'astrological physician' and was extremely popular.[26] He claimed to have seen around 60,000 patients during the 40 years that he practised his art. Meanwhile, the churchwardens of Thatcham in Berkshire consulted a local cunning woman to find out who had stolen their communion cloth. This made the dividing line between religion and magic even more blurred.

The Reformation, which got under way in England in the early sixteenth century, sought to rid society of such superstitious practices, replacing them with the persuasive (but less appealing) idea of salva-tion through faith. An individual should have a direct relationship with God and not rely upon the intercession of intermediaries such as the clergy or saints. Only by appealing directly to God through prayer should a person seek to change or improve their lives. The Reformists thus attempted to take all of the magical elements out of religion.

Declaring the use of rituals and relics to be 'the very practice of necromancy', and the Roman Catholic priests 'the vilest witches and sorcerers of the earth', the Reformists swept away as many vestiges of the old religion as they could lay their hands on.[27] Churches were stripped of their shrines and other such adornments. The Mass was denounced as popish nonsense and replaced by a Communion in which the bread and wine were merely representative of Christ's body and blood.

As the sixteenth century progressed, the Reformist measures became ever stricter, with the notable exception of 'Bloody' Mary Tudor's reign, which saw a brief and ill-fated attempt to bring England back to the papal fold. Her half-sister Elizabeth was more tolerant in matters of religion, famously remarking that she had no wish to 'make windows into men's souls'. Her long reign nevertheless witnessed a series of systematic attempts by her increasingly desperate ministers to eradicate the last vestiges of the Catholic faith.

The eroding of the clergy's 'magical' powers which were believed to keep evil at bay accounts for the sudden increase in witchcraft persecutions during the sixteenth century. Deprived of their traditional recourse to protect themselves against maleficent magic, people had no choice but to take legal action. But centuries of tradition could not be swept away overnight. While the Reformation undoubtedly gave the justice system a powerful new role in the persecution of witches, it did not completely eradicate the old systems of belief. 'Three parts at least of the people [are] wedded to their old superstition still,' lamented a Puritan writer in 1584.[28]

As well as sweeping religious change, the late sixteenth and early seventeenth centuries witnessed an extraordinary series of other revolutions and rebellions. The Thirty Years War, which began in 1618, involved most of the countries of Europe and was one of the most destructive conflicts in its history. Initially fought as a religious war between Protestants and Catholics in the Holy Roman Empire, it gradually became a power struggle between old rivals the Habsburgs and the Bourbons. Such political turmoil tended to unsettle the ruling elite more than the lower echelons of society. Any perceived threat to social order could in turn prompt monarchs, nobles or members of the judiciary to step up their persecution of witches as a means of re-establishing authority.

Although celebrated for their enlightened and benevolent approach towards the local community, the family at Belvoir would prove the truth of this statement.

2

'A continuall Pallace of entertainment'

The Manners family of Belvoir Castle were one of the richest and most distinguished noble dynasties in England.[1] They had risen to prominence under the Tudors, when they had acquired the earldom of Rutland and made substantial profits from the lands of the dissolved monasteries. As well as Belvoir, they also held estates in Yorkshire, Northamptonshire and at Haddon in Derbyshire. The family had been at the heart of court affairs for many years, and during the latter part of Elizabeth I's reign they had begun to cultivate the future king, James VI of Scotland. The 3rd earl had acted as guarantor of the Treaty of Berwick in 1586, greatly impressing the young Scots king. Although the earl took part shortly afterwards in the trial of James's mother, Mary, Queen of Scots, his successor, John Manners, was chief mourner at her funeral the following year, thereby helping to safeguard his family's burgeoning popularity with their future sovereign.

John Manners seemed to have secured the future of the Belvoir estates when he fathered four sons. The eldest, Roger, inherited these upon his father's death in 1588, becoming 5th Earl of Rutland. He was high in favour with the future king, and was sent on an embassy to Denmark during the year of James's accession.

Francis Manners, the second eldest son, was born in 1578, and like his three brothers was educated at Cambridge. At the age of 20, he travelled widely throughout the courts of Europe, possibly accompanied by the celebrated architect Inigo Jones, and was honourably entertained by princes and emperors in France, Italy and Germany. The 'Grand Tour', as it became known, was intended to improve the linguistic, architectural and cultural knowledge of young gentlemen. So far, Francis's upbringing was entirely commensurate with that of any son of a noble family. But soon after his return from Europe, he fell into dangerous company, becoming part of the Earl of Southampton's circle. As such, he befriended the celebrated playwright

William Shakespeare, who was so impressed by the young nobleman that he created an impresa (a device to be painted on a shield for a tournament) for him, and persuaded the actor and theatre manager Richard Burbage to paint it.

A short while later, Francis became embroiled – along with his elder and younger brothers, Roger and George – in the Earl of Essex's rebellion and was imprisoned in the Poultry Counter at Elizabeth I's orders.[2] Francis pleaded his innocence in a letter to Robert Cecil, by then the most powerful man at court, assuring him that he had only been seeking out his brother Roger when he had joined the conspirators at Essex House, and was thereafter 'carried with this sway into London'.[3] It was an unlikely tale and worked little effect upon the authorities. Only the payment of a hefty fine secured the brothers' release, and Francis was committed to the custody of his uncle Roger at Enfield.[4]

Francis's involvement in the Essex rebellion may have been due to more than the hotheadedness of youth, as one family member claimed.[5] Although he was later praised as 'discreet in his words, prudent and just in all his actions . . . faithful to his countrie', there was a darker side to Francis's character.[6] Lamenting his involvement in the affair, Francis confided to his uncle: 'I take it as a punishment from God for the wicked life I have spent, hopinge hereafter he will give me more grace to leade a better life and to serve him duly and truly, for I see without him no man shall prosper in this world.'[7]

Perhaps as part of this resolve, in May 1602 Francis married Frances Knyvett, widow of Sir William Beville of Kilkhampton, Cornwall, and one of the daughters and co-heirs of the wealthy Sir Henry Knyvett of Charlton in Wiltshire. The couple had a daughter, Katherine, in 1603.[8] This year also saw the passing of the mighty Tudor dynasty and the dawn of the Jacobean age in England. The glory days of the Virgin Queen had long since passed, and by the time of her death, as Bishop Goodman observed, 'the people were very weary of an old woman's government'.[9] Elizabeth died in the early hours of 24 March. By the end of the day, James VI of Scotland had been proclaimed King of England. Although trouble had been feared, it was a remarkably peaceful transition from one royal house to another.

Frances Knyvett died of smallpox in 1605, having given birth to no further children. On 26 October 1608, her widower married Cecilia, daughter of Sir John Tufton of Hothfield in Kent, sister of Nicholas, first Earl of Thanet, and widow of the aged Sir Edward Hungerford.

The date of Cecilia's birth is not recorded, but it is likely to have been in around 1587, which would have made her nine years younger than her second husband – an improvement upon her first.[10] We know little of her life before her marriage to Francis, although the patchy evidence that does exist suggests that she was a strong and feisty woman, not content to play the conventional role of the dutiful wife. Raised as part of a large family, she had been given a rudimentary education and was barely literate by the time she reached adulthood. This was by no means unusual: only between 5 and 10 per cent of women could read or write during the period 1580–1640. Even in privileged families, the education of girls was seen as superfluous, provided they were instructed in household management, needlework, and other accomplishments necessary for their future as wife and mother. Women were not admitted to the universities, the function of which was to prepare future statesmen or clergymen. 'Books are part of a man's prerogative,' opined the ill-fated Jacobean courtier Sir Thomas Overbury, who added that too much learning made women mentally unstable.[11] The records suggest that most women did not think to question this situation, having few ambitions beyond the domestic sphere. A well-born seventeenth-century lady Elizabeth Jocelyn wrote detailed instructions for the education of her child, should she fail to survive the birth. While she was clear that a son ought to be prepared for a career in the church, if the child was a girl, she stipulated: 'I desire her bringing up to be learning the Bible, as my sisters do, good housewifery, writing, and good works; other learning a woman needs not.'[12]

Cecilia's first marriage, to Sir Edward Hungerford, had not been a happy one. Sir Edward was many years her senior – old enough to be her grandfather – but he was in desperate need of an heir. Cecilia could not have welcomed this unsavoury prospect, and despite her husband's best efforts, no child resulted from the union. Sir Edward was not a kind husband. He came from a family which would be called dysfunctional in modern parlance. His father had been executed for sodomy, and there had been rumours of involvement in witchcraft. This could have helped foster a fear and hatred of witches in Edward's young wife, which would later find full expression.

Unhappy though it was, the marriage was also mercifully brief. Sir Edward died shortly afterwards – exhausted, perhaps, by his efforts to beget an heir. Cecilia no doubt rejoiced in her freedom, but she had a tremendous battle to secure her jointure of £2,000. Without it, she knew that she could offer only a paltry dowry to a future husband, given that she came from such a large family. Her doggedness in pursuing what was hers by right hints at a ruthless, ambitious side to her nature. She was determined that, having suffered a miserable first marriage, she would secure a much greater one second time around.

Like any man of breeding, Francis Manners was expected to marry not for love but for financial or political gain. With only a daughter from his previous marriage, he needed a son to secure the future of his estate. Sons had proved hard to come by in the Manners family in recent times, the title having passed from brother to brother rather than from father to son. The Puritan writer Daniel Rogers condemned those who were motivated by passion in choosing a wife as 'poor greenheads'. He even argued that marriages based upon passion rather than politics might result in contaminated offspring: 'What a cursed posterity such are likely to hatch . . . what woeful imps proceeded from such a mixture.'[13] Although Francis and Cecilia's marriage was not primarily founded upon love, these words would prove prophetic.

That there was attraction between them is evident from the family papers, which provide some tantalising details about their courtship. Thomas Screven, agent to Francis's elder brother Roger, wrote from London in late October 1608: 'This woing of Sr Francis Manners goeth exceedingly well forward and he applies yt like a good woer.' The Lord Chamberlain visited Sir John and his daughter to enquire how negotiations for the betrothal were proceeding, and he remarked that he 'fyndes all well and her affection strong'.[14] Theirs was more than merely a physical attraction, though: they had a crucial – and controversial – interest in common, for they were devout Catholics – and, it was whispered, secret Papists.

At the time of Francis's marriage to Cecilia, Catholics constituted a small percentage of the population, most of whom (officially, at least) adhered to the Protestant religion espoused by their king. The 'old religion' had become a seigneurial movement, with small groups of Catholics centred upon a local gentleman's house. The recusant gentry tended to intermarry with their co-religionists, as

Francis chose to do, which led to an 'inbred cousinage' of landed families.[15]

Cecilia's sister, Ann, had married the notorious Roman Catholic Francis Tresham, who had taken part in both the Essex rebellion and the Gunpowder Plot of 1605. The fact that Francis Manners was eager to associate himself with the Tufton family is one of several indications that he was of the same faith. Meanwhile, Sir John Tufton heartily approved of the match, the Manners family being one of the most distinguished in England. He suspected, though, that the couple had already agreed to marry before his consent was formally sought.[16] That Cecilia was considered a great prize in the marriage market is suggested by the fact that as negotiations were drawing to a close, another candidate suddenly entered the frame. Screven wrote with all haste to his master, urging him to settle the required sums in order to bring the alliance to a swift conclusion.[17]

Cecilia soon proved that she had been worth her new husband's efforts. Seventeenth-century society prescribed a strict set of conventions for the behaviour and status of wives, and Cecilia seemed to be a textbook example. Gervase Markham's influential book *The English Hus-wife*, which first appeared in 1615, provided a detailed description of an ideal wife. 'She ought, above all things, to be of an upright and sincere religion, and in the same both zealous and constant; giving by her example an incitement and spur unto all her family to pursue the same steps, and to utter forth by the instruction of her life those virtuous fruits of good living, which shall be pleasing both to God and his creatures.' As well as pious, a woman should be 'of great modesty and temperance . . . appearing ever unto him [her husband] pleasant, amiable, and delightful', and her virtue should be beyond question. 'Our English housewife must be of chaste thought, stout courage, patient, untired, watchful, diligent, witty, pleasant, constant in friendship, full of good neighbourhood, wise in discourse, but not frequent therein, sharp and quick of speech, but not bitter or talkative, secret in her affairs, comfortable in her counsels, and generally skilful in all the worthy knowledges which do belong to her vocation.'[18]

But Cecilia was an ideal wife in a more important way than merely her behaviour and piety. Soon after her wedding to Francis, she fulfilled that most basic – and essential – of wifely duties by producing a son and heir to inherit the Belvoir fortune. The boy was christened Henry, possibly as a compliment to the new king, who had chosen that name for his own eldest son and heir. The date of Henry Manners's birth is not known, and neither is that of his younger brother, Francis, but the evidence proves that they must both have been born within the first five years of the marriage.

By the time of his marriage to Cecilia, Francis had already started to make a name for himself at court. He would enjoy greater favour in James's reign than he had in the time of Elizabeth. His first recorded meeting with the new king was on 22 April 1603, when James chose to rest at Belvoir overnight on his long journey south to claim his crown. A contemporary account of the visit described how 'His Highnesse was not only Royally and most plentifully received, but with such exceeding joy of the good Earle [Roger] and his honourable Lady [Elizabeth Sidney], that he tooke therein exceeding pleasure.'[19] After breakfast the following morning, James conferred a number of knighthoods upon the local dignitaries in attendance, including the youngest of the Manners brothers, Oliver. But it was Francis who seems to have made the greatest impression upon the new king, for he soon after became a prominent member of the royal court. He was created Knight of the Bath in January 1605, at the same time as the king's son and heir.

Francis became 6th Earl of Rutland and inherited the Belvoir estates upon the death of his elder brother Roger, who had no children, on 26 June 1612. More titles soon followed. In July the same year, he was made lord lieutenant of Lincolnshire, and soon after he became constable of Nottingham Castle and keeper of Sherwood Forest. An indication of how close he now was to the king was the fact that when, in 1613, he picked a fight with the Earl of Montgomery and Lord Davers in quick succession, James – far from reprimanding him – stepped in to prevent further trouble.[20] In April 1616, Francis was made Knight of the Garter, and Lord Baron Ros of Hamlake three months later, the latter in compensation for unsuccessfully claiming the barony of De Ros of Helmsley – the most ancient baronial title in England – which had been bestowed upon his cousin, William Cecil.[21] An even clearer indication of Francis's growing prestige at court came the following year when he was appointed a privy councillor and soon afterwards accompanied James to Scotland.

In common with other prominent families, the Manners leased a home in London – Bedford House, an impressive mansion on the north side of the Strand. Built in 1586, it boasted at least 45 rooms and was lavishly decorated. An inventory taken in 1643 describes tapestry hangings adorning the walls in the family's apartments, luxurious Turkish carpets in many of the rooms, chairs covered with crimson or green velvet, gilt candlesticks and silver-lined glassware. The most attractive feature of the house from the earl's perspective, though, was the fact that it afforded him easy access to the court. Although she rarely left Belvoir, the countess was very fond of the London house, and when there was a threat of losing it, the earl wrote anxiously to his fellow courtier and politician Sir Edward Conway that his 'Countess will hardly part with Bedford House'.[22]

As well as his official duties, Francis also played a full part in the entertainments of the court, and was often listed as a participant in the increasingly lavish masques that were held there. The earl threw himself into court life with great enthusiasm, lavishing huge sums in order to enhance his prestige with the king. He is recorded as being present at most of the major court occasions, including more official engagements such as the investiture of the king's eldest son, Henry, as Prince of Wales in 1610.[23] The latter occasion was described by King James's well-informed ambassador to the Netherlands, Dudley Carleton, who was enraptured by the glittering spectacle: 'In the Tilt-yeard, there were divers Earles, Barons, and others, being in rich and glorious armoure, and having costly caparisons [a decorative cloth for a horse], wondrous curiously imbroydered with pearls, gould, and silver, the like rich habiliaments for horses were never seene before.'[24]

In contrast to her husband's close contact with the king, Cecilia rarely ventured far from Belvoir. There is no record of her attending the court, although the fact that she knew Bedford House makes this a strong possibility. Mostly, however, she only encountered James and his court when they visited her husband's estate. Neither is there any mention of particular friends or acquaintances: the usual social niceties of a lady of the manor did not seem to interest her. Rather, life at her husband's castle seemed to be all-consuming. She thrived upon the organisation and discipline necessary to maintain a well-ordered household. This was not the case with all aristocratic wives. The surviving diaries of seventeenth-century noblewomen are littered with complaints about their miserable lives. Writing in the middle of the century, the Duchess of Newcastle, who was herself childless, reflected on women's lot: 'All the time of their lives is ensnared with troubles, what in breeding and bearing children, what in taking and turning away servants, directing and ordering their family . . . and if they have children, what troubles and griefs do ensue? Troubled with their forwardnesse and untowardnesse, the care for their well being, the fear for their ill doing, their grief for their sicknesse, and their unsufferable sorrow for their death.'[25]

The new countess would soon know the truth of this statement all too well. But for the moment, the image of her that emerges from the records is of a brusque, highly organised, controlling woman who kept a strict rein on the household at Belvoir. She also closely superintended her sons' upbringing, and took a keen interest in that of her stepdaughter. Given that Katherine was very close to her father and had been indulged by him since her infancy, it is possible that she resented the interference of her new stepmother. Relations between them certainly soured when Katherine reached adulthood, and the two women would become estranged after the earl's death. This gives the lie to the adulatory account written by the family's private chaplain, Richard Broughton, in 1633, which refers to 'a mutuall and long Affection euen from the yonge yeares of the one betwixt Mother and Daughter, as also the united hearts of Wife and Daughter'.[26]

By the seventeenth century, it was customary for children of noble families to be educated at home by a private tutor up to the age of 14. More attention tended to be paid to the education of boys, and they would enjoy (or endure) a strict regime in which there was very little room for playing or other relaxed pastimes. As well as concentrating on religious and classical studies, and the study of Latin, some households would hire an expert in more specialised subjects such as French. Given the importance of the two Manners boys to the future of their father's estate, it is likely that no expense was spared on their education. By contrast, the fact that Katherine grew up to be barely literate suggests that, like Cecilia's own, very little attention was paid to her education.

The Earl and Countess of Rutland lived a life of luxury at Belvoir, which was one of the most magnificent estates in England. Standing on top of 'a very lofty hill', the castle commanded 'a most delicious and pleasing prospect, being accounted one of the best prospects in the land', according to the early-seventeenth-century antiquary William Burton.[27] It dated back to the time of William the Conqueror – whose standard-bearer, Robert de Todeni, founded the castle – and remained a royal stronghold until 1527, when it was granted to Robert, 1st Baron de Roos. It eventually passed into the hands of the earls of Rutland, and was rebuilt by the 5th earl in splendid Gothic style with a central tower that is reminiscent of Windsor Castle.

Much of the castle that Francis and Cecilia Manners would have known was destroyed during the English Civil War. Belvoir was one of the most notable strongholds of Charles I's supporters, and in 1649 the republican Council of State ordered its demolition. The contemporary account books and other papers give some sense of the scale and luxury of the original castle, however. As well as the public rooms, family and guest chambers, nurseries, library and chapel, there was an extensive network of kitchens, cellars, pantries, a buttery and a laundry room.

Francis had inherited a staggeringly large household from his elder brother Roger, who had retained 212 servants and 9 clergy. An extravagant spender to the end, Roger had lavished huge sums on everything from feasts to finery. He had also been a prodigious gambler, and had frittered away between £1,000 and £1,500 a year on this vice. Spending an average of £1,000 or more a year on his clothes, he thought nothing of laying out £64 for the embroidery of sumpter cloths (used to cover goods during transport) with the peacocks of the Manners crest, or £84 on the embroidery of a masque costume in the year of his death.[28] His funeral feast had been prepared by no fewer than 27 cooks.[29] By then, the Manners family was one of the most prestigious in England, with extraordinarily extensive estates which spanned Derbyshire, Nottinghamshire, Rutland, Warwickshire and Yorkshire, as well as Leicestershire and Lincolnshire. But they had a long history of consistently living beyond their means, and Francis – although a little more careful than the rest – was no exception.

The contemporary records attest to the generosity and benevolence of the new earl, describing him as 'charitable to the poor' and 'affable to all'.[30] It was said that he 'proceeded so honourably in the course of his life, as neither displacing Tenants, discharging servants, denying the accesse of the poore, welcoming of strangers, and performing all the duties of a noble Lord'. Little wonder that he was known as a popular lord and master, who 'fastened as it were unto himself the love and good opinion of the Country' and was revered by 'great and small' alike.[31] Cecilia equalled him in kindness and good humour, and was said to 'beare as free a mind'.[32]

By all accounts, the earl and countess enjoyed a 'cheerful' marriage. The earl later said that 'there was never man had a more loving and vertuous wife then she hath beene to mee'.[33] Described as 'an amiable couple', they were generous hosts to servants and guests alike, 'so that Beaver Castle was a continuall Pallace of entertainment, and a daily reception for all sorts both rich and poore'.[34] Another contemporary source concurs that the castle was 'a place, that gives welcome to all', and a later account tells of the Manners's 'magnificent hospitality'.[35]

They and their guests enjoyed many luxuries. Their diet, even on ordinary days, included such rarities as 'straweburies and rapseses', apricots, artichokes, fresh salmon and trout, swan, capon, peacock and partridge.[36] There were numerous fish ponds at Belvoir and the family's other estates which kept them supplied with fresh fish, and beehives so that they might sweeten their dishes with honey.[37] They drank wine from Venetian glass, ate their meals off silver dishes and plates, and their silver cutlery was engraved with peacocks and coronets.[38] The couple also exchanged lavish New Year gifts with the king each January, as tradition dictated for the nobility.[39]

A later account describes the family's sumptuous jewels, which included a gold chain set with 138 small diamonds, a diamond hatband, a 'valentine' in gold, a 'great diamond jewel', and a gold 'moddell' (medal) with a picture of the King of France.[40] The earl even had a pair of gold stirrups made, while a green velvet saddle and scarlet riding coat were commissioned for his daughter Katherine, also a keen horsewoman.[41] There were also numerous payments made for sumptuous new gowns, including 'crymosin velvet for a robe of honour' which was trimmed with ermine, ash-coloured taffeta silk for a new dress, and a pair of nightcaps – one made from gold and silver thread, the other from black silk.[42] Meanwhile, their rooms were furnished with embroidered beds, Flemish tapestries and 'Turkie carpetes'.[43]

The family were regularly entertained by troupes of musicians and actors, including on occasion the queen's own players.[44] The account books include payments for lute strings for Lady Katherine, and repairs to the younger son's 'citron' (cittern, a stringed instrument).[45] The earl was also an avid reader, judging from the number of histories and other books that were purchased for the castle.[46] Rather less refined was the pastime of bear-baiting, which took place at Belvoir on at least one occasion.[47] Like his late brother, Francis was a betting man (although thankfully less voracious), and there were payments for money lost at cards and the horses.[48]

Francis and Cecilia's efforts to establish Belvoir as a 'pallace of entertainment' were intended for more than their own amusement. It brought them to the attention of their pleasure-loving king, who decided to make a return visit to the castle in August 1612. The visit would have profound repercussions for the Manners family. In cultivating James, the earl and countess were not merely enhancing their political standing; they were allying themselves with the most notorious royal witch hunter in Europe.

3

A Storm at Sea

Known as the 'cradle king', James had become the nominal ruler of Scotland at the age of just 13 months, following the enforced abdication of his mother, Mary, Queen of Scots, in 1567. She had subsequently fled to England, where she remained Elizabeth I's captive for almost 20 years, until her execution in 1587.

The lonely and often dangerously volatile childhood that James endured may account for the fearful, suspicious, almost neurotic nature that became increasingly manifest in adulthood. From his earliest infancy, he had endured a series of shocks. Whilst still in his mother's womb, he had been threatened by the murder of his mother's favourite, David Rizzio, which had almost caused Mary to miscarry. At only a few months old, he had survived the murder of his father, the despised Lord Darnley. As a youth, he had narrowly escaped a host of plots and assassination attempts. In 1579, John Stewart, Earl of Mar, younger brother of James III, was accused of 'consulting with witches and sorcerers, in order to shorten the king's days'. Before he could be brought to trial, he was 'bled to death in his own lodgings'.[1] Twelve witches, and three or four wizards, were subsequently accused of being his accomplices and were burned at Edinburgh.

Throughout this turbulent time, James had been taught to revile the weakness and licentiousness of his absent mother, and this deepened into a more general antipathy towards women. His mother's violent death also seems to have inspired a dark fascination with magic. 'His Highnesse tolde me her deathe was visible in Scotlande before it did really happen,' related Sir John Harington many years later, 'being, as he said, "spoken of in secrete by those whose power of sighte presentede to them a bloodie heade dancing in the aire". Hereat, he namede many bookes, which I did not knowe, nor by whom written; but advisede me not to consult some authors which woulde leade me to evile consultations. I tolde his Majestie, "the

power of Satan had, I muche fearede, damagede my bodilie frame;
but I had not farther will to cowrte his friendshipe, for my soules
hurte.'"[2]

A fragile and sickly child, for the first six or seven years of his
life James had been unable to stand up or walk without assistance.
'His legs were verey weake, having as was thought some foule play
in his youth, or rather before he was borne, that hee was not able
to stand at seven yeares of age,' remarked one of his earliest biog-
raphers.[3] As a young man, he had been able to indulge his love of
riding only by being tied on to his horse, and throughout his life
he tended to walk while leaning on the shoulder of an attendant.
Little wonder that he had always preferred studying to physical
pursuits.

Although far short of being a great intellectual, James's mental
abilities compensated to some degree for his physical deficiencies. He
was a product of the strict Scottish Reformation. From an early age
he was trained by scholars of the Protestant faith, and he grew up
with a strong aversion to Catholicism. Because the latter was closely
entwined with sorcery in the minds of many of his contemporaries,
it was perhaps natural that the King of Scots should develop a deep-
seated suspicion of witchcraft. The scholarly nature of his burgeoning
interest in the subject was attested to by a contemporary, who
described how he was 'ever apt to search into secrets, to try conclu-
sions, as I did know some who saw him run to see one in a fit whom
they said was bewitched'.[4]

In 1589, beset by political turmoil at home and abroad, James
resolved to strengthen his position by making an advantageous alliance
with a foreign bride. His choice fell upon Anne of Denmark, and on
18 June his earl marshal left Scotland on a mission to Copenhagen to
arrange the contract. The marriage was celebrated by proxy on
20 August, and Anne set sail for her new country. But three weeks
later, there was still no sign of her fleet approaching Scotland. On
12 September, Lord Dingwall, one of James's closest advisers, arrived
at Leith with grave news. He told how he had 'come in company
with the Queen's fleet three hundred miles, and was separated from
them by a great storm: it was feared that the Queen was in danger
upon the seas'. Upon hearing the news, King James, who had been
waiting anxiously at Seton House, overlooking the Firth of Forth,

became 'very impatient and sorrowful for her long delay', and ordered a fast to be held to ensure his bride's safe arrival. When October arrived with no further tidings of the lost fleet, James dispatched Colonel Stewart to Norway 'to see what was word of the Queen'. Keen to play the romantic hero, he wrote an impassioned letter for the colonel to give to Anne, in which he spoke of 'the fear which ceaselessly pierces my heart' and his longing to see the object of 'all his love'.[5]

It did not take Colonel Stewart long to reach Norway, and he soon sent word back to James that Queen Anne's fleet had been battered back by violent storms. With the onset of winter, her sailors had decided to abandon the voyage until the weather turned more clement. In a display of uncharacteristic bravery and decisiveness, James immediately declared that he would sail across the North Sea and collect his bride himself. The reason for his haste had less to do with romantic notions than a determination to prove his masculinity. Rumours were abounding about his relationship with his new favourite, Alexander Lindsay, who was whispered to be the King's 'nightly bed-fellow'.[6] In a letter to his subjects written shortly before his departure, James lamented that 'the want of hope of succession bred disdain. Yes, my long delay bred in the breasts of many a great jealousy [suspicion] of my inability, as if I were a barren stock.' He thereby justified his sudden departure, assuring his people: 'I am known, God be praised, not to be intemperately rash nor conceity [flighty] in my weightiest affairs, neither use I to be so carried away with passion as I refuse to hear reason.'[7]

The Scottish king reached Norway without incident, and finally met his bride in Oslo on 19 November. The Danish nobles who had assembled to greet him observed that he was 'a tall, slim gentleman thin under the eyes', very richly dressed in red and gold velvet. They looked on in astonishment as, without hesitation, James strode up to Anne and gave her 'a kiss after the Scots fashion at meeting, which she refused as not being the form of her country'. Desperate to avoid further humiliation, James urgently whispered some words of encouragement in her ear, which evidently had the desired effect, for shortly afterwards 'there passed familiarity and kisses', and the encounter was declared 'a joyful meeting on all sides'.[8] The couple were married four days later.

Now in the midst of a Scandinavian winter, James had no intention of braving the seas again until the weather grew warmer. He therefore spent a pleasant few months with his new wife at Elsinore Castle in Denmark, where he 'made good cheer and drank stoutly till the springtime'.[9] But the Scottish king's visit was not all about revelry and overindulgence. On his travels through his wife's native land, he met a number of intellectuals and philosophers, including a leading Danish theologian named Niels Hemmingsen. As well as being a staunch Calvinist, Hemmingsen was also a noted demonologist. He and James had a lengthy debate about theological issues, and the Scottish king afterwards confessed to being so impressed by the elderly theologian that their meeting stood out as one of the highlights of his visit. Similarly influential was James's meeting with Tycho Brahe, a renowned astronomer. Brahe was a fervent believer in the existence of witchcraft, and attempted to convince James of its dangers. Witches were actively hunted out in Denmark, where the theory of a demonic pact had been widely accepted. The Scottish king was apparently greatly inspired by the Danish example, and it was during this visit that the seeds of his own witch hunting fervour were sown.

James's pleasant sojourn in Denmark could not last for ever, and with the onset of spring he could no longer ignore the calls of his advisers to return to Scotland and bring order to the rebellious subjects who had made the most of his absence. But despite the milder weather, the crossing was once more to prove difficult. The royal fleet was battered by violent storms and one of the ships was lost. James immediately placed the blame on witches, claiming that they must have cast evil spells upon his fleet. Thenceforth, his fascination with witchcraft deepened into a dangerous obsession.

Witchcraft had been on the Scottish law books since 1563, but until now it had gone virtually unprosecuted. All of that changed with James's return from Denmark. Fired up by the likes of Hemmingsen and Brahe, he was determined to introduce similarly harsh measures against witches in his native land. His turbulent sea voyage presented him with the perfect opportunity. With bewildering speed, a hundred suspected witches were arrested and examined, and their 'devilish' plot to drown the Scottish king and his new wife was uncovered.

During the course of the interrogations, one of the prisoners, Agnes

Sampson, alleged that the plot had been masterminded by James's deadliest enemy, Francis Stewart, Earl of Bothwell. A staunch Roman Catholic, Bothwell had a strong bloodline to the Scottish throne because his father was the illegitimate son of James V. But his claim was only valid while James remained without an heir, so the earl had good reason to prevent the passage of the king's new wife. According to Sampson's account, Bothwell had promised 'gold and silver and victual' to all those who agreed to help bring about the King's death.[10] He was also said to have been a skilful necromancer who held frequent communication with witches.

Rumours of witchcraft had long been employed to do away with political opponents, as Elizabeth Woodville and Anne Boleyn had found to their cost, and Bothwell's enemies at court seized upon Sampson's testimony as an ideal opportunity to be rid of him. He was duly called before the Privy Council on 15 April 1591, and although he stoutly denied the charges against him, he was summarily imprisoned in Edinburgh Castle. He escaped two months later, and the Privy Council put out an urgent appeal for his capture, declaring that the earl had 'had consultation with necromancers, witches and other wicked and ungodly persons, both without and within his country, for bereaving of his Highness's life'. Moreover, he had given himself 'over altogether in[to] the hands of Satan, heaping treason upon treason against God, his Majesty and this his native country'.[11] But Bothwell had considerable support across Scotland, and not only evaded escape, but turned from prey into predator, terrifying James by raiding the royal palaces of Holyroodhouse and Falkland while the king was in residence. On one such occasion, James heard a disturbance in the chamber next to his own. Rushing to see what had happened, he was aghast to discover his mortal enemy kneeling next to his sword – a sign that Bothwell considered he had control of the palace but would not use his power to harm the king. Paralysed by fear, James (who believed the earl had satanic powers) screamed that Bothwell might take his life, but he would never have his immortal soul. Upon the arrival of some courtiers, the king regained his composure and bargained with the earl. It was agreed that Bothwell would be tried for his offences, but then acquitted and released into exile.

The women with whom he was said to have conspired were less fortunate. They had been arrested and interrogated as soon as the 'conspiracy' had come to light. At the same time, arrests had been made in Denmark. Soon after James and Anne's departure, an investigation had been launched into why her first attempt to embark for Scotland had failed. Peter Munk, the admiral of the fleet, was questioned by the authorities. He was quick to deflect the blame on to Copenhagen's governor, Christoffer Valkendorf, for failing to keep the navy in order, and took his complaint to Denmark's supreme court. The latter found in favour of Valkendorf and declared that gales had been the cause for the fleet's aborted voyage. However, the governor pointed out that these gales may have been generated not by nature but by witchcraft. At around the same time, an English spy in Copenhagen reported that Munk 'hathe generated five or six witches to be taken in Coupnahaven, upon suspicion that by their witche craft they had staied the Queen of Scottes voiage into Scotland, and sought to have staied likewise the King's retorne'. The threat or implementation of torture was used to wring confessions out of all of the women, who admitted to sending demons to climb aboard Anne's ship and pull it under the waves.[12] They were sentenced to death.

Meanwhile, in Scotland, the first to confess was a young woman named Geillis (or Gilly) Duncan, a servant in the house of David Seaton, deputy bailiff of the small town of Tranent on the shores of the Firth of Forth, about nine miles east of Edinburgh. She had recently gained renown for her skill in curing diseases, 'and for doing other things which gave rise to the belief that the agency by which she worked was something more than natural'.[13] Her master's suspicions were further aroused when he discovered that she was secretly leaving his house every other night. Together with some of his acquaintance he interrogated Geillis and subjected her to 'grievous torture', which included the use of 'pilliwinks' – a device similar to thumbscrews.[14]

Geillis subsequently made a full confession. According to her testimony, she had been part of an extensive network of witches – the names of 70 conspirators are listed in the records – who had plotted the king's death and that of his new bride. They included Agnes Sampson, described as 'a woman not of the base and ignorant sort of witches, but matron-like, grave, and settled in her answers'.[15] She confessed that one All Hallows' Eve 'she was accompanied . . . with a great many other witches, to the number of two hundred, and that all they together went to sea, each one in a riddle or sieve, and went into the same very substantially, with flaggons of wine, making merry and drinking by the way, in the same riddles or sieves, to the kirk of North Barrick, in Lowthian, and that after they had landed, took hands on the land, and danced this reel or short dance, singing all with one voice, "Comer go ye before, comer go ye / If ye will not go before, comer let me."[16]

On another occasion, after hearing that the new queen had embarked for Scotland, they had undertaken a gruesome ritual which involved taking a cat and christening it with the name of their intended victim (presumably either Queen Anne or King James) and then binding the severed genitalia and limbs of a dead man to each of its legs. The witches then sailed out to sea and tossed the cat into the waves, whereupon 'there did arise such a tempest in the sea, as a greater hath not been seen'.[17] They had used similar means to impede James's voyage to Denmark, and when both he and Anne had finally embarked for Scotland, Satan himself had appeared to the witches and 'promised to raise a mist, and cast the king into England, for which purpose he threw into the sea a thing like a foot-ball'. One witness claimed to have seen 'a vapour and smoke rise from the spot where it touched the water'.[18]

King James himself presided over the interrogation of Agnes Sampson at Holyroodhouse in Edinburgh. When she 'stood stiffly in denial' of the charges against her, she 'had all her hair shaved off, in each part of her body, and her head thrawn [wrenched] with a rope according to the custom of that country, being a pain most grievous'. All of this continued for an hour, while the king looked on with 'great delight'. There then followed the most dramatic moment of the interrogation when James, responding to something that Agnes had said, leapt up in fury and declared her a liar. But she calmly took him to one side and convinced him of her magical powers by telling him certain 'secret matters' that had passed between him and his new wife on their wedding night. Whether she made a calculated guess or had genuine psychic ability, James was astounded at her revelation. 'The King's Majesty wondered greatly, and swore by the living God, that he believed all the devils in hell could not have discovered the same, acknowledging her words to be most true, and therefore gave the more credit to the rest that is before declared.'[19] He immediately ordered that the torture must stop, for he was now convinced that she was telling the truth. This had no doubt been the purpose of Agnes's audacious ploy. Even the prospect of death was more welcome than the prolonged agony and humiliation of torture. Although she escaped the horror of burning, which a number of her co-conspirators had suffered, her fate was hardly less appalling. She was taken to the castle hill in Edinburgh and bound to a stake, then 'wirreit' (strangled) until she was dead. Her remains were then burned to ashes.[20]

Barbara Napier, another woman who was implicated in the case, was rather more fortunate. As the crowds gathered to witness her execution in May 1591, her friends made the claim that she was pregnant. This was enough to bring proceedings to a halt until such time as it could be proved whether Barbara really was in this condition. The jury refused to find her guilty of treason on the grounds that there was insufficient evidence. When he heard of this, James was so enraged that he called for a new trial against her and began legal proceedings against the jury members themselves. He instructed his agent: 'Try by the mediciners' oaths if Barbara be with bairn or not. Take no delaying answer. If you find she be not, to the fire with her presently', adding that she should be first disembowelled so that the crowds might see that she had not been with child.[21] There is no record of Barbara ever having been executed, so either she really was pregnant and by the time she gave birth the king's wrath had cooled, or his advisers persuaded him that, legally speaking, he was on shaky ground. The affair rankled with James, and he was quick to point out that he himself had almost lost his life as a result of this witchcraft conspiracy, warning his subjects: 'If such troubles were in breeding whilst I retained my life, what would have been done if my life had been taken from me?'[22]

The trial of the North Berwick witches made a profound and lasting impression upon the young king. Agnes Sampson had testified that the Devil hated him 'By reason the king is the greatest enemie hee hath in the world'.[23] This cast James in the role of avenging knight of the Christian faith – a role that he wholeheartedly embraced. He became convinced that the more vigorously he persecuted those suspected of conspiring with the Devil, the less power the Devil would have over him or his kingdom. By setting himself up as God's chief advocate on earth, he acquired a dangerously free hand to hunt down witches with as much severity as he wished. The speech that he made at the acquittal of Barbara Napier made this ominously clear: 'As I have this begun, so purpose I to go forward; not because I am James Stuart, and can command so many thousands of men, but because God hath made me a King and judge to judge righteous judgement.'[24]

With all the passion of a religious zealot, James set about convincing his subjects of the evil that lay in their midst. As soon as the North Berwick trials had ended, he commissioned *Newes from Scotland*, a pamphlet that relayed the whole saga in scandalised language aimed at whipping up popular fear of witches. Cases of witchcraft became increasingly prevalent in Scotland from the late sixteenth century, to the extent that it was 'an object of more universal and unhesitating belief than in almost any other country'.[25] King James VI was said to have taken an 'extraordinary interest' in all of them.[26]

The Scottish king's growing obsession with witches led him to incite his subjects to be ever more watchful for signs of 'devilish practises' in their local communities. Others went a step further by making up cases in order to gratify the king's curiosity. Even men of high rank became involved, such as in 1596 when John Stewart, the master of Orkney, was accused of having employed witches to bring about the death of Patrick, Earl of Orkney. This case, like so many others, was probably motivated by ambition or revenge, but the involvement of such prominent persons gave credence to the growing belief in the existence of witches.

The following year, James VI became the only monarch in history to publish a treatise on witchcraft. The book was the result of painstaking and meticulous work on James's part, and must have taken years to complete. Early versions of the manuscript still survive and show more than a hundred amendments made by the king's own hand. The finished version, *Daemonologie* (literally, the science of demons), was an 80-page quarto which went through several editions and was later translated into Latin, French and Dutch. Although lacking in original or profound ideas, the fact that it had been written by a king made it enormously influential.

The book masqueraded as an intellectual debate on the likelihood of the existence of witches, being written as a dialogue between two educated and informed men, but it was clear that the Scottish king was already a devout believer. In the preface, he declared that he wished to convince the 'doubting hearts of many' that the 'assaults of Satan are most certainly practiced'. He spoke of 'the fearful abounding at this time, in this country, of these detestable slaves of the Devil, the witches or enchanters', and accused those who had attempted to disprove their existence as being 'of that profession'.

The lengthy debate between 'Philomathes' (the doubter) and 'Epistemon' (the believer) begins with the latter – who is clearly a mouthpiece for James's own views – setting out his reasons for believing in the existence of witches. He claims that witchcraft is 'clearly proved by the Scriptures . . . and by daily experience and confessions'.[27] There follows a detailed discussion about the various magical arts, and how witchcraft differs from necromancy, astrology from astronomy, and so on. This proves (as it was no doubt intended to) the impressive array of works that James had consulted, which made him one of the leading authorities on the subject.

Although James tried to mask his maniacal obsession with witchcraft by constructing an apparently calm and rational debate between two intellectuals, the hatred and terror that he felt towards the 'instruments of Satan' becomes increasingly apparent as the book progresses. In particular, his description of witches' power verges on the hysterical, as he lays virtually all of the evils of the world at their door. Not only could they 'make men or women to love or hate [each] other', they could 'lay the sickness of one upon another . . . bewitch and take the life of men or women . . . raise storms and tempests in the air . . . make folks to become frantic or maniac . . . make spirits either to follow and trouble persons, or haunt certain houses . . . And likewise they can make some to be possessed with spirits, and so to become very demoniacs.'[28] His hysteria proved dangerously infectious. Anyone who read and was influenced by the book (and there were many) would henceforth look with suspicion upon their neighbours when even the slightest misfortune befell them. Moreover, the king made it plain that the only way to rid the world of such evils was to hunt down, arrest and execute the perpetrators. By offering their life as a 'sacrifice' to God, the authorities would lift the curse placed upon the witches' victims.

As well as to convince those who doubted the existence of witchcraft, the purpose of *Daemonologie* was to inspire those who persecuted witches in Scotland and England with new vigour and determination. James described witchcraft as 'high treason against God', which meant that all manner of horrors were justified in wringing confessions from them and meting out punishments.[29] Realising that some might be reluctant to prosecute witches for fear of recrimination, James cleverly argued that this would only happen if they were not severe enough in their punishments. 'If he [a magistrate] be slothful towards them, God is very able to make them instruments to waken and punish his sloth,' he claimed. 'But if he be the contrary, he according to the just law of God, and allowable law of all nations, will be diligent in examining and punishing them, God will not permit their Master [Satan] to trouble or hinder so good a work.'[30]

One of the most dangerous pieces of reasoning in the book concerned the condemnation of those accused of witchcraft. According to James, 'God will not permit that any innocent person shall be slandered with that vile defection.'[31] In short, an accusation was a sufficient proof of guilt. Moreover, he argued that even those who were suspected of being present at sabbats – which the magistrates and members of the jury knew to be imaginary – should be condemned and executed because God would not have allowed them to be accused of being present unless they really had been. Little wonder that under his direction the witch hunts gathered such terrifying momentum, and the atmosphere of fear and suspicion within local communities soon reached fever pitch.

Upon the subject of how a convicted witch should be punished, James was emphatic: 'They ought to be put to death according to the law of God, the civil and imperial law, and municipal law of all Christian nations.' His personal preference was for death 'by fire', but he admitted that the method of execution depended upon the laws and customs of each country. None should be spared, except children – for, James argued, 'they are not that capable of reason as to practice such things'. Otherwise, a prince or magistrate should not hesitate to exact the ultimate punishment. James warned that 'not to strike when God bids strike, and so severely punish in so odious a fault and treason against God . . . is not only unlawful, but doubtless . . . comparable to the sin of witchcraft itself'.[32]

By the time that *Daemonologie* was published, witchcraft had already been a statutory crime in Scotland for over 30 years. It was a capital offence to use spells and invoke the power of the Devil, who 'will attend them in some familiar shape of Rat, Cat, Toade, Birde, Cricket etc.'.[33] James now established a commission to hunt out witches in his kingdom. Before long, an ever-increasing number of women were being summarily arrested and tried, and almost half of them were executed – often on the flimsiest of evidence. His subjects were actively encouraged to inform upon those whom they believed to be witches. Inside every church was a wooden box or chest into which anyone could post a scroll of paper with the name of the person they suspected, together with a few cursory details of their crime. These chests were opened every 15 days by officials specially appointed to the task, and action would duly be taken against the persons named therein. The system was praised by the notorious French witch hunter Jean Bodin, who claimed that otherwise 'poor simple people fear witches more than they do God or all the magistrates, and do not dare to come forward as accusers, or as informers'.[34] But the image of a community too terrified to name the evildoers in their midst did not bear much relation to reality. The anonymity of the Scottish system tempted many men and women to make accusations not just against suspected witches, but against neighbours with whom they had quarrelled or any other members of the community against whom they bore a grudge. The potential for abuse was therefore considerable.

With such incentives to concoct a case against members of the community, it is little wonder that many thousands of innocent people were accused and tried as witches. Even George Gifford, one of the most influential witchcraft writers of the late sixteenth and early seventeenth centuries, admitted that the general climate of fear, suspicion and vengeance was likely to produce many false accusations: 'These things taking root in the hearts of the people, and so making them afraide of Witches, and raising up suspitions and rumors of sundry innocent persons, many giltles.'[35]

Although the witch hunts gathered a terrifying momentum from the mid sixteenth to the mid seventeenth centuries, they had their origins much earlier in history. The Bible contains many references to witches, sorcerers, necromancers and other practitioners of the dark arts. One of the most striking episodes is in the first Book of Samuel, which tells how, on the eve of a great battle, King Saul of Israel sought out a woman who was known to communicate with the dead. Rather than obtaining the hoped-for guidance from her, his

encounter merely invoked the wrath of Samuel's ghost, who berated
Saul for consulting with a witch.[36] There are many other illustrations
of witchcraft in the Old Testament. 'In the tyme of Moses it was
very ryfe in Egypt,' claimed one source. 'The Devill was exceeding
crafty from the beginning. Alwaies labouring to seduce and deceive
after the woorst manner.'[37] The punishments for witchcraft
prescribed by the Bible were of the severest kind. According to
Exodus: 'Thou shalt not suffer a witch to live.' Meanwhile, Leviticus
urged: 'A man or also a woman that hath a familiar spirit, or that
is a wizard, shall surely be put to death. They shall stone them with
stones; their blood shall be upon them.'[38]

    The beginning of serious official action against witches was signalled
by a papal bull issued in December 1484 by Pope Innocent VIII.[39] The
bull, which was widely printed and circulated, decried those who had
'abused themselves with devils, incubi and succubi, and by their incantations, spells, conjurations, and other accursed superstitions and
horrid charms, enormities and offences, destroy the offspring of
women and the young of cattle, blast and eradicate the fruits of the
earth, the grapes of the vine and the fruits of trees'. In order to
eradicate such evil, Innocent VIII gave great powers to the inquisitors
responsible for rooting out such 'heretical depravity', urging them to
employ 'the necessary, appropriate and legally ordained inquisition
into and punishment, correction, castigation and improvement of such
excesses, crimes and misdeeds.'[40]

    The significance of the bull was that it declared that witchcraft was
heresy. Until then, witches had been viewed merely as magicians who
could command special powers to do good or evil. But now they were
condemned as Devil-worshippers who had rejected God and the
Christian faith in order to serve Satan. This was a crime against the
church which must not be left unpunished. It was easy to justify this,
thanks to the various references within the Bible to the importance
of doing away with sorcery of all kinds. The fact that the Bible
appeared to sanction the persecution of witches gave enormous power
to those who sought to eradicate them from society. It also proved
one of the most enduring justifications for the witch hunts. Even as
late as the mid eighteenth century, the Methodist preacher John Wesley
claimed that 'giving up witchcraft is, in effect, giving up the Bible'.[41]

    Although there was ample justification for the bull, it is unlikely that Innocent VIII was acting out of a genuine concern for the evil that witches might inflict upon the population. It is no coincidence that the great witch hunt coincided with the Renaissance, a period in which the church's authority was severely threatened. By whipping up a climate of fear and suspicion, and setting itself up as the chief means of protection against the powers of darkness, the papacy and its representatives spied its best chance of survival.

Significant though it undoubtedly was, the papal bull only related to Germany. However, it was closely followed by the publication of *Malleus Maleficarum* (*The Hammer of Witches*), an enormously influential work which used the bull as its justification to spearhead a great witch hunt across the Continent. Written by two Dominican friars in Cologne, Heinrich Kramer and Jacob Sprenger, the book was reprinted 13 times by 1520, and a further 16 times by 1660. Echoing the words of the bull, the authors whipped up popular fear and suspicion of the 'very many persons' at large in communities across Europe who were intent upon committing 'unspeakable superstitions and acts of sorcery' against men, women, children, animals and crops. These malcontents would not rest until they had 'killed, suffocated and wiped out' anyone who was unfortunate enough to cross their path.[42]

The idea that witches did not work alone but were part of a wide-spread anti-Christian sect struck terror into the hearts of all those who read the book – just as the authors intended. At this time, there were many who doubted the existence of witches, a fact that Kramer and Sprenger confronted head on as 'obstinacy' and 'heresy'. Among them was the leading light of the Italian Renaissance, Leonardo da Vinci. Although he did not altogether rule out the possibility that witches existed, he claimed that only the uneducated really believed in them: 'Undoubtedly if this necromancy did exist, as is believed by shallow minds, there is nothing on earth that would have so much power either to harm or to benefit man.'[43] By creating the idea of a witchcraft conspiracy, the authors cleverly lent a new urgency to the eradication of the dark arts. It was one thing to have a troublesome old woman in the community whose curses, spells and potions might or might not be effective; quite another to imagine her as part of a mass conspiracy led by the Devil which aimed at the destruction of Christianity. The idea was quick to take hold. After all, did not the Bible teach that 'rebellion is as the sin of witchcraft'?[44]

As well as providing a comprehensive and extraordinarily detailed account of the various forms of witchcraft and sorcery, the *Malleus Maleficarum* also set out the methods that the ecclesiastical and secular authorities should employ to punish the crime. The exact wording that judges should use in beginning proceedings was stipulated, as well as the number of witnesses required, how their statements should be recorded, and the means by which the accused should be interrogated – including the methods of torture to be employed if they proved unwilling to confess.[45]

The *Malleus Maleficarum* was in effect a step-by-step guide to the successful hunting down and prosecution of witches, which made it easy – indeed, essential – for those in authority to reach a guilty verdict. Although it became enormously influential on the Continent and ran into many editions, its significance should not be overstated. It did not, on its own, spark the witch craze of the sixteenth and seventeenth centuries. Neither was its influence on the same scale in every country: it would be a full century before its potential was realised in England. There were also those (albeit small in number) who refused to adhere to its 'silly and godless absurdities'.[46] But from the late sixteenth century, it became an invaluable source of reference for all those involved in the arrest, interrogation and trial of witches. Its contents were devoured by the pamphleteers and polemicists of the late Elizabethan era, who used it as an inspiration for their own works.

Stoked by the *Malleus Maleficarum* and other incendiary publications aimed at whipping up public fear and suspicion, the witch craze rapidly took hold in Continental Europe. Between the early fifteenth and mid seventeenth centuries, as many as 100,000 people were tried as witches, of whom at least 40,000 were executed. Around half of these lived in German lands within the Holy Roman Empire, which formed the epicentre of the European craze. Mass executions of literally hundreds of witches took place in Germany and France, and one notorious trial in northern Spain lasted for five years and involved a staggering 7,000 cases.[47]

The 'Grand Tour' of Europe that Francis Manners had undertaken as a young man coincided with the very peak of the witch hunts. He had also visited the two countries where the persecutions were so intense that they served as a model for the rest of Europe to follow. In frequenting the courts of Germany and France, Manners could not fail to have encountered evidence of witch hunts, interrogations and trials. Given that witch-burnings were popular spectator sports, he may well have taken his place among the audience. The German witch hunt, in particular, was notorious for its brutality, as one contemporary observed: 'That Nation was so carried away with that darksome Idolatrous opinion of Witches power, that seldom came any thing cross, but some were accused to have occasioned it as Witches.'[48]

The effect of this experience upon Francis is not recorded in any of his letters or papers. Was he revolted by the barbarity of the torture and executions, or did they inspire in him a dangerous fervour to bring such women to justice in his own country? The horrific events that would unfold at Belvoir Castle suggest it was the latter. He certainly harboured a fascination with witchcraft from that time forwards. Among the archives at Belvoir Castle are papers from 1582 and 1591 relating to the trial of Richard Bate, a surgeon from Burton upon Trent, who was accused of making wax effigies of his mother-in-law and her children (except his own wife) so that he might cause them to perish and thus inherit their property.[49] That these should be preserved at Belvoir, despite their not being connected to the estate, perhaps reflects the family's interest in the subject.

James, too, was heavily influenced by Continental demonology, and his kingdom adopted strikingly similar means of interrogation and execution of suspected witches. The number of executions in Scotland is difficult to ascertain, but scholars have estimated that the figure was as high as 4,000 during the period from the mid sixteenth to the mid eighteenth century.[50] This was striking for such a small country, and was more than double the execution rate in England. Those women who were convicted met the hideous death of burning at the stake, apparently to prevent the resurrection of the body. The Earl of Mar was so traumatised by witnessing a mass burning in 1608 that he recounted it to the Privy Council in all its horrific detail. Describing the 'sic ane crewell maner' in which some of the women died, he told how others of them had broken free of the fire 'half brunt' before being captured and cast back into the flames to meet their deaths.[51]

A similarly harrowing tale was of the elderly and confused Janet Horne, the last witch to be executed in Scotland, who was seen warming herself by the fire that she was to be burned in, thinking it had been lit for her comfort.

Burning was also the common form of execution on the Continent, where many thousands of people went to the flames. However, with the exception of Spain and Italy, most witches were garrotted at the stake before the flames had consumed their bodies. Even this horrific death was considered insufficient punishment by the authors of the *Malleus Maleficarum*. They noted, rather regretfully, that most of those convicted were burned at the stake, rather than being 'thrown to wild beasts to be devoured by them'. The reason for this 'milder' punishment was that 'the majority of them are women'.[52]

Shocking though it is, the total number of executions does not convey the intensity of the witch hunt. In addition to the official trials and executions, there were possibly many thousands of other people who suffered a more random form of justice at the hands of neighbours through assaults, lynchings and summary executions. Neither does it account for the thousands more who endured the terror of living under suspicion of witchcraft or who were ostracised by their local community. Any woman – particularly if she was old and poor – must have felt like a hunted animal. Even children were not exempt. The records attest that a child as young as three was imprisoned on suspicion of witchcraft, and the youngest person to be executed was just eight years old. Witchcraft was therefore a much more common feature of life in communities across Europe than the formal statistics suggest.[53] The influential French magistrate Pierre De Lancre declared himself to be 'horrified' by 'the multiplicity and infinite number' of witches in the Pays de Labourd in southwest France. 'They estimate that there are thirty thousand souls in this country of Labourd,' he wrote, 'and that among all these people there are very few families who do not come into contact with witchcraft in one way or another.'[54]

Neither do the official figures take account of the scores of people who were accused, driven into exile, given lesser penalties or who died in prison.[55] Even those who were acquitted were often blighted for life by their experience – either physically or psychologically. As well as suffering the terror of interrogation and torture, they were all too often treated as social pariahs for ever afterwards.

> If therefore a witch has been convicted as a witch, she will always be known as a witch, and consequently presumed guilty of all the impieties that witches are well known for. And even if the sentence is not carried out, the accusation, her reputation and the widespread rumour will be enough to establish a strong presumption and the infamy of the deed. For if the law requires that a woman accused of wantonness but released remain with a bad record for the rest of her life, how much more ought one to regard than a woman ill-famed and dishonoured who has the reputation of being a witch? For it is a most powerful presumption that when a woman is reputed to be a witch, she is one.[56]

There are numerous examples of women whose lives were blighted by such dangerously skewed logic. A Hertfordshire woman named Jane Wenham was described as having 'become so odious to all her neighbours as to be deny'd in all probability the common necessaries of life . . . The more firmly her neighbours believed her to be a witch . . . the worse they would use her.'[57] When 'Goodwife Gilnot' of Barham in Kent was acquitted in 1641, she returned to a miserable existence in her local community, vilified by her neighbours and deprived of her livelihood. 'If she be esteemed such a kind of creature everybody will be afraid of her,' remarked an unsympathetic contemporary, 'and nobody set her a-work, inasmuch as truly she will be utterly undone.' Another accused witch, Sarah Liffen of Great Yarmouth, was said to have died alone and miserable, being 'so forlorn and wretched a person as she labour'd under the imputation of being a witch, and the youth and other rude folks in the town . . . did often insult and affront her as she walk'd, and at her own house'. Others suffered worse torments. In 1612, Mary Sutton was beaten with a cudgel 'till she was scarce able to stir'.[58] Life was little better for the surviving relatives of a convicted or reputed witch. When a young couple in Lorraine were both accused of witchcraft, it emerged that they had decided to marry after attending the execution of their respective parents, 'so that they would have nothing to reproach one another with'.[59]

The onset of the Protestant Reformation in the early sixteenth

century, and the Counter- (or Catholic) Reformation which followed,
provided a dangerous new impetus to the witch hunts. Both movements sparked an increased awareness of the presence of the Devil
in the world, and a determination to wage war against him. Despite
being directly opposed on matters of doctrine, the leaders of the two
reformations were equally vociferous on the need to eradicate the
evils of witchcraft. Martin Luther, who spearheaded the Protestant
Reformation, declared that all witches were the whores of the Devil
and should be burned. Another Protestant reformer, John Calvin,
quoted Exodus in insisting that witches 'must be slain'.[60] As active
preachers who regularly addressed large crowds of people, men such
as these were enormously influential in whipping up popular fear and
suspicion.

The gulf between the saved and the damned seemed to be growing
ever greater. In a society increasingly preoccupied by attaining salva-
tion through conforming to strict standards of piety and moral behaviour, the pursuit of individuals who were believed to be intrinsically
evil was given a new urgency. Helping to hunt down and condemn
suspected witches relieved people's anxiety about their own destiny,
and gave them confidence in their own moral sanctity and ultimate
salvation. The events that were soon to be played out at Belvoir Castle
would prove just how dangerously true this was.

James's accession to the throne of England provided a new outlet for
his witch hunting fervour. From the moment that he was proclaimed
king, anticipation among his new subjects at the prospect of meeting
'the bright starre of the North' reached fever pitch.[61] 'Manie have
beene the mad caps rejoicinge at oure new Kynges cominge,' observed
the celebrated courtier and gossip Sir John Harington.[62] As soon as
James arrived in his new kingdom, he was subject to intense scrutiny.
Some praised his ready good nature and sharp intellect. Roger
Wilbraham, a London lawyer, enthused: 'The King is of the sharpest
wit and invention, ready and pithy speech, an exceeding good memory;
of the sweetest, pleasantest and best nature that ever I knew.' The
Venetian ambassador, Scaramelli, was more circumspect. Marvelling
at how James's councillors stood about him 'almost in an attitude of
adoration', he could not resist adding that 'from his dress he would
have been taken for the meanest of courtiers'. Others agreed that, in

sharp contrast to the late queen, James lacked 'great majesty' and 'solemnities'.[63] Although 'crafty and cunning in petty things', he lacked astuteness in 'weighty affairs', which led one contemporary to coin the famous description of him as 'the wisest foole in Christendome'.[64]

After half a century of being under the authority of queens, the people greeted the accession of a king with enthusiasm in many quarters, but James hardly presented a very manly figure. Of little above average height, he had remarkably soft white skin, and his beard was sparse. His large eyes held a look of vacant intensity, which often deepened into suspicion or apprehension. One observer remarked that his eyes were 'ever rowling after any stranger came into his presence, in so much, as many for shame have left the roome, as being out of countenance'.[65] At the same time, his tongue seemed too large for his mouth, which made his already broad Scottish accent even harder to understand, and his act of drinking very ungraceful. '[It] made him drinke very uncomely, as if eating his drinke, which came out into the cup of each side his mouth,' observed one contemporary with some distaste.[66] Physically weak and uncoordinated, 'his walke was ever circular, his fingers ever in that walke fidling about his codpiece'.[67] A recent commentator has described James as 'the dribbling, bulbous-eyed, bandy-legged king'.[68] Upon his arrival at the court in London, he already had his arm in a sling thanks to falling from his horse. He also complained of having been 'very ill' with a heavy cold ever since coming to England, and he was still grumbling about it almost two years later.[69] Although the king appeared somewhat corpulent, this was because he wore a heavily quilted doublet for protection against assassins. 'Naturally of a timerous disposition', he had long cherished an intense fear of bared weapons and had once dissolved in panic when his own queen had come towards him with a sword in her hand, ready for a ceremony of knighting.[70]

James's 'unmanly' nature extended to his private life. Although he had fathered five children by Anne of Denmark, their marriage was one of politics, not passion. They lived separate lives at court, and it was noted that they did not 'converse' together.[71] 'He was ever best, when furthest from the Queen,' remarked Sir Anthony Weldon, one of the earliest historians of James's reign, who concluded that this was the reason for James's constant 'removes' from court.[72] The king had long been rumoured to be a closet homosexual, and throughout his reign – both in Scotland and in England – he surrounded himself with a succession of beautiful young men. Each of these was rapidly promoted to an exalted position at court, and then just as rapidly dropped when a younger, more attractive man came along. In the very public world of the court, nothing remained a secret for long, and the king's sexuality was soon whispered about in the capital and beyond. One of his subjects recorded in his diary a conversation he had had with a friend: 'Of things I discoursed with him that were secret as of the sin of sodomy, how frequent it was in this wicked city', and added: 'we had probable cause to fear, a sin in the prince [James] as well as the people'.[73] Sodomy was at that time a capital felony, but the king was said to have personally intervened to save a Frenchman who was arrested for the crime from the usual punishment of death. That the celebrated Virgin Queen should be succeeded by a sexual deviant was too much for some of James's subjects to bear.

The new king took full advantage of the other diversions that the court had to offer. Indeed, so fond was he of revelry, masques, feasting and other such pastimes that he soon began to neglect the business of government. Upon his accession, there had been high hopes that he would prove an able and decisive ruler, and no matter how dazzlingly effective Elizabeth had shown herself to be in matters of state, there was still a feeling of relief among many councillors that a man had returned to the helm at last. 'Our virtuous King makes our hopes to swell,' declared Thomas Wilson, a protégé of Robert Cecil, 'his actions suitable to the time and his natural disposition.' But within a few short weeks, a disappointed Wilson was forced to admit: 'Sometimes he comes to Council, but most time he spends in fields and parks and chases, chasing away idleness by violent exercise and early rising, wherein the sun seldom prevents him.' The waspish Scaramelli observed with relish how quickly things had unravelled: 'The King, in spite of all the heroic virtues ascribed to him when he left Scotland and inculcated by him in his books, seems to have sunk into a lethargy of pleasures, and will not take heed of matters of state. He remits everything to the Council, and spends his time in the house alone, or in the country at the chase.'[74] This was no bias on the part of a foreign ambassador, for there were plenty of Englishmen who agreed. Among them was John Chamberlain, a well-connected

London gentleman who made it his business to find out the latest gossip from court and report it to his friends overseas. He confided to his friend Ralph Winwood: 'The King . . . finds such felicity in that hunting life, that he hath written to the Councill that it is the only means to maintaine his health, which being the health and welfare of us all, he desires them to take the charge and burden of affairs, and foresee that he be not interrupted or troubled with too much business.'[75]

But there was one matter of state in which James took a keen and active interest. According to one source, he 'carried his hatred of witches with him into England, and with his reign in the latter country began the darkest period of the history of witchcraft in the southern parts of our island'.[76]

The English were a good deal more ambivalent than their northern neighbours, and indeed the rest of Europe, on the subject of witchcraft. Although there had been periods of intense witch hunting during Elizabeth's reign, the laws and punishments were less severe. The earliest known reference to witchcraft in civil law was in the time of King Wihtraed (690–731). Anyone found guilty of making 'an offering to devils' would simply be fined. Religious leaders, meanwhile, recommended fasting for anyone found guilty of killing someone through witchcraft. The law did become progressively harsher towards suspected witches, however, and by the reign of King Ethelred in the late tenth century, it was decreed that they 'be driven out of this country' or else 'totally perish'.[77]

For several centuries afterwards, witches were classed as heathens or heretics and dealt with by the ecclesiastical courts. By the fourteenth century, witchcraft had gained enough notoriety to be referenced by Chaucer in the Friar's Tale. From that time onwards, most English monarchs found themselves subject to what have been termed 'treason-cum-sorcery' plots. Alice Perrers, the avaricious mistress of Edward III, was accused of winning the king's favour by 'wicked enchantments'. In 1406, Henry V wrote to the Bishop of Lincoln expressing anxiety about the many sorcerers in his diocese, 'who perpetrate daily many horrible and detestable crimes to the damage of the people and scandal of the church, and directing him to seek them out, examine them, and detain them until they repent'.[78]

But it was during the reign of his son, Henry VI, that witchcraft

really gained notoriety, when Margery Jourdemayne, the so-called
Witch of Eye, was found guilty of conspiring with others to bring
about the king's death through sorcery. She was burned at the stake
at Smithfield, and later immortalised by Shakespeare.[79] One of her
co-conspirators, Eleanor, Duchess of Gloucester, was found guilty of
using witchcraft to supplant the king with her ambitious and powerful
husband. She escaped death, but after performing a public penance
spent the rest of her days as a prisoner.

Eleanor's sister-in-law, Jacquetta, was said to have used witchcraft
to ensnare Edward IV into secretly marrying her widowed daughter,
Elizabeth Woodville. The marriage caused a scandal because Elizabeth
was a commoner, and her enemies claimed that as a result England
suffered 'many murders, extortions and oppressions'.[80] Edward's
brother, Richard, Duke of Gloucester, used the rumour to justify
declaring Edward's sons illegitimate and thus open the way for his
seizure of the throne in 1483.

Witchcraft cases became a matter for secular jurisdiction with the
passing of the first and most stringent English witchcraft statute by
Henry VIII in 1542, although church courts continued to try cunning
folk, sorcerers and fortune-tellers. The 1542 Act had possibly been
prompted by another treasonous plot involving sorcery. There is no
evidence that it was ever enforced, and it was repealed just five years
later at the beginning of Edward VI's reign.

A new statute 'agaynst Conjuracions Inchantments and Witche-
craftes' was passed in 1563. This was another time of uncertainty for
the reigning monarch. Elizabeth I had been on the throne for just five
years but was already surrounded by plots to supplant her. Concern
had also recently been expressed by John Jewel, Bishop of Salisbury,
about the 'witches and sorcerers' who, he said, had 'marvellously
increased within this your grace's realm'. He warned: 'These eyes
have seen most evident and manifest marks of their wickedness. Your
grace's subjects pine away even unto the death, their colour fadeth,
their flesh rotteth, their senses are bereft.'[81] Just over a year later,
Edmund Grindal, Bishop of London, urged the Privy Council to take
action against a priest who, as well as being a suspected papist, was
much addicted to 'magic and conjuration'. Grindal pointed out that
the law made inadequate provisions to deal with such offenders.[82]

The 1563 Act prescribed the death penalty for 'Invocacon of evill and wicked Spirites, to or for any Intent or Purpose', and for using 'Witchecrafte Enchantment Charme or Sorcerie, whereby any p[er] son shall happen to bee killed or destroyed'.[83] Any accomplices of the main perpetrator were also to 'suffer pains of death as a felon or felons'. The least severe punishment for witchcraft was a year's imprisonment, but the conditions in many gaols were so dire that this often equated to a death sentence.

The first major English witch trial took place in 1566, at Chelmsford in Essex, and resulted in the first recorded hanging for this crime. A rush of similar trials followed, reaching their peak in the mid to late sixteenth century, which coincided with the beginning of the second and most severe period of continental persecutions. The rising 'witch panic' was accentuated by the discovery in 1578 of a plot to kill the queen and two of her advisers by maleficent magic. A full-scale investigation was launched by the Privy Council when three wax figures were found hidden in a dunghill, one of them marked with the name 'Elizabeth' on its forehead. The panic felt at the heart of government rapidly filtered down to the rest of society. Belief in witches had become so prevalent that one contemporary remarked with some alarm: 'There is scarse any towne or village in all this shire, but there is one or two witches at the least in it.'[84] This may not have been an exaggeration. Compared to other crimes, it was clear that cases of witchcraft increased significantly during the period. They did so at a steady rate, rather than in a series of periodic scares. A study of three Essex villages in the late sixteenth century shows that they were less common than theft, assault, sexual misdemeanours and failing to attend church, but more frequent than murder, drunkenness, marital disputes, quarrelling, breaking the Sabbath and misbehaviour on church premises.[85] In total, witchcraft cases represented 13 per cent of all criminal business, but more than half the villages in this county were involved in the prosecution of witches at one time or another.

The method of execution was less barbaric in England than in Scotland and on the Continent. Only if witchcraft was bound up with crimes of heresy, poisoning, treason or petty treason (such as if a woman murdered her husband) would the perpetrator suffer death by burning – or, an equally hideous prospect, by 'boylynge'.[86] Instead, as in other cases of felony, the gallows provided the means of execution, as one contemporary pamphleteer observed: 'They are beyond God's grace and the best thing to do with them is hang them.'[87] Any member of the aristocracy found guilty of the crime might be beheaded. The seventeenth-century commentator William Dugdale noted that this means of execution was 'very antient' as a punishment for felony in England.[88] Others decried the fact that witches did not suffer a crueller death. The notorious witch hunting magistrate Brian Darcy lamented that 'An ordinary felon . . . is throttled: a sorcerer, a witch . . . defying the Lord God to his face . . . is [also] stifled.' He openly condemned this 'inequality of justice' and declared that a convicted witch deserved a death that was 'much the more horrible'.[89]

By the end of Elizabeth's reign, the number of witchcraft trials and executions had declined significantly. There was also a growing scepticism about the existence of witches. Even as early as 1578, a Norwich physician named Dr Browne was accused of 'spreading a misliking of the laws by saying there are no witches'.[90] The most outspoken sceptic, though, was Reginald Scot, who poured scorn upon the existence of witches in his detailed and lengthy tract, The Discoverie of Witchcraft. He lamented that the 'fables of Witchcraft have taken so fast hold and deepe root in the heart of man', and that 'the world is now so bewitched and over-run with this fond error, that even where a man shuld seeke comfort and counsell, there shall hee be sent (in case of necessitie) from God to the divell; and from the Physician, to the coosening witch'.[91] Scot courted such notoriety that King James himself denounced his 'damnable opinions' and ordered that all copies of his book be burned.[92] The English philosopher Thomas Hobbes was similarly sceptical about witchcraft, but he nevertheless believed that the guilty should be punished: 'As for witches, I think not that their witchcraft has any real power. Even so, they are justly punished for falsely believing that they can do such mischief, joined with their purpose to do it if they can, their trade being nearer to a new religion than craft or science.'[93]

Meanwhile, the author and scholar Robert Burton, whose most celebrated work was published two years after the Flower women gained notoriety, agreed that old age and melancholy played tricks on the minds of those women who were suspected of witchcraft.

All those extraordinary powers which old witches were supposed to exercise, and pretended to possess; such as bewitching cattle to death, riding in the air upon a coulstaffe, flying out of the chimney top, transforming themselves into the various shapes of cats and other animals, transporting their bodies, suddenly and secretly, from place to place . . . and other 'supernatural solicitings' of the like kind, are all ascribed to the corrupted fancy, which is engendered by that morbid, atrabilious melancholy matter, attendant upon moping misery and rheumed age.[94]

Even on the Continent, where the witch hunts were still in full swing, there were some dissenting voices. The Dutch physician Johann Weyer was one of the first to publish a treatise against the existence of witchcraft. *De Praestigiis Daemonum* (*On the Tricks of Devils*) first appeared in 1563, and claimed that witches were really just confused old women, suffering from various mental and physical disorders. Likewise, that the sickness and death they were believed to inflict were the result of natural causes. Referring to witchcraft as a 'vicious seed' and 'the old snake [which] stirs the fire', and to those who believed in it as 'dull-witted' and 'absurd', Weyer urged: 'Daily experience teaches us what cursed apostasy, what friendship with the wicked one, what hatred and strife among fellow creatures, what dissension in city and in country, what numerous murders of innocent people through the devil's wretched aid, such belief in the power of witches brings forth.' He went on to assert that a witch's power existed only in her imagination. 'Witches can harm no one through the most malicious will or the ugliest exorcism . . . their imagination – inflamed by the demons in a way not understandable to us – and the torture of melancholy makes them only fancy that they have caused all sorts of evil.' He ended with a plea to those who dispensed justice not to 'impose heavy penalties on perplexed, poor old women' but to demand proper evidence.[95]

All of this was anathema to James. He was determined to drown out every dissenting voice within his new kingdom. It is no coincidence that *Daemonologie* was reprinted twice during the year of his accession.

This prompted a rash of similar pamphlets aimed at whipping up popular fear of witches. Heartily though James approved of these publications, he was determined to do more in his crusade against witches. In his view, English law was by no means strict enough in prosecuting the crime. Barely a year after his accession, he therefore ordered that the Elizabethan statute on witchcraft be replaced by a much harsher version. Until now, those who practised witchcraft were severely punished only if they were found to have committed murder or other injuries through their devilish arts. In short, it was the crimes caused by witchcraft, not the practice itself, that had been the object of concern. James, however, wanted the practice of any form of magic to be severely punished, regardless of whether it had caused harm to others. His new statute made hanging mandatory for a first offence of witchcraft, even if the accused had not committed murder. And if the accused was found to have the Devil's mark on their body, this too was enough to condemn them to death. The Act stipulated: 'If any person or persons . . . shall use practise or exercise any invocation or conjuration of any evil or wicked spirit, or shall consult, covenant with, entertain, employ, feed, or reward any evil and wicked spirit to or for any intent or purpose . . . [they] shall suffer pains of death.'[96] James's determination to stamp out witchcraft in all forms was brutally apparent: 'All manner of practise, use or exercise of Witchcraft, Encantement, Charme or Sorcerie should be from hencefoorth utterly avoyded, abolished, and taken away.'[97]

The all-encompassing nature of the 1604 Act meant that the vast majority of witchcraft cases were now dealt with by secular rather than ecclesiastical courts. This in turn made the prospect of severe punishment far stronger. Many of those previously found guilty of witchcraft in the church courts had been ordered to do public penance in front of the other villagers. This usually took place on a Sunday, and the accused would be made to wear a white sheet, carry a white wand and 'penitentlie confesse that she is hartelie sorrie for that she hath geven vehement suspicion of wichecrafte and wicherie'.[98] Now, a suspect faced the grim choice of a year's imprisonment or death. 'His Majesty found a defect in the statutes made before his time, by which none died for Witchcraft but they only who by that means killed, so that such were executed rather as murderers than as Witches,' reported Edward Fairfax, who, believing his daughters to be victims of witchcraft, was a staunch supporter of the harsher regime. 'But his Highness made a new law against the sin itself, which in itself is so abominable, and therein showed his zeal for the honour of God.'[99]

A testament to how eager James's new subjects were to curry favour with him by echoing his hatred of witches came the same year that the new Act was passed. Christopher Marlowe's dark morality play, *The Tragicall History of the Life and Death of Doctor Faustus*, had first been performed in around 1588, five years before the playwright's death. But it was not until 1604 that it was published – the very year that James I began his crusade against witchcraft in England. This was no coincidence: the play was one of the most shocking portrayals of witchcraft ever to be performed on stage. Its central character makes a pact with Lucifer, whereby the latter promises Dr Faustus unlimited knowledge and power for a number of years, at the end of which period Faustus will give his soul to his satanic master. The play ends with a devil coming to claim the doctor's soul and drag him off to hell. Audiences were so aghast at the horrors that unfolded before them that some were said to have been driven mad by it, and on occasion real devils were reported to have appeared on stage, 'to the great amazement of both the actors and spectators'. As well as terrifying people into avoiding any dabbling with necromancy, the play also intensified their hatred and fear of witches.

Other playwrights were quick to follow suit. Ben Jonson devised a number of masques for the entertainment of the king and his court. The 'antimasque' to his *Masque of Queens* included the presentation of a group of witches who represented 'the opposites to good fame'. The playwright had clearly done a great deal of research, for he referenced a range of current and classical demonological works as his sources. He set out detailed instructions for the staging of the antimasque, describing the entering on stage of 11 witches 'some with rats on their head; some on their shoulders; others with ointment pots at their girdles; all with spinales, timbrels, rattles, or other venefi-call instruments, making a confused noyse, with strange gestures'. One of their number was 'naked arm'd, bare-footed, her frock tuck'd, her hayre knotted, and folded with vipers; in her hand a torch made of a dead man's arm, lighted; girded with a snake'.[100]

Jonson's description of the performance of the play at Whitehall in February 1609 gives a sense of the impact that it must have had upon the king, queen and assembled courtiers.

> His Majesty, then, being set, and the whole company in full expectation, the part of the scene which first presented itself was an ugly Hell; which, flaming beneath, smoked unto the top of the roof . . . these Witches, with a kind of hollow and infernal music, came forth from thence . . . I prescribed them their properties of vipers, snakes, bones, herbs, roots, and other ensigns of their magic, out of authority of ancient and late Writers . . . These eleven Witches beginning to dance, (which is an usual ceremony at their convents or meetings, where sometimes also they are vizarded and masked), on the sudden one of them missed their Chief, and interrupted the rest with this Speech . . .

> > The weather is fair, the wind is good,
> > Up, Dame, on your horse of wood;
> > Or else tuck up your gray frock,
> > And saddle your goat, or your green cock.[101]

But the most famous of all the literary works inspired by witchcraft, winning widespread acclaim in its day and ever since, was Shakespeare's *Macbeth*. It is deliberately short in length, as James was known to have little patience for sitting through long plays; it is also significant that the occasion of its inaugural performance was a visit by Queen Anne's brother, the King of Denmark, in 1606, given that it was James's voyage to his wife's native land that had prompted his obsession with witchcraft. Shakespeare wove in several references to this voyage in the play, such as when the First Witch claims that she set sail in a sieve, just as one of the North Berwick witches was accused of doing. The line 'Though his bark cannot be lost, / Yet it shall be tempest-tossed' almost certainly alluded to James's near-death experience.

All the leaders of the English judiciary would have been present at this important state occasion, and this was exactly the sort of play that would inspire them with the same witch hunting fervour as their royal master. The drama centred around Macbeth and Lady Macbeth, who murdered King Duncan to seize the throne of Scotland after three witches prophesied Macbeth's succession. Whether the witches thus caused the overthrow of the natural succession, or merely brought out Macbeth's inherent evil, was left to the audience's imagination. Either way, the play both confirmed and introduced new elements to the stereotypical view of a witch, with her spells and familiars. It also spawned two of the most quoted lines in English literary history:

> Double, double, toil and trouble;
> Fire burn, and cauldron bubble.[102]

Macbeth instilled fear among those watching that witchcraft was not just a satanic confederacy, but a conspiracy against the state. The latter notion was all too readily accepted in England at this time because the play was performed just a few short months after one of the most notorious conspiracies in history.

Even though Catholicism had become increasingly sidelined in the religious and political life of England, many of those who on the surface conformed to the new Anglican faith held tight to the old traditions, ceremonies and relics of their Catholic past. Thus it was noted that many still had their 'beades closely handeled' in church, and were in the habit of crossing themselves 'in all their actions'.[103] If Elizabeth I had turned a blind eye to such things, James insisted upon a much stricter observance of the Protestant faith. When it became clear that the new king had no intention of following his predecessor's policy of toleration, Robert Catesby and his co-conspirators hatched a plan to blow up the House of Lords during the state opening of Parliament on 5 November 1605. This was intended to be the prelude to a popular revolt in the Midlands, during which James's nine-year-old daughter, Elizabeth, would be installed as the Catholic head of state. It was only thanks to an anonymous letter to the authorities, received in late October, that the king and his Protestant regime were not wiped out. The House of Lords was searched at around midnight on 4 November, just hours before the plot was due to be executed, and Guy Fawkes was discovered with 36 barrels of gunpowder – more than enough to reduce the entire building to rubble.

'The meanes how to have compassed so great an acte, was not to be performed by strength of men, or outward violence, but by a secret conveyance of a great quantitie of gunpowder in a vault under the Upper House of Parliament,' wrote a shocked Earl of Salisbury, 'and soe to have blowne up all at a clapp, if God out of His mercie and just revenge against so great an abomination had not destined it to be discovered, though very miraculously, even some twelve hours before the matter should have been put in execution.'[104] Sir Edward Hoby was similarly aghast at the audacity of a plot that had so nearly succeeded. 'The plot was to have blown up the King at such time as he should have been set on his Royal Throne, accompanied with all his Children, Nobility, and Commoners, and assisted with all Bishops, Judges, and Doctors,' he told the English ambassador in Brussels, 'at one instant and blast to have ruin'd the whole State and Kingdom of England.'[105] All the conspirators were eventually rounded up, and those who were not killed in their attempt to flee met the traitor's death and were hanged, drawn and quartered.

Although it had been thwarted, the Gunpowder Plot had seriously destabilised the Jacobean regime, ushering in a period of intense paranoia and suspicion, particularly towards Catholics. Parliament responded by passing the 'Act for the better discovery of Popish Recusants', whereby Catholics became liable to imprisonment and forfeiture of property for refusing an oath of allegiance. The repercussions of the plot were also stipulated in a handbook for Justices of the Peace published in 1618, which urged that 'Popish Recusants (especially such as have bin reconciled to the Pope, or drawne to the Popish Religion, since the Gunpowder Treason, for these are by his Maiestie accounted most dangerous)' should be dealt with strictly according to the statute book.[106] In practice, though, central government did little, beyond a few recusancy fines, to bring Catholics under state control.

Since the link between Catholic or 'papist' practices and witchcraft had always been strong, the king's war on witches was given a fresh impetus in the wake of the Gunpowder Plot. 'The late divilish conspiracy did much disturb this part,' reported Sir John Harington. 'We know of some evil-minded catholics in the west, whom the prince of darkness hath in alliance; God ward them from such evil, or seeking it to others. Ancient history doth shew the heart of man in divers forms: we read of states overthrown by craft and subtilty.' Before long, a widespread Catholic conspiracy was feared. 'These designs were not formed by a few: the whole legion of catholics were consulted; the priests were to pacify their consciences, and the pope confirm a general absolution for this glorious deed, so honourable to God and his holy religion. His Majesty doth much meditate on this marvellous escape, and blesses God for delivering his family, and saving his kingdom, from the tryumphs of Satan.'[107]

Tensions remained high in the months that followed. In March 1606, it was rumoured that James had been murdered on a hunting trip. 'The news spread to the city and the uproar was amazing,' reported the Venetian ambassador. 'Everyone flew to arms, the shops were shut, and cries began to be heard against Papists, foreigners and Spaniards.'[108] Even seven years later, the atmosphere was still highly charged. At the notorious Pendle witch trial, it was alleged that the accused had hatched their own gunpowder plot to blow up Lancaster Castle. This was almost certainly a tale invented by the examining magistrates to make an example of their prisoners and heighten public interest. It is significant that the author of the trial pamphlet, Thomas Potts, a clerk of the Lancashire Assizes, dedicated it to Thomas Knyvett (uncle of Francis Manners's first wife) – the man credited with arresting Guy Fawkes and thus saving the life of the king.

The theme of a satanic conspiracy was taken up by other pamphlet-eers, notably William Perkins. 'The most notorious traytor and rebell that can be, is the witch,' he opined. 'For shee renounceth God himselfe, the king of kings, shee leaves the societie of his church and people, shee bindeth herself in league with the devil.'[109] Meanwhile, Thomas Cooper's extensive treatise of 1617 drew a direct correlation between the Gunpowder Plot and the dark arts: 'Hath not the Lord enabled mee to discover the practice of Antichrist in that hellish plot of the Gunpowder-treason?'[110]

This same belief in the existence of a witchcraft conspiracy accounted for the rapid spread of the witch hunts across Europe. An accused witch would be asked to name her co-conspirators, and under torture would do so. Alonso de Salazar Frías, one of the judges in the notorious mass trial which began in 1609 in Navarre, northern Spain, was aghast at how quickly panic could spread once the word 'witch' had been whispered in a community: 'There were neither witches nor bewitched in a village until they were talked about and written about.'[111]

Between 1610 and 1612, there was a sudden prevalence of accusa-tions of sorcery across most of the Continent. The celebrated eighteenth-century philosopher Voltaire estimated that there were as many as 100,000 victims of the witch craze. Only the lands of the Orthodox church in the east and the Dutch republic in the west offered any sanctuary. The situation was mirrored in England, where one of the leading intellectuals of the day, William Perkins, warned his readers in 1608 that 'Witchcraft is a rife and common sinne in these our daies, and very many are intangled with it.' His contemporary, Chief Justice Anderson, agreed – 'They abound in all places' – and cautioned that without swift preventative action they would 'in short time overrun the whole land'.[112]

By the time James visited Belvoir Castle in August 1612, the witch craze had reached fever pitch in both England and Europe. The king was accompanied by his son and heir, Prince Henry. It would be one of the prince's last public appearances, for he died of typhoid three months later. Cultured and charismatic, Henry was adored by the English people, and there was widespread mourning when news of his death was announced. A contemporary had noted disapprovingly that, given Henry's poor health, 'the greatnesse of the journey' and 'the extreme and wonderfull heat of the season', he ought to have been excused the long trip to Belvoir.[113] But the castle had become a favoured retreat and 'principal feature' of the king's progresses around his kingdom, and he and his son were rewarded with 'verie honourable Entertainment' for several days by the Earl of Rutland.[114]

The visit in 1612 was part of the king's traditional summer progress. This annual event constituted an extraordinarily complex operation. The itinerary would be published in late spring, and the nobility of the land would find out who would have the dubious (and often cripplingly expensive) honour of hosting the king and his court. James and his sprawling entourage of councillors, courtiers, attendants and servants afforded an impressive – if slow-moving – spectacle as they made their way through the shires of England. The king and his courtiers would travel on horseback, flanked by liveried footmen. Next came the ladies of the court seated in large square coaches, bumping and jolting along the roads which in dry weather were little better than hardened, cracked mud tracks – and were considerably worse after a wet spell. Behind the ladies was a vast train of between 400 and 600 carts, loaded with baggage, tents and other paraphernalia considered essential for the visits. Hundreds of servants would either ride on top of these or walk alongside. This unwieldy, cumbersome cavalcade wound its way slowly along lanes and tracks, pausing for dinner at inns and country houses, and covering no more than 12 miles a day.

The agonisingly slow pace of the progresses accounts for the fact that they never reached the more remote parts of the kingdom. Rather, they traditionally focused upon the southern circuit, encompassing Surrey, Hampshire and Wiltshire, or a Midlands circuit including Bedfordshire, Northamptonshire, Leicestershire and Nottinghamshire. James preferred the latter circuit, and Belvoir was always the highlight of it. He expected to be entertained royally and made his displeasure felt if the hospitality was in any way lacking. In a rather half-hearted gesture to reduce the financial burden on his hosts, he limited the number of his retinue, although it was still considerable. Those houses, like Belvoir, which the king particularly favoured could face ruin as a result of his frequent visits. When Bishop Lancelot Andrewes of Winchester entertained the royal party in magnificent style at Farnham Castle in 1620, the bill exceeded £2,400, which is equivalent to around £230,000 today. Little wonder that some hosts occasionally begged to be spared a visit.

Despite the heavy burden on his estate, the Earl of Rutland was careful to show no sign of reluctance to welcome James and his court. The king evidently enjoyed the Rutlands' famed hospitality in 1612, because he made five more visits during the years that followed. The household accounts give a sense of the magnificence – and cost – of these visits. As well as orders for vast quantities of venison, ox, veal, lamb, capon, salmon and wine with which to feed the king and his court, there are also payments for silver plate and gilt cups, gold-embroidered cloth, the stabling of horses and the 'mending of heighe ways against the Kinge's Majestie's coming to hunt'.[115] The king was fond of hunting, and the Vale of Belvoir provided some of the best hunting grounds in the country.

James's visits to Belvoir were about politics as much as pleasure, however. The conversations over dinner or during the chase would have been dominated by state affairs. As a fierce advocate of the Protestant faith, James could not abide what he scathingly referred to as the 'rotten religion' of the papists.[116] Yet he could not have failed to be aware of Francis Manners's devout Catholicism. The earl and countess employed a renowned Catholic, Richard Broughton, as their private chaplain. In a book dedicated to his patrons, Broughton described them as 'constant supporters of holy Catholike Religion'.[117] Francis had also amassed a significant collection of works at Belvoir by professors of that religion.[118] Some astonishment had been expressed by contemporaries when the earl had been honoured with the Garter in 1616, given that Roman Catholics were barred from public office.[119] Moreover, as a member of the House of Lords, a privy councillor and a lord lieutenant of Lincolnshire, he had been obliged to take the Protestant oath of allegiance to the Crown.

That the king turned a blind eye to the earl and countess's Catholicism is an indication of the high favour in which they stood. Francis also suppressed his more extreme papist beliefs in the interests of political gain. However, as his career at court developed, he increasingly clashed with other members of the Council. John Chamberlain, who had a detailed knowledge of court events, was dismayed by how much favour the king showed Rutland, 'in regard that the wife of the former [Cecilia] is an open and knowne recusant, and he is saide to have many daungerous persons about him'.[120] In an age dominated by suspicion and fear, the Catholic faith became synonymous with plots and conspiracies. Francis and Cecilia Manners were thus playing a dangerous game in expressing their faith so openly and – apparently – surrounding themselves with a group of like-minded people.

Despite the difference in their religious beliefs, James and Francis enjoyed a great deal of common ground in other areas – none more so than the need to obliterate the evils of witchcraft. In 1611, the Authorised Version of the Bible, with its condemnation of witches, was republished under the king's watchful eye and distributed throughout the kingdom. Then, in the summer of 1612 – less than two weeks after James's visit to Belvoir – there occurred one of the most notorious witch trials in history.

The household at Belvoir would have been well aware of this trial, for the 12 suspects had been arrested in early 1612, and their case had attracted a great deal of attention. They hailed from the area around Pendle Hill in Lancashire, and were charged with the murders of 10 people by witchcraft. Among them were three generations of the same family. The first trial, at which two of the accused were convicted, was held at York on 27 July, and the rest were brought before the Lancaster Assizes on 18 August. In total, 10 were found guilty and hanged, one was found not guilty and another died in prison. The account of the case, written by Thomas Potts, was one of the most popular works of the day and helped secure the Pendle Witches' place in history. The Earl of Rutland could not have guessed that he would soon find himself at the centre of an even more notorious trial.

4

'Witches three'

Among the beneficiaries of the Earl and Countess of Rutland's famed generosity were Joan Flower and her two daughters, Margaret and Phillipa, who hailed from nearby Bottesford. A contemporary source notes that the three women 'dayly found reliefe' from the castle, presumably in the form of money or provisions.[1] But the noble couple evidently felt that such temporary help was not enough, for they offered all three positions as charwomen, or daily house servants. The date of their employment is not known. Possibly they were brought in to assist with preparations for the royal visit of August 1612 – it was common for great houses such as Belvoir to swell the ranks of their servants in order to cope with such occasions. The Flower women must have impressed their masters, for their employment continued well beyond the king's visit. Joan's younger daughter, Margaret, was particularly favoured, because she was given the dual responsibility of working in the wash house and looking after the poultry. Better still, she was invited to live in the servants' quarters at the castle.

Another contemporary source numbers Joan among the 'auncient people' who lived near to the Belvoir estate.[2] Her two daughters are afforded much less attention in the contemporary sources: they are very much supporting actresses in the drama surrounding their mother. The ballad that was later written about the family claims that they had 'lived long' in Bottesford.[3] An attractive cottage close to St Mary's church is still known as the Witch's House today, but although it dates from the right period, its connection to the Flower women is unauthenticated. Given that most of the residents of Bottesford were tenants or servants of the Earl of Rutland, though, it is likely that Joan and her daughters lived in the village itself, rather than in the poorer dwellings scattered around the countryside nearby.

The Flower family had been connected to the earls of Rutland since at least the middle of the sixteenth century. In their heyday, the women of the Flower family had enjoyed the privileged position of lady-in-waiting to the countesses of Rutland, and had retained servants of their own. The archives at Belvoir Castle contain a handful of tantalisingly brief references to the favour that they enjoyed there. Among the earliest is a receipt dated 24 December 1557 for 13s.3d paid to 'Maistres Flower', one of the gentlewomen of the lady of the house, for her wages. The Flower family evidently enjoyed the same status throughout Elizabeth I's reign, for in around 1603 the then countess, wife of the 5th earl, made a payment of five shillings to a servant of Mrs Flower 'for presenting her Ladyship with a cake'.[4]

This Mrs Flower was almost certainly Joan. By the time the sources record anything more than the most cursory details of her life, she had fallen upon hard times and was looking after her daughters alone. Although there is no clear reference to her having been married, the contemporary records suggest that she was a widow rather than an unmarried mother. The records at Belvoir contain a few references to there being a male member of the Flower family. In 1604, Thomas Flower was a prominent enough parishioner to be among only eight men to pay the national grant of tax, the lay subsidy, to the Crown. But we know for certain that he was not Joan's husband, because he was married to Elizabeth Fairbairn, who hailed from another long-standing Bottesford family. It is more likely that Joan had been married to the John Flower who is mentioned as a servant of Sir Charles Manners, a relative of the 5th earl, in June 1608. A little under three years later, in January 1611, a 'Mr Flowar's man of Hucknall' is recorded as having delivered a dozen pigeons to the castle. The fact that he had a servant might suggest that he was very affluent, but this was an age when most households – except the very poorest – retained at least one servant.[5]

Compared to the destitution that they would later endure, Joan was in a stable position until at least 1611. Soon after the mention of John Flower's gift to the Earl of Rutland, though, she suffered a sudden and dramatic loss of status. The archives at Belvoir contain a note of a payment made to 'goodwyfe Flower'.[6] The change from 'mistress' to 'goodwife' is significant. The latter was a term of address for a woman of low social status, whereas 'mistress' often meant 'lady of the house' or head of a household. Joan's demotion was probably caused by the death of her husband. Married women had no independent wealth or property, and their fortunes were inextricably bound up with those of their husband. The luckier ones found that widowhood gave them not only welcome independence after years of subservience to their husband, but considerable wealth and property. The law dictated that widows were entitled to a third of their late husband's property. It also allowed them to continue their husband's business, provided they did not have a grown son who could do so.

However, this evidently was not the case for Joan. Any property or business that she did inherit was not enough to support herself and her daughters, and they were soon forced to seek menial employment in order to survive. It may have been their sudden loss of status that prompted the increasing ostracisation that the Flower family suffered in the local community. The sources imply that they had never been popular with their neighbours, but their connection to the Manners family had ensured that they were at least tolerated. Now, they found themselves the subject of increasingly malicious gossip and rumour.

One of the many factors that set Joan Flower and her daughters apart from the rest of the Bottesford community was that they apparently failed to attend church. Joan was described as 'a monstrous malicious woman, full of imprecations irreligious, and for any thing they saw by her, a plaine Atheist'.[7] In this most God-fearing of ages, the fact that the women were not churchgoers was enough to spark deep-seated suspicion, hatred and fear among their neighbours. The religious fervour of the Reformation was still strong in the early seventeenth century. Anyone who chose not to worship was not just ostracised by their neighbours; they risked persecution by the state. It was also interpreted as a sign of confederacy with the Devil. Many suspected that witches were religious Nonconformists. The records of ecclesiastical courts for the period show that a number of convicted witches had previously been named for such crimes as non-attendance at church, Sabbath-breaking and cursing or blaspheming. Others had been convicted of fornication, prostitution and adultery.

The Flower women's morals were also called into question. It was whispered that their home was little better than a 'bawdy house'.[8] Margaret and Phillipa were both described as 'abandoned and profligate women; who scrupled not at the means, by which to satisfy their inordinate desires.'[9] Phillipa, who according to the contemporary ballad was the elder of the two daughters, 'was well knowne a Strumpet lewd'.[10] The fact that Joan chose not to remarry intensified the rumours. Without a man to govern her morals and those of her daughters, their natural licentiousness would continue unchecked.

As women who had tasted the pleasures of the flesh, widows were thought likely to seek other sexual partners either within or outside marriage. Most men found this notion both disturbing and repugnant. As the great Renaissance philosopher Marsilio Ficino rather bluntly put it: 'Women should be used like chamber pots: hidden away once a man has pissed in them.'[11] Such women were also assumed to be more susceptible than their married counterparts to being seduced by the Devil. In the minds of most contemporaries, there was thus a dangerously thin dividing line between widowhood and witchcraft.[12]

Joan's frequent 'irreligious' outbursts, and her hostile, combative nature, meant that she could hardly have been further from the contemporary image of an ideal widow. The latter was expected to be meek, obedient and submissive. Shakespeare's King Lear was made to remark: 'Her voice was ever soft, gentle, and low, an excellent thing in a woman.'[13] Convention dictated that widows should devote the rest of their lives to the memory of their late husbands, living in quiet and devout solitude. Failure to do so could result in social ruin. The seventeenth-century moralist Richard Braithwaite warned: 'Great difference then is there betwixt those widows who live alone, and retire themselves from public concourse, and those which frequent the company of men. For a widow to love society . . . gives speedy wings to spreading infamy . . . for in such meetings she exposeth her honour to danger, which above all others she ought incomparably to tender.'[14]

Far from being pitied, widows attracted widespread suspicion, tending to find themselves on the periphery of society soon after their husband's death. The natural order of society dictated that women should be subject to the authority of men – be they fathers, husbands or sons. It was inconceivable that a woman might wish to make her own way in the world, unfettered by paternal or marital ties. The few who did, either by choice or circumstance, were viewed with suspicion, even fear, by the other members of their community. Single women were derided as freaks of nature, and a contemporary ballad claimed that women who died as virgins 'lead apes in hell'.

Interestingly, although most of the sources suggest that the Flower family were poor, a contemporary document refers to their 'extraordinary ryot and expences'.[15] This might indicate that Joan had not adjusted to the decline in her status and therefore consistently lived beyond her means. More likely is that the claim was intended to emphasise the general ill repute of their household. The rumours rapidly gathered pace and became ever more shocking. Joan was described as being an unkempt woman with a 'strange' countenance – 'a woman full of wrath'. A contemporary claimed that her eyes were 'fiery and hollow' and her demeanour 'strange and exoticke'.[16] She was, in short, becoming every day more like a witch.

Writing at the close of Elizabeth's reign, Samuel Harsnett, an English bishop, referred to a witch as 'One that hath forgotten her pater noster, and hath yet a shrewd tongue in her head, to call a drab, a drab.'[17] Older women in particular, no longer beholden to fathers or husbands, often felt freer to speak their minds, and rapidly gained reputations as scolds or blasphemers as a result. This was the case with Joan Flower, who was the head of her own household (such as it was) and had no man to answer to. Scolding was considered a serious offence and was punished by the 'scold's bridle', which locked the victim's head inside an iron cage that drove spikes through her tongue, as well as by the ducking stool, by which the accused was plunged underwater in a stagnant pond or cesspool. Persistent offenders risked having their tongue cut out as a punishment.

The systematic character assassination suffered by Joan Flower and her daughters was not something from which they could easily recover. In a male-dominated world, a woman's reputation was her power base. If this was called into question by members of her community, it all too often set her on the path to ruin. And it needed little foundation to become whispered about as established fact.

Even without the ostracisation that Joan and her daughters suffered, they faced an inordinate struggle to find their way in the world. The early seventeenth century was a time of economic hardship and chronic underemployment, with between a third and a half of the population living a hand-to-mouth existence. Moreover, the career options open to women in this period were on the whole of low status, badly paid and unreliable: in short, a good deal less advantageous than those available to men. Almost all rural women kept gardens, cared for domestic animals, preserved and cooked food, chopped wood, transported water, cared for and educated children, nursed the sick and prepared the dead for burial. But all of these were merely part of their expected domestic duties, and unless they were able to sell some of their produce at local markets, they gained no income from them.

Women could secure paid employment as seamstresses, lacemakers, milliners, weavers, spinners, tavern keepers, cooks, midwives, wet nurses and farm labourers at harvest time. The other career open to unmarried women was prostitution, and the fact that the Flower women's morals were frequently called into question suggests that they may also have resorted to that. Isott Wall, a widow from Somerset, was hauled before the courts on suspicion of prostitution, and shamelessly boasted that 'she would open her door at any time of the night either to a married man or a young man'.[18] Other widows were known to pay in kind for the manual labour that would formerly have been carried out by their husbands.

But it may have been the work that Joan chose to pursue first and foremost that paved the way to her downfall. It certainly intensified the suspicions of her neighbours. Joan had an impressive knowledge of plants and herbs, and gradually built up a reputation as a cunning woman. Wise or cunning folk had been an integral part of the village community for many hundreds of years.[19] They often had a thorough knowledge of herbs and other natural medicaments, and as such they made up for the shortcomings of the official medical practitioners of the day.

Seventeenth-century medical science offered little relief for those suffering from sickness or disease. Its practitioners were still guided by the principles set down by the ancient Greek physicians Hippocrates, Aristotle and Galen. These taught that the human body was made up of four 'humours' (blood, phlegm, yellow bile and black bile), and that any ailment sprang from an imbalance between them. The principal task of a physician was therefore to establish which of these four humours was out of line, and to rid the body of its excess by either bloodletting (often by applying leeches) or the use of purges and emetics. If the patient improved as a result, it was more by luck than judgement. 'Many diseases they cannot cure at all, as apoplexy, epilepsy, stone, strangury, gout . . . quartan agues; a common ague sometimes stumbles them all,' sneered the early-seventeenth-century scholar Robert Burton.[20] James I was equally scornful, and made little secret of the fact that he regarded academic medicine as useless.

The ineffectiveness of physicians was of little concern to the majority of the population, however, because only the rich could afford them. Most other people had to rely on the services of their local cunning man or woman – who were, arguably, more successful anyway. Thomas Hobbes claimed that he would 'rather have the advice or take physic from an experienced old woman that had been at many sick people's bedsides, than from the learnedst but unexperienced physician'.[21] He was not alone. 'Charming is in as great request as physic, and charmers more sought unto than physicians in time of need,' observed the polemicist William Perkins in 1608.[22] In vain did George Gifford urge his readers: 'He which seeketh helpe in sicknes at the hands of a Phisicion, doth that which is lawfull being ordeyned of God. For he hath given the nature & properties unto things, which shall serve for medicine. Shall a man therefore hold it lawfull to seeke helpe at the devil.'[23]

As well as enjoying higher rates of success than traditional physicians, cunning folk were also considerably cheaper. Most did not charge a fee per se (perhaps fearing accusations of fraud if their remedies did not work), but made it clear that a 'donation' was expected. Even so, it was hardly a lucrative profession – donations varied enormously, and sometimes payment was conditional upon success. Most cunning folk therefore practised their arts alongside other occupations. Only those who succeeded in gaining an excellent reputation and a wide client base, or who were fortunate enough to win the patronage of a member of the aristocracy, could hope to secure a substantial income from the profession. The real lure of the trade was the prestige. One early-seventeenth-century commentator scathingly noted that such people were 'fantastically proud' and boasted of 'their gift and power'.[24]

Far from being a threat to their neighbours, cunning folk were an indispensable part of the community: there were precious few doctors in rural areas during this period, so the help and advice of cunning folk was actively sought. As well as healing with potions or spells, they delivered babies, performed abortions, cured male impotence and female infertility, foretold the future, located thieves or lost property, made or removed curses, advised the lovelorn and made peace between neighbours. Their popularity was due to the fact that they tended to the soul as well as the body, and could provide objective, impartial and (mostly) confidential advice. 'Out of question they be innumerable which receive helpe by going to the cunning men,' observed an influential writer on witchcraft.[25] One particularly renowned cunning woman was said to have forty clients a week. Often people would travel considerable distances – even beyond their county boundary – in search of a cure from such practitioners.

Even churchmen were known to consult cunning folk, although in theory they sat on different sides of the spiritual divide. 'She doeth more good in one yeare than all these scripture men will doe so long as they live,' observed one contemporary of his local wise woman.[26] Despite being viewed as rivals, there was a great deal of overlap between cunning people and churchmen, at least during the pre-Reformation period. The former often prescribed the use of liturgical chants to rid a patient of their ailments. In 1528, a healer named Margaret Hunt was questioned by the authorities and required to describe the methods she used in detail. She told them that her first recourse would be to kneel and pray to the Blessed Trinity to heal her patients. She would then advise them to recite for nine consecutive nights a series of Paternosters, Aves and Creeds.[27] Even after the Reformation, the chanting of Catholic prayers in Latin remained a key ingredient in the treatment of illness by magical means. The seventeenth-century astrologer William Lilly recorded a popular formula for curing dental problems. The patient had to write the following verse three times on a piece of paper: 'Jesus Christ for mercy sake / Take away this toothache.' They were then advised to repeat the verse aloud and burn the paper.[28] As the witch hunts gathered ground in the later sixteenth and early seventeenth centuries, some of those accused claimed that they had healed not by magic, but by seeking God's intervention through prayer.

Cunning men and women also advised their clients to hang passages from the Bible around their necks (the first chapter of St John's Gospel was particularly popular), or to carry certain holy objects, such as communion wafers, holy water or a crucifix, in order to protect against evil and bewitchment. In 1590, James Sykes, a healer from Yorkshire, confessed to curing horses by writing prayers on fragments of paper and hanging them in their manes.[29] Religious charms and incantations were employed for every conceivable ache and pain: 'the stinging of serpents, bleeding at the nose, blastings, inflammations, burnings with fire, scalding with water, agues, toothache, cramps, stitches, prickings, ragings, achings, swellings, heart burnings, flowings of the head, &c.'[30] The notion that such ailments were a foreign or evil presence in the body that needed to be exorcised or conjured out was an ancient one, and many of the practices of local healers had been handed down through generations since the Dark Ages.

The effectiveness of these cunning folk varied widely. Those who had a detailed knowledge of the healing properties of certain plants and minerals no doubt provided a much more reliable alternative to conventional medicines than those who veered towards 'magical' cures such as spells and incantations. Paracelsus, considered the 'father of modern medicine', burned his text on pharmaceuticals in 1527, declaring that he 'had learned from the Sorceress all he knew'. A century later, William Perkins, the leading English Protestant thinker of his day, claimed that on visiting cunning folk, 'the meanes are received, applied, and used, the sicke partie accordingly recovereth, and the conclusion of all is, the usual acclamation; Oh happie is the day, that ever I met with such a man or woman to helpe me!'[31] Reflecting on his life in the 1630s, Adam Martindale described how a local wise woman had proved far more effective than members of the medical profession at curing an unpleasant skin condition:

A vehement fermentation in my body . . . ugly dry scurfe, eating deep and spreading broad. Some skilfull men, or so esteemed, being consulted and differing much in their opinions, we were left to these three bad choices . . . in this greate straite God sent us in much mercie a poore woman, who by a salve made of nothing but Celandine and a little of the Mosse of an ashe root, shred and boyled in May-butter, tooke it cleare away in a short time, and though after a space there was some new breakings out, yet these being anointed with the same salve . . . were absolutely cleared away, and I remain to this day ever since perfectly cured.[32]

Some of the herbal remedies used by the healers can still be found in modern pharmacology. They include ergot to relieve labour pain and belladonna to prevent miscarriage. Others, such as boiling hair and eggs in urine, have – thankfully – disappeared. Perhaps because of their seemingly miraculous nature, conception and childbirth tended to attract the greatest range of magical treatments. Wearing amulets containing powders could either enhance or prevent conception; herbs wrapped in linen and worn around the neck were used as contraceptives, as was a bizarre concoction of the ashes of a female mule's hoof mixed with wine. Meanwhile, women who wished to conceive without having sex were given horse's semen to drink, and a prolonged labour could be brought to a swift conclusion by opening doors or chests within the patient's house. George Gifford was deeply suspicious of the cunning folk's potions and practices, claiming that 'Satan . . . teacheth them to make poisons: whereupon this is cleere that the greeke woord Pharmakeia is used as a generall name for witchcraft & sorcery.'[33]

Psychology was a major factor. A local healer knew her neighbours intimately and could therefore act as an effective therapist and comforting adviser. As such, she was a precursor to the modern-day psychiatrist in making the connection between physical and mental well-being. The attention that she gave each patient, often enlisting the support of other family members, eased their minds and might in itself have led to healing. Faith was another important factor. One cunning man was said to have urged his clients: 'you must beleeve it will helpe, or els it will doe you no good at all'.[34] The pamphleteer Richard Bernard concurred: 'These witches profess that they cannot heal such as do not believe in them.'[35]

Most people were all too willing to place unquestioning trust in their healer. After all, they presented a much more appealing option than contemporary doctors, with their purges, leeches and – worst of all – barbaric surgical procedures. In any case, failure by a cunning man or woman could be easily explained away by saying that the client had left it too late to seek help, had performed the prescribed rituals ineffectively, or had lacked faith in their efficacy. The fact that even as late as the nineteenth century common people across Europe clung to these cunning folk in preference to other medical practitioners is a testament to how highly valued they were.

An important aspect of the cunning person's art was to cultivate a sense of mystery, keeping their patients in ignorance of the precise formula of the herbs or incantations they were using. Although contemporary charm books survive, they were never printed and published, except by those wishing to expose them as fraudulent. During the early years of Elizabeth I's reign, a woman named Alice Prabury was investigated by the church authorities, who found that she 'taketh upon her to help by the way of charming, and in such ways that she will have nobody privy of her sayings'.[36] In this respect, there was little distinction between cunning folk and conventional medical practitioners. 'We go to the physician for counsel, we take his recipe, but we know not what it meaneth; yet we use it, and find benefit,' observed William Perkins. 'If this be lawful, why may we not as well take benefit by the wise man, whose courses we be ignorant of?'[37]

Many cunning folk enhanced their mystique by wearing strange costumes, or filling their consulting rooms with weird and wonderful objects. Mirrors and crystal balls were favoured devices for discovering the identity of a thief or other culprit. Elizabeth I's favourite astrologer, John Dee, was said to have a crystal 'as big as an egg: most bright, clear and glorious'.[38] One victim of theft consulted the local cunning man, who 'browghte with him a looking glass (about vii or viii inches square), and did hange the said glasse up over the benche in his said hawle, upon a nayle, and bad the said examinate look in yt, and said as farre as he could gesse, he shulde see the face of him that had the said lynnen'.[39]

A host of other props, costumes, potions and paraphernalia were employed by these 'white witches'. Johann Weyer, physician to the Duke of Cleves, scathingly described

the entire category of tricks and illusions by means of which these malefic or evildoers . . . produce phantasms and apparitions while fraudulently vaunting their many 'miracles'. They usually employ sorcerers' enchantments, absurd conjurings, illicit pagan sacrifices, imprecations, a naming of divine names, the recitation of sacred or barbarous words, and mutterings of all sorts. On occasion they irrelevantly introduce plants, animals, and parts of animals – whether for superstitious reasons or by way of deceit. Sometimes too they employ special perfumes, lights, eye-salves, and periapts or objects affixed to the person by binding or suspension; they also employ metals, artificial bodies, statues, little images, rings, and seals; they make various objects; they likewise employ mirrors and similar monstrosities and tools of the magic art.'[40]

As well as healing the sick, cunning folk enjoyed impressive rates of success in the detection of theft and other crimes. When their methods are scrutinised, it becomes clear that they cleverly combined mystical objects and devices with real detective work. Any investigation would begin with the cunning man or woman asking their client to produce a list of suspects. The client proved all too willing to cooperate, given that they often bore a grudge against someone in the community and saw this as an ideal means of gaining the upper hand. Armed with this information, the healer would employ various rituals to determine who the guilty party was. A popular method was to hang a sieve by the point of some shears and read out the names of the suspects. When the guilty person was named, the sieve would spin around. Given that the client had already revealed who they thought the prime suspect was, it was easy for the healer to make the sieve spin at the right moment. 'Many other pretie knackes hee glorieth in,' sneered one cynic, 'as if he had attained great wisedome.'[41]

In such cases, the role of the cunning folk was less to identify the thief than to strengthen their client's resolve to prosecute him. Not everyone was taken in by their powers. The author of the Belvoir witch pamphlet criticised 'the conceit of wise-men or wise woemen, that they are all meerely coseners and deceivers; so that if they make you beleeve that by their meanes you shall heare of things lost or stolne, it is either done by Confederacy, or put off by protraction to deceive you of your money'.[42] He warned that their artifice was born of malicious intent: 'However the professors aforesaid practise murther and mischiefe, yet many times they Pretend cures and preservation; with many others, carrying the shew of great learning and admired knowledge; yet have they all but one familier tearme with us in English called Witches.'[43]

Cunning folk also played an important role in bringing the guilty party to light through intimidation. As well as detecting the thief, murderer or other criminal, they were known to have magical recipes which could inflict pain or injury upon the culprit, or paralyse him so that he could not escape. In small, insular communities such as Bottesford, where everyone knew everyone, the fact that the local cunning person had been enlisted to solve a crime would be widely known and talked about. The criminal, too, would hear about it. Many either returned the stolen goods, confessed their guilt or fled in panic – such was the strength of belief in the power of cunning folk. George Gifford described a typical scenario: 'A man hath a silver cup missing, all corners are sought but yet it cannot be found . . . He enquireth secretly where there is a cunning man of great fame. Thether he hasteth. Home he returneth and in very deede findeth the cup.'[44] Even when the wrong person was identified, that person would have a strong interest in proving their innocence by finding the real culprit, so the role of the cunning man or woman still proved ultimately effective.

Cunning folk often pedalled charms and sigils to perform all manner of other beneficial functions: from securing victory in battle to winning at cards or excelling at the lute. Such charms were believed to contain familiar spirits that would work their magic at the propitious moment. They were favoured by rich and poor alike; even kings and queens were not averse to using them. Elizabeth I sent a protective amulet to her favourite, the Earl of Essex, when he embarked upon his expedition to the Azores in 1597. Meanwhile, Thomas Wolsey and Thomas Cromwell were both said to have used magic rings in order to win Henry VIII's favour.

Many of those who bought charms from cunning folk did so to remove some impediment in their love lives, whether it was unrequited passion, impotence or unsatisfactory intercourse. Goodwife Swan of Margate in Kent boasted in 1582 that she could make a drink 'which, she saith, if she give it to any young man that she liketh well of, he shall be in love with her'.[45] During the investigation into the murder of Sir Thomas Overbury in 1613, it emerged that Frances, Countess of Essex, and her confidante, Anne Turner, had consulted an astrologer and magician to secure the love of the Earl of Somerset and Sir Christopher Mainwaring. In other cases, the use of magic was blamed for things going wrong in a relationship. Thus, when the 5th Earl of Sussex abandoned his wife for his mistress during James I's reign, the countess's friends attempted to prove that she had lost her husband because of maleficent magic. But the countess was hardly blameless: as well as 'enterteininge the unlawfull affections of other persons', she was said to have 'secretly professed and practized the unlawfull and damnable artes of witchcrafte' in order to bring about her husband's death.[46] Meanwhile, in 1619 a gentlewoman tried to disguise the shame of her daughter's elopement with a local ploughboy by attributing it to 'diabolical sorcery'.[47]

The other most popular service performed by cunning folk was to predict the future. They employed a variety of means to do so, from gazing into a crystal ball to listening to the croaking of frogs, or simply claiming that they had the natural gift of foresight and regularly witnessed 'visions' of what was to come. Others used a combination of fraud and psychology, secretly listening in on conversations and then startling their clients with how much they knew about their personal circumstances, or asking leading questions during the consultation. Often people sought out a fortune-teller at times of crisis in their lives. In such cases, the cunning folk could help them to reach a decision, or strengthen their resolve if they already half knew the course of action they wanted to take. When he fell from James I's favour, the Earl of Somerset was rumoured to have consulted a wizard about how to regain his former position. At around the same time, Mrs Suckling, a doctor's wife from Norfolk, sought the help of a renowned Norwich palmist to find out when her husband would die. The answer evidently did not prove satisfactory, for Mrs Suckling went on to offer the wise woman money to poison him.[48]

Despite the inevitable patchiness of the cunning folk's success, the fact that they offered a 'one-stop shop' for a whole range of ills afflicting society made them an indispensable part of any community. By the late sixteenth century, one leading authority on magic and witchcraft wrote that there was a 'miracle worker' in every parish, and that some places had as many as 18. At the same time, Henry Holland, a Cambridgeshire preacher, scornfully remarked upon 'the continual traffic and market which the rude people have with witches'. Johann Weyer was aghast that 'the frenzy of this satanic profession has so pervaded the minds of these men that they believe that their every desire is accomplished by such demonic impostures, that new powers are conferred upon the nature of things, or former powers taken away, weakened, or enlivened, or that the course of nature is changed, lightning bolts stirred, thunderclaps, winds, and rains unexpectedly roused or quelled, serpents stripped of their savagery and violence, untamed beasts brought under control, iron broken, diseases inflicted and cured, shades and spirits of the dead called up'.[49] George Gifford was similarly confounded by their popularity: 'Is Satan become a weldoer? Is hee so charitable and so pitifull that hee will releeve mens miseries? . . . Some man will replye that this is a common thing and well tried by experience, that many in great distresse have bin releaved and recovered by sending unto such wise men or wise women, when they could not tel what should els become of them, and of all that they had.' But Gifford warned that there was a high price to pay for such healing: 'For Satan . . . healeth the bodie, to the end he may the more fully possesse and destroy the soule . . . O wretched men so relieved: they do imagine that the devill is driven out of them, and he hath entred in deeper.'[50]

Belief in the powers of cunning folk remained just as strong in the early seventeenth century. Robert Burton echoed the earlier view that there was a cunning man in every village, and in 1621 the future Bishop of Lincoln lamented that it was 'scarce credible how generally and miserably our common ignorants are besotted with the opinion of their [cunning folk's] skill; and how pitifully they are gulled by their damnable impostures, through their own foolish credulity'.[51]

For all their popularity, cunning folk were not immune to suspicion and malevolence from members of their community. In theory, they harnessed the powers already at work in the universe, whereas witches drew upon evil powers within themelves. But as the witch hunts gathered momentum, the dividing line between beneficial magic such as this and the maleficium of 'black' witches became dangerously blurred. 'It is indifferent to saie in the English toong; she is a witch; or she is a wise woman,' declared Reginald Scot.[52] His contemporary, George Gifford, agreed: 'God saith . . . that such persons as seeke unto Conjurers and Witches, doe goe a whoring after devilles.'[53] Because women were not permitted to study conventional medicine, it became widely accepted that the only way they could acquire the necessary skills and knowledge was from the Devil. 'If a woman dare to cure without having studied, she is a witch and must die,' the church proclaimed.[54]

Ironically, although many cunning folk were later prosecuted as witches, they were also responsible for fanning the flames of the witch hunting fervour. 'If they doe suppose that one is bewitched, they enquire after a wise man or a wise woman, to learne who hath done the deede,' observed George Gifford. 'There be none more extreme haters of witches, then such as be infected with a kinde of witchcraft themselves.' But he warned that such folk were carrying out the Devil's work, just as surely as the 'witches' whom they accused. 'A man is sicke, his sicknesse doth linger upon him. Some doe put into his head that he is bewitched. He is counselled to send unto a cunning woman. She saith he is forspoken indeede, she prescribeth them what to use, there must be some charme and sorcerie used. The partie findeth ease, & is a glad man, he taketh it that he hath made a good market, it was a luckie hower when he sent to that woman. For doubtlesse he did thinke that if he had not found so speedie a remedie, the Witch would utterly have spoyled him.'[55] In this way, cunning folk would regularly diagnose bewitchment – something that more orthodox physicians often refused to do. If a series of disasters befell a community, then either its members or the authorities would routinely consult the local cunning man or woman to find out who was responsible. Although they pretended to use mystical powers to discover the suspect, the name of anyone believed to be dabbling in the dark arts would already have been given to them by previous clients: they were, after all, the chief repositories of gossip, rumour and information in the community.

Sometimes, though, the cunning folk were responsible for initiating suspicions by planting the idea in a client's mind that their ailment or misfortune was the result of maleficium on the part of a hostile member of the community. The mid-seventeenth-century commentator Thomas Ady claimed that cunning folk 'will undertake to tell them [their clients] who hath bewitched them, who, and which of their Neighbours it was'.[56] In 1619, it was said of William Walford, a cunning man from Cold Norton in Essex, that 'his order is, when he comes to visit any sick neighbour, to persuade them that they are bewitched, and tells them withal [that] except they will be of that belief they can very hardly be holpen of their disease and sickness'.[57] Others shied away from actually naming the suspect, but dropped such heavy hints that their client was left in no doubt. When his wife fell grievously ill in 1645, a desperate Essex man sought the advice of his local cunning woman, who told him 'that his wife was cursed by two women who were neere neighbours to this Informant, the one dwelling a little above his house, and the other beneath his house, this Informants house standing on the side of an Hill: Whereupon he beleeved his said wife was bewitched by one Elizabeth Clarke'.[58]

Indispensable though they may have been, therefore, the position of the cunning man or woman in their local community was a potentially dangerous one. By meddling in local disputes, failing to satisfy their clients, or simply knowing too much about an individual's business, they could arouse feelings of suspicion and paranoia. Joan Flower would soon know the truth of this all too well.

5

'Busie-bodies and flatterers'

Although life in their local community was becoming increasingly uncomfortable for Joan and her daughters, the favour that they enjoyed with the Manners family afforded them valuable protection. It was most likely Joan who had been instrumental in securing employment at Belvoir, and she must have been triumphant at having successfully re-established her family's connection to the castle.

However, such good fortune stoked the jealousy of their disapproving neighbours, and also caused resentment among the other servants at Belvoir. Household positions in noble families were often virtually hereditary, with generations of the same family serving as valet, cook or housekeeper to a lord and his entourage. The Flower women might therefore have been viewed with suspicion as unwelcome outsiders – particularly if, as the records suggest, Joan adopted an attitude of superiority, harking back to her family's former status. Complaints against them were said to have begun 'many yeares' before any action was taken.[1]

Even if it began well, the relationship between master and servant was often fraught with difficulty. In an age long before the drawing up of formal employment contracts, the arrangements for hiring and keeping servants proved a fertile breeding ground for tensions and grudges. People were generally wary of accepting anyone of questionable reputation into their household, and even the children of such individuals were sometimes rejected on the grounds that they might be tainted by association. Likewise, if a servant – once hired – was badly treated, or punished or dismissed for a perceived failing, then bitter conflicts could arise.

Although it was unusual for a servant to be accused of anything worse than pilfering or carrying on illicit relations with other members of the household, older servants were vulnerable to charges of witchcraft if any ill fortune befell the family whom they served. A late sixteenth-century case involved a Frenchwoman named Mengeotte le Compaing. She soon became deeply unpopular with the other servants, who blamed her for various illnesses which beset the household. Matters came to a head when her mistress's three-year-old daughter died, and Mengeotte found herself accused of maleficent witchcraft. She steadfastly denied any wrongdoing, but soon found herself dismissed from service.[2]

But it appeared that the Flower women need fear no such dangers. Their favour with the earl and countess seemed so secure that nothing could threaten their position at the castle. Their enemies put this down to deception on Joan's part. It was said that thanks to her 'monstrous' cunning, she was able to fool the earl and his family that she and her daughters were loyal servants of good character, so that 'all things were carried away in the smooth Channell of liking and good entertainment on every side'. The family whom they served was even said to 'love' them.

Joan herself apparently enjoyed particular favour with the earl, and a contemporary account refers to the 'familiarity and accustomed conferences he was wont to have with her'.[3] It may have been her reputation for healing that first brought her to his attention. Francis sought her advice on many occasions, and the pair seemed to enjoy a 'close confederacy', spending many hours discussing natural remedies. Among the state papers of James I is a letter which implies that the earl also had a reputation for unorthodox methods of healing. Nicholas Burton wrote from court that he 'has cured many persons of the stone, by misletoe'.[4] Mistletoe was believed to have restorative and cleansing powers, and was therefore used by herbalists and cunning folk to treat a variety of ills.

The Flower women were reported to have carried out their duties effectively and 'continued with equal correspondency'.[5] Quite how long they enjoyed a life of stability at the castle is not certain. One seventeenth-century account claims that they were employed at Belvoir for 'several years' before trouble began to flare up.[6] However, the contemporary pamphlet which tells their story implies that rumours of misconduct began to circulate among the other servants within a matter of months. Piecing together the fragmentary evidence, the latter seems more likely.

It was probably in early 1613 that the servants at Belvoir lodged a formal complaint about the Flower women with Cecilia, who, as countess, was responsible for the management of the household. The author of *The Wonderful Discoverie of the Witchcrafts of Margaret and Phillippa Flower, Daughters of Joan Flower* was at pains to point out that while 'honourable persons' never lacked 'busie-bodies, flatterers, malicious politicians, underminers, nor supplanters one of anothers good fortune' to serve their own ends by whispering malicious tales, this was not the case with the servants at Belvoir.[7] The latter were motivated only by a simple desire to serve the earl and his lady and to uphold their honour. The fact that what followed was less a straightforward account of the Flower women's misconduct than a complete character assassination gives the lie to this statement.

At the crux of the accusations was that Margaret Flower had begun to steal provisions from the castle and hasten with them to her mother's house late at night, when she believed the rest of the household was asleep. These provisions were 'unbefitting for a servant to purloyne' and were used to 'maintaine certaine deboist [debauched] and base company which frequented this Joane Flowers house the mother, and especially her youngest Daughter'.[8] One source disapprovingly noted that 'people of no good reputation' also came to visit Phillipa at all hours of the night.[9] Among them was Thomas Simpson, presumably a local man, who claimed that she had bewitched him, 'for hee had no power to leave, and was as he supposed marvellously altered both in minde and body since her acquainted company'.[10]

Joan herself, despite her age, was said to have just as many lovers as her daughters. They included a Mr Peake or Peate, who was a long-term servant of the earl. When he wronged her in some way, she took up with another, Mr Vavasour. He is recorded as having given her 'a paire of gloves', presumably as a token of affection.[11] His identity is not known for certain. It is possible that he was a member of the Vavasor family of Husbands Bosworth, some 35 miles south-west of Belvoir, who were connected with the Manners family because of their Catholic sympathies.[12] More likely he was drawn from the Vavasour family who had been long-term gentry servants of the castle. Vavasour soon abandoned her company, 'as either suspicious of her lewd life, or distasted with his onn [own] misliking of such base and poor Creatures'. In her frustration, Joan complained to the earl about her former lover, Peake, but her confidence in his support was misplaced:

'wherein she conceived that the Earle tooke not her part, as shee expected, which dislike with the rest, exasperated her displeasure against him, and so she watched the opportunity to bee revenged'.[13]

As the rumours about them gathered ground, Joan and her daughters may have been influenced by their neighbours' perceptions. They were believed to be evil, and therefore might have begun to live up (or down) to their reputation. They were not alone. Reginald Scot described how dangerous village gossip could be in this respect: 'These miserable wretches are so odious unto all their neighbours, and so feared, as few dare offend them, or denie them anie thing they aske. As a result, they imagine that they can do things quite beyond the ability of human nature.'[14] Moreover, religious beliefs dictated that a tendency to think bad thoughts or commit bad deeds was a sign that a person was possessed by the Devil. Many of those who stood accused of witchcraft may have therefore believed that their less charitable thoughts or actions were the result not of their own free will but of a satanic master.

So far, if the rumours are to be believed, it seems that the Flower women were little more than petty thieves whose morals did not bear close scrutiny. The tales of Margaret's 'lewd and filching prankes' might have been easily dismissed by the earl and countess, particularly as they cherished a high opinion of the women – thanks, it was said, to the latter's 'cunning observance and modest carriage toward them'.[15] Even if they themselves did not believe the rumours, though, they must have been aware of how disruptive an influence the Flower women had become in their household, so they decided to act. According to a contemporary account of the controversy, it was Cecilia who first took the matter in hand. She was said to have discovered some 'undecencies' on the part of Margaret Flower, as well as 'neglect of her businesse'.[16] This was more than enough to justify dismissing the girl, and Margaret left Belvoir shortly afterwards, having been commanded 'never [to] returne unto their sight'.[17]

Margaret later claimed that her dismissal was due to the countess 'growing into some mislike with her', but Cecilia may have acted more to keep the peace in her household than out of a genuine belief in Margaret's guilt.[18] This is suggested by the fact that she gave her an extremely generous parting gift of 40 shillings (as much if not more than a year's pay), together with a bolster and a wool mattress. The latter would have enabled the girl to sleep in a good deal more comfort than she was used to at home, for most poor people were obliged to sleep on mattresses made of straw, which often became infested with mice and other vermin. Nevertheless, Margaret's dismissal gives the lie to the assertion earlier in the Belvoir witch pamphlet that the earl and countess were model employers, 'neither displacing Tenants [nor] discharging servants'.[19]

Quite who had played a part in Margaret's disgrace and that of her family must remain a matter for conjecture. They certainly had a number of enemies within the local community. It is easy to imagine a coterie of resentful servants concocting a tale of the women's crimes in order to be rid of their unwanted presence. Equally, a former lover or betrayed spouse may have been determined to exact revenge. The earl himself may even have been responsible by seducing one of the Flower women and then creating a counteraccusation in order to cover his tracks. The fact that Margaret was given such a generous settlement hints at some guilt on the Manners's part.

Although it no doubt immediately relieved the tension in the household at Belvoir, according to a later testimony Margaret's dismissal set in chain a tragic series of events that would blight the earl and countess's family for years to come. It also had devastating consequences for the Flower women themselves.

According to the contemporary account of the controversy, as soon as Margaret Flower had been dismissed from service, her 'hatefull mother witch' immediately began plotting revenge with her 'darlings' and 'terrified them all with curses and threatning of revenge, if there were never so little cause of displeasure and unkindnesse'.[20] Margaret later admitted that Joan had 'grudged at it [her daughter's dismissal] exceedingly, swearing in her heart to be revenged'.[21] Together with her daughters, she was said to 'use frightful imprecations of wrath and malice towards the objects of their hatred'.[22] The fact that the accusations against them had been so easily believed by the local community 'did turne her [Joan's] love and liking toward this honourable Earle and his family into hate and rancor: whereupon despighted [maliciously indignant] to bee so neglected, and exprobated [upbraided] by her neighbours for her Daughters casting out of doors, and other conceived displeasures, she grew past all shame and woman-hood, and many times cursed them all that were the cause of this discontentment, and made her so loathsome to her former familiar friends and beneficial acquaintance'.[23]

If Joan and her daughters had really been so indiscreet in voicing their displeasure against the earl and his family, they would live to regret it. A common feature of witchcraft cases was that the accused had uttered curses against members of the community, and that these same people were subsequently struck down by sickness or other misfortune. As one contemporary observed: 'Then they, upon whom such adversities fall, weighing the fame that goeth upon this woman (hir words, displeasure, and cursses meeting so justlie with their misfortune) doo not onelie conceive, but also are resolved, that all their mishaps are brought to passe by hir onelie meanes.'[24] William Perkins claimed that one of the surest means of discovering and condemning a witch was 'if after cursing there followeth death, or at least some mischief'.[25] The author of the Belvoir witch pamphlet agreed: 'There bee certaine men and women gronne [grown] in yeares, and ouer gronne with Melancholly and Atheisme, who out of a malitious disposition against their betters, or others thriuing by them; but most times from a heart-burning desire of revenge, having entertained some impression of displeasure, and unkindnesse, study nothing but mischeife, and exoticke practises of loathsome Artes and Sciences.'[26] Witches were people of 'ill natures, of a wicked disposition, and spitefully malicious', claimed one contemporary of the Flower family, while another described them as 'full of revenge, having hearts full of rancour'.[27]

The Book of Isaiah notes that to 'speak inwardly and to mutter' is a sign of necromancy, and this belief endured throughout the proceeding centuries.[28] That it was possible for one person to inflict harm upon another by the use of hostile words was a strong conviction throughout medieval times. The pre-Reformation church had played a key role in this, with its emphasis upon chants and incantations as a means of promoting good or dispelling evil. But it was not just churchmen whose words held special powers. Ordinary men and women could ill-wish their enemies with well-chosen words and ancient spells. Part of the evidence against Joan Page, an Essex woman accused of witchcraft, was that she was said to be 'develishe of her tonge'.[29] In 1602, a man named Owen ap Rees was charged as 'a common curser of certain of his neighbours, going upon his knees, wishing their houses burnt and other losses unto them'. Likewise, Agnes Browne, one of the witches of Northamptonshire accused in 1612, was described as being of 'an ill nature and wicked disposition,

spightfull and malitious', and 'hated, and feared among her neighbours'.[30] Five years later, Joanna Powell, of Westhide in Herefordshire,
was brought before the authorities because she 'did curse John Smith,
one of the churchwardens, upon Thursday last, in Welsh language,
kneeling down upon her bare knees and holding up her hands, but
otherwise the words he could not understand'.[31]

Joan Flower had long been regarded by her neighbours as a
'monstrous', ungodly woman who did not flinch from using foul
language and blasphemous oaths. But according to the account of her
downfall, she now became utterly possessed by evil. 'Her very countenance was estranged, her eyes were fiery and hollow, her speech fell
[savage] and envious, her demeanour strange and exoticke, and her
conversation sequestered; so that the whole course of her life gave
great suspition that she was a notorious Witch, yea some of her
neighbours dared to affirme that she dealt with familiar Spirits.'[32] In
an age when people believed that a witch could inflict harm 'by malitious and wrie looks in anger and displeasure', this was significant. As
one authority opined: 'There proceed out of the eye with the beams,
noysome and malignant spirits, which infect the ayre, and doe poison
or kill, not onely them with whom they are daily conversant, but
others also whose companie they frequent.'[33]

It was apparently now, fired up by a sense of injustice and a desire
for revenge, and encouraged by their three associates, that Joan and
her daughters resolved to employ the dark arts to achieve their ends.
According to the contemporary account of their case: 'When the
Divell perceived the inficious [corrupted or wicked] disposition of this
wretch, and that she and her Daughters might easily bee made instruments to enlarge his Kingdome, and bee as it were the executioners
of his vengeance; not caring whether it lighted upon innocents or no,
he came more neerer unto hem, and in plaine tearmes to come quickly
to the purpose, offered them his service, and that in such a manner,
as they might easily command what they pleased.' The Flower women
were said to have readily agreed to exchange their souls for the power
to inflict evil upon those who had wronged them. The pact was sealed
with 'abominable kisses, and an odious sacrifice of blood', and Joan,
Margaret and Phillipa 'much rejoyct' in their 'cunning and artificial
power, to doe what mischeife they listed'.[34]

Joan and her daughters were alleged to have wasted no time in exercising their newly gained powers. Suddenly, the blame for every misfortune that befell the community of Bottesford was laid at their door. A contemporary ballad claimed:

> They did forespeake [foretell], and Cattle kild,
> that neighbours could not thrive,
> And oftentimes their Children young,
> of life they would deprive.[35]

It is astonishing how quickly a suspected witch could become a scapegoat in this way. Bishop Samuel Harsnett warned:

> Looke about ye, my neighbours; if any of you have a sheepe sicke of the giddies, or an hogge of the mumps, or an horse of the staggers, or a knavish boy of the schoole, or an idle girl of the wheele, or a young drab of the sullens, and hath not fat enough for her porridge, nor her father, and mother, butter enough for their bread; and she have a little helpe of the Mother, Epilepsie, or Cramp, to teach her to role her eyes, wrie her mouth, gnash her teeth, startle with her body, hold her armes and hands stiffe, make anticke faces, girne, mow, and mop like an Ape, tumble like a Hedgehogge and can mutter out two or three words of gibridg, as *obus*, *bobus*: and then with-all old mother Nobs hath called her by chaunce, idle young huswife, or bid the devil scratch her; then no doubt but mother Nobs is the Witch: the younge girle is Owle-blasted, and possessed.

Thus, he concluded: 'there be two grand witches in the world, that seduce the soules of the simple, & lead them to perdition: Lying wonders, and Counterfeit zeale'.[36]

The virulence of popular hatred against suspected witches such as the Flower women was extraordinary. Many believed that they were the architects of every misfortune, every grief, every suffering. 'She is the very pestilence of the earth,' claimed George Gifford in one of his impassioned tracts on the subject. 'All calamity is brought upon men by her. Shee killeth men and beastes. Shee tormenteth men, & she destroyeth mens goods. No man can be in safety so long as shee liveth. Woe bee unto him which doth displease her, thrise happy are they which do not meddle with her.'[37]

Rumour had it that in tormenting their neighbours by killing their crops or animals, Joan Flower and her daughters were merely practising for their real mission: the downfall of the Manners family. It was said that they had determined to stop at nothing to 'blast the branches of that house, and undermine the root'. The unsuspecting earl and his family would suffer 'the burthen of a terrible tempest, which from these Divellish devises fell uppon him'.[38]

Did the Flower women, and others like them, genuinely believe that they could harness the powers of evil? In an age dominated by superstition, it is quite possible that they believed in witchcraft as strongly as did their accusers – the only difference being that they were its instruments, not its victims. The author of *The Wonderful Discoverie* was in no doubt that they, and others like them, were 'transported with an opinion of their owne worth, and prevailing in this kinde'. He scorned the fact that they 'hath so prevailed with divers, that they have taken upon them indeed to known more than God ever afforded any creature, & to performe no lesse than the Creator both of Heaven and earth; making you beleeve with Medea, that they can raise tempests, turne the Sunne into blood, pull the Moone out of her Spheare, and saile over the Sea in a cockleshell'.[39] Likewise, Reginald Scot, who was one of the few writers in the sixteenth century to dismiss witchcraft as superstition, described how the devil could take hold in the 'drousie minds' of old and infirm women, 'so as, what mischeefe, mischance, calamitie, or slaughter is brought to passe, they are easilie persuaded the same is doone by themselves; imprinting in their minds an earnest and constant imagination hereof . . . They are . . . so firme and steadfast in their opinions, as whosoever shall onelie have respect to the constancie of their words uttered, would easilie beleeve they were true indeed.'[40] The mid-seventeenth-century writer Arthur Wilson agreed: 'They themselves, by the strength of fancy, may think they bring such things to pass which many times unhappily they wish for and rejoice in when done, out of the malevolent humour which is in them: which passes with them as if they had really acted it.'[41]

At least some of those who confessed to crimes of witchcraft could have been delusional, hysterical, schizophrenic or otherwise mentally instable. Given that so many women from the poorer classes were ill nourished, overworked and almost continually pregnant, it would not have been suprising if their mental state was fragile, to say the least. But the sheer number of those convicted for practising maleficent magic, and the striking similarity of the descriptions they provided in their confessions, makes it highly unlikely that most were suffering from mental illness. Moreover, this was an age when the vast majority of people believed in mystical forces, ghosts, imps, fairies and demons. The fact that witches tried to harness such forces did not make them any more mentally unstable than their fellow men.

Another theory is that those who practised magical arts, including the use of spells and potions, experienced drug-induced hallucinations. The ingredients of certain witches' salves included nightshade, which contains belladonna. Historians – and even some contemporary commentators – have suggested that, if used in sufficient quantities, such salves might well produce the sensation of flight. A number of those convicted of witchcraft mentioned this salve in their confessions. Among them was Elizabeth Style, who recounted: 'Before they are carried to their meetings, they anoint their Foreheads and Hand-wrists with an Oyl the Spirit brings them (which smells raw) and then they are carried in a very short time.' Meanwhile, a Somerset witch named Ann Bishop told how 'her Forehead being first anointed with a Feather dipt in Oyl, she hath been suddenly carried to the place of their meeting . . . After all was ended, the Man in black vanished. The rest were of a sudden conveighed to their homes.'[42] The applying of the ointment before the sabbat was recognised as part of the witch's ritual, and inspired a number of contemporary works of art, notably François Queverdo's Le Départ au Sabbat and Frans Francken's The Witch's Kitchen.[43] But as the salve was prescribed to clients, as well as being used by the witch herself, this theory is not entirely satisfactory.

A similar explanation for the fanciful descriptions of flights on broomsticks, nocturnal orgies and pacts with devils is the eating of mouldy rye bread by the peasantry. This apparently resulted in ergot poisoning, the symptoms of which included hallucinations, mania and convulsions. It could thus account for the actions of both the witches and their victims. It is an unlikely theory, and one which is easily contradicted by scientific evidence. Neither was the witch craze likely to have been caused by the arrival of syphilis as an epidemic disease. Such theories are temptingly simple, but in reality the witch hunts resulted from a series of complex social, religious and economic conditions which varied from country to country and region to region.

Even if a suspected witch did not claim she had supernatural powers at the time of her arrest, in the terror and confusion of imprisonment and interrogation she might come to believe that this was the case. A play inspired by the trial and execution of Elizabeth Sawyer in 1621 presented her as a product of society rather than an enemy of it. The author put the following words into her mouth:

> Some call me witch,
> And being ignorant of my self, they go
> About to teach me how to be one; urging,
> That my bad tongue (by their bad language made so)
> Forespeaks their cattle, doth bewitch their corn,
> Themselves, their servants, and their babes at nurse.
> This they enforce upon me; and in part
> Make me to credit it.[44]

Perhaps the Flower women's only real crime had been to attempt to wield power in a man's world. As three unmarried women, they had not been subject to the traditional male authority that the vast majority of women were confined by. They had even dared to flout the earl's right to rule their lives. But their quest for power in a deeply misogynistic society was doomed to failure. Unable to cope with the notion of women who might wish to live without the guidance and authority of a man, society condemned them. And it did so by twisting their quest for independence so that it was not their own wits upon which they relied, but a despicable pact with the Devil. He, not they, was the source of their power.

Whether or not the Flower women had intended harm against the Manners family, shortly after Margaret's dismissal a calamity befell the household at Belvoir. In late summer 1613, their elder son, Henry, Lord Ros, suddenly 'sickened very strangely', and 'did lingring, lye tormented long'.[45] To his parents' horror, he never recovered. He died in September and was buried at Bottesford church on the 26th of that month. The family accounts include a payment of £8 dated the following day to 'defraye the chardges of my late Lord Rosse's

funerall'.[46] This was a fraction of the sum lavished upon Roger
Manners's funeral the previous year. But the passing of an earl was
an occasion for ostentatious reverence, particularly as it was usually
arranged by his successor. That the young Lord Ros's funeral was a
much smaller affair suggests an altogether more private and poignant
occasion, marked by genuine grief on the part of the earl and his
wife.

As well as the funeral expenses, the household accounts contain a
receipt for three legacies bequeathed by the family's former agent,
Thomas Screven, to Countess Cecilia, Lady Katherine and 'my Lord
Roos'. This was received after 29 September 1613. It is possible that
Screven made the bequest before Lord Ros's death, but more likely
is that it was intended for the younger son, Francis, who inherited the
title upon his brother's death.

The death of the elder son and heir to the Manners fortune ushered
in a period not just of grieving, but of profound unease for Francis
and Cecilia. The future of their estates now rested upon their younger
son, Francis. Their anxiety was entirely understandable. Some of the
most ancient and distinguished noble families in the region had disappeared through either debt or bad genetic luck. Among them was Sir
Vincent Fulnetby, who had been so proud of his lineage that he had
ordered that his tomb in Rand church be decorated with 23 coats of
arms. But his ancient pedigree was no guarantee of future security:
he died without a male heir, and his estate was carved up between
his three daughters. There were always new families waiting in the
wings to take over an heirless or debt-ridden estate, and with it the
local offices and privileges that had been enjoyed by the former owner.

To his parents' dismay, not long after Henry's death, young Lord
Francis fell sick with the same terrifying symptoms that had afflicted
his elder brother during his final days, being 'severely tormented by
them; and most barbarously and inhumanely tortured by a strange
sicknesse'. To make matters worse, it was reported that Lady Katherine
also fell gravely ill 'and many times in great danger of life, through
extreame maladies and unusuall fits'.[47] To complete the catastrophe,
the earl and his wife were also afflicted with 'sicknesse and extraordinary convulsions'.[48]

Terrifying though this sudden sickness was, it was by no means
unusual for a family to be struck down in this way. Death and disease

were regular visitors to families at all levels of society, and children under the age of five were most vulnerable. The rudimentary knowledge of obstetrics and child health meant that many perished in infancy. The contemporary records do not contain a single reference to a sick baby receiving any kind of treatment except 'unwitching'.[49] Doctors simply did not know how to treat them: it was pure chance whether they lived or died. As well as natural diseases such as pneumonia or meningitis, which could produce sudden and violent symptoms, infants were also subjected to child-rearing practices which weakened or damaged their health. Babies were tightly swaddled in order to keep their limbs straight. They were weaned on 'pap', a sort of flour paste, and were given adult food at a dangerously young age. As they grew older, they were dressed in coarse, restrictive garments which could cause infections, not to mention discomfort.

None of this was understood to have any bearing upon the fact that so many children perished. Instead, the high rates of infant mortality were attributed by a deeply superstitious and religious society to children being too young to protect themselves with prayers or incantations. It was therefore the primary responsibility of a mother to keep her children in health and to protect them from 'evil spirits'. She would trim a baby's nails with her teeth, and the trimmings would be carefully burned or buried. Human waste such as this was seen as raw material for witches, who were believed to use them to inflict harm upon the bodies that they came from. Teething pain was relieved by giving the child a piece of coral to suck, which had the added benefit of being a charm against witches. An infusion of poppies was another common pacifier, and although some herbal remedies proved effective, many were poisonous and fatal. Hygiene – even in richer households – was disregarded as being of secondary importance, contact between humans and animals was an everyday occurrence, and sewage and water supplies were not always adequately separated. The potential for disease was therefore dangerously high.

Nevertheless, the servants at Belvoir were quick to point the finger of blame at 'the old malitious feend', Joan Flower, and her evil daughters. Despite being their 'victims', the earl and countess refused to listen to such allegations. Their loyalty to the Flower women is admirable, particularly as Joan had apparently made no secret of her fury against the family for Margaret's departure 'in such vile disgrace' a short time before, and was said to have uttered many oaths and curses against them. Her anger had been at least partially justified: she had lost her livelihood at the hands of one of the wealthiest men in England. But in expressing it, she had helped to seal her doom, and that of her daughters, for the vast majority of witchcraft cases required the existence of prior animosities in order to secure a conviction. Joan had therefore played right into the hands of her hostile neighbours.

By now, gossip was rife throughout Bottesford that Katherine Manners and her half-brother had been 'set upon by their [the Flower women's] dangerous and divellish practises'.[50] A contemporary ballad even claimed that they both died of their illness.[51] Interestingly, though, while the family archives are littered with doctors' bills and other references to the two boys being ill, there is no evidence that Katherine ever fell sick – or certainly not seriously enough to warrant the attention of physicians. She seems to have been added to the sorry tale of bewitchment almost as an afterthought, as if to prove that the Flower women were determined to exact their revenge against the whole Manners family, not just the young boys.

It may seem outlandish that contemporaries were so quick to ascribe the sickness of the Manners children to bewitchment, but in this pre-Enlightenment age, medical knowledge and practices were rudimentary. Often, when a physician was unable to find the cause of an illness – or, indeed, to cure it – he would deflect criticism by claiming that the patient had been possessed by evil spirits or was a victim of witchcraft. 'Every disease whereof they neither understand the Cause, nor are acquainted with the Symptoms must bee suspected for witchcraft,' claimed John Gaule.[52] The seventeenth-century physician Thomas Ady shared his scepticism. He scorned the readiness with which an 'ignorant physician' would diagnose bewitchment to 'cloak' his lack of knowledge: 'When he cannot find the nature of the disease, he saith the party is bewitched.'[53]

Meanwhile, the Italian scholar Francesco-Maria Guazzo helped propound such beliefs by producing a list of 20 symptoms of bewitchment, covering almost every eventuality. For example, he stated that a sure sign of evil forces at work was if 'the sickness does not lessen, but rather increases and worsens'. Symptoms could range from a fever and convulsions to fatigue, loss of appetite and impotence.[54] Even the Royal College of Physicians was prepared to countenance such beliefs.

When a man named John Parker fell dangerously ill in 1623, the College ruled that witchcraft might have played a part, 'by the strangeness of the sick man's infirmities'.[55]

In his inflammatory pamphlet, *The Triall of Witch-craft*, John Cotta described a range of more bizarre illnesses which were caused by bewitchment. 'In the time of their puroxismes or fits,' he claimed, 'some persons have beene seene to vomit crooked iron, coales, brimstone, nailes, needles, pinnes, lumps of lead, waxe, hayre, strawe, and the like, in such quantity, figure, fashion and proportion, as could never possibly passe downe, or arise up thorow the naturall narrownesse of the throat, or be contained in the unproportionable small capacity, naturall suscep-tibility and position of the stomake.' He went on to describe how other victims had 'in the time of the exacerbations of their fits, spoken languages knowingly and understandingly, which in former time they did never know, nor could afterward know againe'.[56]

Such bizarre symptoms aside (which owed more to the frightened onlookers' imaginations than to reality), it is easy to imagine how some ailments, such as epilepsy, paralysis and high fevers – all of which could produce sudden and terrifying symptoms – were mistaken for bewitchment. Possession by the Devil or other evil spirits was believed to result in wild convulsions and contortions – as if the victim was being attacked by some invisible creature – as well as hysterical fits, paralysis and strange ravings. Children were thought to be particularly susceptible to being 'visited with diseases that vex them strangelie: as apoplexies, epilepsies, convulsions, hot fevers . . . which by ignorant parents are supposed to be the vengeance of witches'. Their opinions would subsequently be confirmed by 'unskilfull physicians'. Thus, said Scot, 'witchcraft and inchantment is the cloke of ignorance.'[57] Equally sudden and terrifying in their effects, strokes were often attributed to bewitchment. The notorious case of the Pendle witches began with a pedlar, John Law, refusing to give Alice Device some pins because she had no money. No sooner had he set off on his way than he 'fell down lame in great extremitie', robbed of speech and with his left side paralysed.[58]

Accusations of infanticide became a regular feature of witchcraft trials. Suspected witches were often accused of taking revenge upon a person for a real or perceived slight by robbing them of their most precious possession – their child. Such was the case with a Suffolk woman who was hauled before the authorities in 1645 and subjected to three nights' sleep deprivation. She confessed that she had 'cursed 2 children of Parkers and that they languished immediately . . . and concerneinge one fulcher's child that . . . she went and touched the child in the cradle and imediately it sprung up in the cradle and beinge taken with strange fits and imediately died.' As well as lack of sleep, the woman had also been subjected to a humiliatingly intimate examination, for her interrogator added that 'her imps hange in her secret parts in a bag'.[59] Other accounts tell of children being bewitched by toads, plagued by invisible wasps and breaking out in agonising sores.[60] Such cases were believed to result from jealousy on the part of the witch, who was perhaps childless herself, had been frustrated in love, or had otherwise fallen short of social expectations. 'A woman usually becomes a witch after the initial failure of her life as a woman,' observed one recent authority.[61]

Among the cases of infanticide was that of Ellen Smythe, a spinster who was prosecuted at the assizes in Essex for bewitching a four-year-old child to death. Ellen was the daughter of a notorious Maldon witch, and allegedly attacked young Susan Webbe as a punishment for arguing with her own daughter. According to the account of her trial, she 'gave here a blowe on the face, whereupon so soone as the child came home she sickened, and languishyng two daies, cried continually, awaie with the Witche, awaie with the Witch, and so died'. Ellen's own son, aged 13 years, testified against her, describing her familiars in great detail. Another Essex woman, Margery Stanton, was brought before the assizes for causing a woman to swell so that she looked pregnant and nearly burst. She was also said to have cast a spell upon a child so that it 'fell into suche shrickyng and staryng, wringyng and writhyng of the bodie to and fro, that all that sawe it, were doubtful of the life of it'.[62]

Midwives as well as cunning folk were also susceptible to accusations of witchcraft. A certain amount of professional male jealousy was involved here, because fertility and childbirth were a predominantly female domain. Outlandish claims of midwives seizing newly born infants and 'baptising' them in the name of the Devil before the local priest could arrive testify to the fear and suspicion that surrounded these healers. Some midwives were even accused of eating the babies they had delivered. One suspected witch from Lorraine described how she had killed a small child, whose corpse she later dug up and took with her to be eaten at a sabbat.[63] Meanwhile, a German midwife named Walpurga Hausmännin was convicted of killing more than 40 children, and was burned at the stake for her crimes in 1587.[64] It was thus with some confidence that the influential demonologist Jean Bodin asserted: 'There is nothing more normal for witches than to murder children.'[65]

For the Flower women, being accused of the murder of one child and the attempted murder of two others was not the end of it. They would also be blamed for the fact that the countess failed to fall pregnant after the birth of her second son. The contemporary account of the controversy claims that immediately after the children fell ill at the hands of the Flower women, both the earl and countess were 'brought into their snares' and prevented from having any more children. It was common in European trials for a witch to be accused of destroying a couple's fertility. This seems to have been one of their most feared powers, and it was referred to in Pope Innocent VIII's edict of 1484: 'These wretches . . . hinder men from generating and women from conceiving, whence neither husbands with their wives nor wives with their husbands can perform the sexual act.'[66]

Perhaps more than any other branch of medical science, fertility and conception seemed so mystical and subject to unseen influences that it was common for witches to be blamed for any difficulties that arose. As Cecilia Manners knew all too well, married women – particularly those in noble or royal families – were under pressure to fulfil that most critical of wifely functions by bearing their husband plenty of heirs. Those who failed to conceive, or suffered miscarriages or stillbirths, must have been tempted to cast the blame elsewhere rather than be deemed an inadequate wife. The local wise woman or witch provided the perfect scapegoat. When Fleuratte Chappouxat was proposed as a midwife for the town of Le Vivier in the south of France, a local couple, Mengeon and Agathe Colin, objected on that grounds that she had a reputation as a witch. Someone else was duly chosen, but when Agathe went on to suffer three successive stillbirths, she blamed it upon Fleuratte's malice.[67] The embarrassing problem of male impotence was also commonly blamed upon witchcraft. A practitioner need only perform a simple trick, such as tying a knot in some lace during the marriage ceremony, to bring this about.

One of the most influential works on witchcraft went into great detail about the various ways in which the Devil, working through 'sorceresses', could hinder conception. These included rendering a couple suddenly 'loathsome' to each other, 'suppressing the hardness of the member suitable for propagation', removing or 'hiding' a man's penis, or 'closing off the seed's paths to prevent it from going down to the vessels of procreation'. The authors urged that such witchcraft constituted murder because it prevented the formation of human life, and should be punished accordingly.[68]

The fact that Francis and Cecilia Manners would indeed have no more children raises the question of whether they came to believe so strongly that they had been bewitched that it had a damaging psychosomatic effect. There are several well-documented witchcraft cases where anxiety apparently led to illness. Among them was the case in 1602 against an Essex witch, Barbara Pond, who was said to have quarrelled with one of her neighbours, 'wherupon the woman fell lame & p[er]swaded her self she was bewitched by her the same Barbara Pond'.[69] Given the negative impact that stress can have upon conception, it is not beyond the realms of possibility that the Mannerses' belief in Joan's 'curse' was enough to render it effective. Otherwise, at 31, Cecilia was still more than capable of bearing children, assuming there had been no complications with the birth of her younger son. Or did she and her husband so firmly believe that they had been cursed that they simply stopped trying to beget another heir? It made little difference either way for Joan and her daughters, whose crimes were now believed to be so heinous that they were vilified throughout the local community.

That the community at Belvoir was so eager to believe that Joan and her daughters were witches was due to more than straightforward malice. The Flower women – Joan in particular – shared a startling number of characteristics with others suspected of 'wicked practises' at this time. For a start, a witch was likely to be a mature female, and often elderly or solitary. The average age of those accused of witchcraft was between 50 and 70, although some 'old' women who were convicted were little more than 40. The records do not reveal how old Joan herself was when she was first accused of witchcraft, but the fact that she was described as 'auncient' suggests that she fell within the usual age bracket of the accused. It was generally believed that the longer a witch lived, the greater her power became. When a mother and daughter were both accused of witchcraft in 1564, the younger woman claimed that her mother was 'the stronger witch'.[70]

The Elizabethan commentator Reginald Scot described a typical witch as 'commonly old, lame, bleare-eyed, pale, foul, and full of wrinkles'.[71] His contemporary, Bishop Harsnett, agreed that the 'true Idea of a Witch' was 'an old weather-beaten Croane, having her chinne, & her knees meeting for age, walking like a bow leaning on a shaft, hollow eyed, untoothed, furrowed on her face, having her lips trembling with the palsie, going mumbling in the streetes'.[72] A century later, Joseph Addison was still able to report:

> When an old woman begins to dote and grow chargeable to a parish, she is generally turned into a witch and fills the whole community with extravagant fancies, imaginary distempers and terrifying dreams. In the meantime, the poor wretch that is the innocent occasion of so many evils, begins to be so frighted at herself and sometimes confesses secret commerces and familiarities that her imagination forms in a delirious compassion, and inspires people with a malevolence towards those poor decrepit parts of our species, in whom human nature is defaced by infirmity and dotage.[73]

As well as being the most vulnerable and dispensable members of society, elderly women (and men) were also more prone to eccentric or antisocial behaviour, which tended to make their neighbours uncomfortable and prompt accusations of witchcraft. The likelihood of senility also increased with age, which made it much easier for interrogators to extract confessions of Devil worship or other such evil practices. Writing in the mid seventeenth century, the French dramatist Cyrano de Bergerac observed: 'She was old: age had weakened her reason. Age makes one gossipy: she invented the story to amuse her neighbours. Age weakens the sight: she mistook a Hare for a Cat. Age makes one afraid: she thought she saw fifty instead of one.'[74] Anne Whittle, one of the Pendle witches tried in 1612, was described as 'a very old, withered, spent and decrepit creature, her sight almost gone . . . Her lips ever chattering and walking: but no man knew what.'[75] A century later, Francis Hutchinson offered a number of sound reasons why the elderly tended to be prone to believe themselves witches:

> Old women are apt to take such fancies of themselves, and when all the country was full of such stories, and she heard the witch-finders tell how familiar the devil had been with others, and what imps they had, she might begin to think that a beggar-boy had been a spirit, and mice upon her mother's bed had been her imps; and, as I have heard, that she was very harmless and innocent, and desirous to die, she told the story to any body that desired it; and besides, as she was poor, and mightily pitied, she had usually money given her when she told the story.[76]

One of the oldest recorded women to be accused of witchcraft was Agnes Fenn, a 94-year-old Norfolk widow, who had been set upon by a group of local gentlemen for apparently bewitching various members of the community. She told how when she had refused to confess her crimes or beg their forgiveness, they 'punched her . . . with the handles of theire daggers and haveinge prepared a stoole in the which they had stoke daggers and knives with sharpe poyntes upwards they often tymes stroke her downe uppon the same stoole whereby she was sore pricked and greeviousely hurt'. Her terrifying ordeal grew even worse when her tormentors then 'tooke upp fier brandes and cast Gunpowder and flashed it in her face cryinge in most terrible and fearefull manner that they woulde burne her for a witch threateninge to cut of her heade and flinge her out of the windowe . . . and then stabbed her in the face with a knife whereby she blede to the quantitie of a quarte'.[77]

In an age that worshipped outward beauty and equated it with inner virtue, it was only natural to conclude that old, ugly women must be inherently evil. A contemporary of the witch hunts of the mid seventeenth century, led by the notorious Matthew Hopkins, observed that suspicion fell upon 'every old woman with a wrinkled face, a furr'd brow, a hairy lip, a gobber tooth, a squint eye, a squeaking voyce, or a scolding tongue'.[78] Witches were also said to be 'foul-smelling'. As Jean Bodin opined: 'Thus one can conclude that women, who naturally have a sweet breath very much more than men, by intimacy with Satan become hideous, doleful, ugly and stinking to an unnatural degree.'[79]

But no matter how inherently evil such women were believed to be, many contemporaries scorned the notion that an elderly, ugly crone could wield any power over her neighbours. Rather, they held that the real power sprang from the Devil himself. Central to this was the belief that most witches made a pact with Satan, relinquishing their mortal soul in return for earthly rewards. Even though witches were undoubtedly wicked, therefore, many experts on the subject believed that they were merely Satan's hand puppets. The author of the Belvoir pamphlet described the 'monstrous subtilty of the Divell' in persuading witches 'to give away their soules to be revenged of their adversaries bodies'.[80] Writing in the late sixteenth century, George Gifford declared that 'witchcraft and conjuration are to bee nombred among these filthy sinnes which are most abominable and odious in Gods sight', but added that 'the fowlest sinnes do spring and flow from the moste unclean fountain, though men be corrupt by nature and very vile, yet the Devils are muche worse. They bee the authours and devisers of sinne . . . The Devill allureth and seduceth men to be a servaunt unto the Witch, but shee is his servaunt.' He scorned the idea that witches were anything other than Satan's 'bond-slaves': 'Shall a silly old creature scarce able to bite a crust in sunder, give autority to the prince of darkness.'[81] A later commentator agreed: 'It is confessed on all hands that the Witch doth not worke the wonder, but the Devill onely.'[82] Most of the accused would confess their Satanic dealings after undergoing torture (or the threat of it). In his influential tract *A Discourse of the Damned Art of Witchcraft*, William Perkins criticised all those who doubted that such pacts were made, citing as proof the fact that so many convicted witches 'have confessed with one consent, that the very ground-worke of all their practises in this wicked art, is their league with the devill'.[83]

As well as being old and ugly, the accused was also likely to be quarrelsome towards her neighbours, and refuse to conform to social mores – including regular attendance at church. Many witches were believed to be secret papists, which set them even further apart from the largely Protestant society of Jacobean England. Lamenting the prevalence of sorcerers, George Gifford described them as 'the fruites of Poperie, which hath remooved away the light, and left the people in the dark to be deluded by the devill'.[84] A later authority thought it no coincidence that 'where Poperie and prophanenesse, with

contempt of preaching, there such miscreants are rife'.[85] Anne Baker
and Joan Willimot, two wise women who were known to Joan Flower
and her daughters, were alleged to have uttered 'Popish prayers' as
part of their craft.[86]

Like Joan Flower and her daughters, those women who were
suspected of witchcraft were often poorer than the rest of the
community, and certainly more so than those who accused them.
The sixteenth-century Italian physician Jerome Cardan described
witches as 'miserable old women, beggars, existing in the valleys on
chestnuts and field herbs'. Meanwhile, the famous French witch hunter
Nicolas Remy claimed in his treatise of 1595 that witches were 'for
the most part beggars, who support life on the alms they receive'.[87]
In the minds of the educated classes, poverty was bound up with
ignorance. As one contemporary put it: 'they are of the meanest and
basest sort both in birth and breeding, so are they the most uncapable
of any instruction to the contrary, and of all good means to reclaim
them'.[88] 'Almost all [are] very miserably poore,' observed one contemporary writer, 'the basest sort of people, both in birth and breeding.'[89]

Old age and poverty went hand in hand. The notion that the older
members of society were looked after by their children or other relatives has little basis in fact. Very few parents lived with their married
children. Moreover, a series of Tudor statutes – notably the Poor Law
of 1601 – meant that the traditional system of church or manorial
welfare for the poor was replaced by compulsory rates levied on
members of the community. There were far more women than men
at the bottom of the social scale, and the image of the poor old
woman lacking income or support became the subject of popular
revulsion. 'The bodies of aged persons are impure', opined William
Fulbeck in his witchcraft tract of 1618, and claimed that they were
'apt for contagion'.[90]

It is easy to see how witchcraft may have appealed to such women.
A pact with the Devil was believed to offer untold riches and pleasures
on earth – far beyond what these women could otherwise hope to
attain. Little wonder that some may have pledged their soul to him
in the genuine hope of rescue from their miserable lives. 'The pore
old hagge thinketh her selfe strong,' scoffed the pamphleteer George
Gifford, 'as she may seme to plague such as she is offended withall.'[91]
Even the great witch hunter James I acknowledged that people sought

to become witches either to alleviate their poverty, or for the promise of power and revenge on their enemies. He was also struck by how often those accused of witchcraft were elderly women. The court gossip Sir John Harington related a conversation that he had had with the king: 'His Majestie did much presse for my opinion touchinge the power of Satane in matter of witchcraft; and askede me, with muche gravitie, – "If I did trulie understand, why the devil did worke more with aunciente women than others?" I did not refraine from a scurvey jeste, and even saide (notwithstandinge to whom it was saide) that – "we were taught hereof in scripture, where it is tolde that the devil walketh in dry places".'[92]

Disturbingly, what made many of those accused of witchcraft stand apart from their contemporaries was the fact that they had a physical or mental disability. A popular handbook on the subject warned readers to 'beware all persons that have default of members naturally, as of foot, hand eye, or other member; one that is crippled'.[93] In *The Witch of Edmonton*, a popular play which appeared in 1621, the protagonist laments: 'Why should the envious world throw all their scandalous malice upon me? 'Cause I am poor, deformed and ignorant, and like a bow buckled and bent together.'[94] One of the defendants in the much-publicised Lancashire witch trials of 1612 was described as an 'odious witch [who] was branded with a preposterous mark in nature, even from her birth: her left eye stood lower than the other, the one looking down, the other looking up, she was so strangely deformed that the best that were present in that honourable assembly and great audience affirmed that they had not often seen anything like it'.[95] The influential scholar William Perkins asserted that most witches were 'aged persons, of weake braines, and troubled with abundance of melancholie'. He went on to describe how this could lead them to 'confesse of themselves things false, and impossible; that they are carried through the Aire in a moment, that they passe through Keyholes, and cleffs of Doores, that they be sometimes turn'd into Cats, Hares, and other Creatures, and such like, all which are meer Fables'.[96] Even Reginald Scot, who was sympathetic towards the women who were accused of witchcraft, described them as 'leane and deformed, shewing melancholy in their faces, to the horror of all who see them'.[97]

There was another, more basic characteristic that Joan, Margaret and Phillipa Flower shared with thousands of other suspected witches. The vast majority (around 92 per cent in England) of those accused of witchcraft in the sixteenth and seventeenth centuries were women.[98] As a modern authority on the subject put it: 'witch hunting is to some degree a synonym for woman-hunting'.[99] Others have described it as a 'holocaust against women'.[100] There is ample justification for this view. As early as the twelfth century, the authorities in one Russian district ordered that the entire female population be rounded up because they were anxious about the prevalence of witchcraft. Three centuries later, all but two of the adult women in Langendorf in the Rhineland were arrested. One influential commentator excused men altogether from involvement, thanking God for having 'preserved the male sex from so great a crime'.[101] Those men who were prosecuted were almost always related in some way to a female suspect or had committed some additional crime. However, this had not always been the case. A papal bull of 1484 had referred to 'many persons of both sexes' who practised witchcraft.[102] In the numerous references to witchcraft found in the Bible, male witches or 'wizards' are given greater prominence than their female counterparts.[103]

The seventeenth-century author John Stearne interpreted such references rather differently. He claimed that God's law against witches, laid down in Exodus, was set in the feminine gender. Likewise, Saul urged: 'Seeke one out, a woman that hath a familiar spirit.'[104] An influential fifteenth-century publication on witchcraft went further still by claiming that there was ample proof in the Bible for woman's fundamental wickedness. It cited passages such as: 'It will be more pleasing to stay with a lion and a serpent than to live with an evil woman', 'Every evil is small compared to the evil of a woman', and 'What else is a woman but the enemy of friendship, an inescapable punishment, a necessary evil, a natural temptation, a desirable disaster, a danger in the home, a delightful detriment, an evil of nature, painted with nice colour.'[105] The authors also quoted various classical writers, such as Publilius Syrus, who asserted: 'When a woman thinks alone, she thinks evil thoughts.'[106] Reginald Scot was virtually the only one of the polemicists to claim that there was little Biblical justification for the witch hunts: 'But as for our old women that are said to hurt children with their eies, or lambs with their lookes, or that pull downe the moone out of heaven, or make so foolish a bargaine, or doo such homage to the divell; you shall not read in the bible of any such witches, or of any such actions imputed to them.'[107]

The prevalence of women as victims of the witch hunt was not entirely due to misogynistic beliefs. Indeed, women played almost as active a part in the hunting down and prosecution of witches as they did as victims of the hunts. Evidence from the Home Counties assize circuit suggests that women were up to 15 times more likely to give evidence in witchcraft trials than in other felony cases.[108] Many of the men who bore testimony were doing so at the prompting of their wives. Moreover, the majority of those who were employed as 'witch prickers' were women. An account of a trial in 1579 tells how the jury directed that 'half a dozen honest matrons' be employed in this task, and many more similar cases could be cited.[109] Women also played a key role in generating accusations of witchcraft in the first place. In the insular world of the village community, rumour and gossip were a favoured pastime, and it was usually the womenfolk who spearheaded it. Inter-female rivalries were also a common feature of rural life. Far from there being a sense of sisterhood, hostilities between women could be much more intense and malicious than those involving the menfolk. Women were generally less tolerant of those of their sex who got above themselves or otherwise did not conform to strict village hierarchies – as Joan Flower and her daughters discovered. In this way, witchcraft accusations became one of the most effective means by which women could exercise power in a society dominated by men.

That there were so many female witches can also be partly explained by significant demographic changes which occurred during the sixteenth century. People married later in life and a higher number than before chose not to marry at all. The number of women in convents also declined, notably (but not exclusively) because of the Reformation and the dissolution of religious houses. The women who no longer followed a religious calling tended to remain celibate. The proportion of women who never married was around 20 per cent, and between 10 and 20 per cent were widows. This meant that as many as 40 per cent of women lived without the legal and social protection of husbands. Some of these found a home with brothers, sons or other male family members, but many others – like Joan and her daughters – chose to live alone. Such women often became lonely, isolated, impoverished and unhappy, complaining about their lot and cursing the society that had brought them so low. They thus became easy targets for accusations of witchcraft.

Many contemporary works on witchcraft claimed that women were naturally more vulnerable to the Devil's wiles because of the malleability of their character and body. William Perkins certainly believed this to be the case. 'The woman beeing the weaker sexe, is sooner intangled by the devills illusions with this damnable art, then the man. And in all ages it is found true by experience, that the devill hath more easily and oftener prevailed with women, then with men. Hence it was, that the Hebrews of ancient times, used it for a proverb, "The more women, the more witches."'[110] Others referred to women's 'credulous nature', which made them 'apt to bee misled'.[111] It was widely believed that their frailty derived from the means of their creation. One authority used as evidence the fact that, according to the Bible, woman was made from the rib of a man, and argued: 'A rib is a crooked thing good for nothing else, and women are crooked by nature.'[112] It is no surprise that the misogynistic James I agreed wholeheartedly with such reasoning: 'As that sex is frailer than man is, so is it easier to be entrapped in these gross snares of the Devil, as was overwell proved to be true by the Serpent's deceiving of Eve at the beginning which makes him the friendlier with that sex since then.'[113]

Single women were particularly vulnerable because it was believed that without the guidance of a husband they did not have the intelligence or willpower to resist the wiles of the Devil. Naturally lacking in intellect, women were believed to be barely educable. Cecilia Manners's education and that of her stepdaughter Katherine was entirely typical of that received by the vast majority of women during the sixteenth and seventeenth centuries. Most formal education was reserved for men, and about half as many women as men were literate. Not only was this used as an explanation for women's susceptibility to witchcraft, but as the vast majority of demonological pamphlets were written by men, it was all too easy for this myth to be propounded.

Women were also believed to have more fiery and passionate natures than men, which made them more vulnerable to bewitchment. 'They have such an unbrideled force of furie and concupiscence naturallie,' claimed one contemporary, 'that by no means is it possible for them to temper or moderate the same. So as upon everie trifling occasion, they (like brute beasts) fix their furious eies upon the partie whom they bewitch. Hereby it commeth to passe, that whereas women having a mervellous fickle nature, what greefe so ever happeneth unto them, immediatlie all peceablenes of mind departeth; and they are so troubled with evill humors, that out go their venomous exhalations, ingendred thorough their ilfavoured diet, and increased by meanes of their pernicious excrements, which they expel.'[114] Likewise, a pamphlet of 1615 warned: 'The malice of a beast is not like the malice of a wicked woman, nor that there is nothing more dangerous than a woman in her fury.'[115]

Women's natural discontent and implacability were also thought to make them 'more malicious, and so more apt to revenge according to their power, and thereby more fit instruments for the Devill'.[116] According to Alexander Roberts, a contemporary of Joan Flower and her daughters, women's tendency to gossip was also to blame: 'They are of slippery tongue, and full of words: and therefore if they know any such wicked practises, are not able to hold them . . . and so the poyson is dispersed.'[117] His views were enormously influential, and were repeated by many of his contemporaries – including the author of the Belvoir witch pamphlet. Richard Bernard, who penned his famous *Guide to Grand Jury Men* in 1627, agreed that as well as being 'more malicious, and so more apt to bitter cursing', women were also 'more tongue-ripe, and lesse able to hide what they know from others'.[118]

Another key trait which made women more likely than men to turn to witchcraft was their voracious sexual appetite, over which they apparently had no control. Constantly driven by the need to copulate, they would indiscriminately seduce husbands (their own and other people's), as well as other women and even animals. This was why so many fell prey to the temptations of the Devil, who saw that he could use the promise of untold sexual pleasure to ensnare them to his will. Many of the contemporary tracts on witchcraft describe the sexually deviant acts which resulted. An influential fifteenth-century manual on witchcraft claimed: 'All witchcraft comes from carnal lust, which is in women insatiable.'[119]

One authority referred to the 'many filthy carnal acts' in which women engaged, claiming that these resulted from their 'defective' and 'imperfect' physical nature. 'Everything is governed by carnal lusting,' it went on, 'and for this reason they even cavort with demons to satisfy their lust.'[120] The French jurist and politician Jean Bodin agreed. 'When we read the books of those who have written about witches, it is to find fifty female witches, or even demoniacs, for every man,' he asserted. 'It is the power of bestial desire which has reduced women to extremities to indulge these appetites, or to avenge themselves . . . For the internal organs are seen to be larger in women than in men, whose desires are not so violent: by contrast, the heads of men are much larger, and in consequence they have more brains and prudence than women.'[121] Again, there is a parallel here with the Flower women. Joan and her daughters had been accused of having loose morals and seducing several members of the local community.[122]

In decrying the promiscuity of women accused of witchcraft, James I had claimed that the 'most part of them [are] altogether given over to the pleasures of the flesh, continual haunting of company, and all kinds of merriness, both lawful and unlawful'.[123] Another authority agreed that those who who led a 'lewd and naughty kind of life' were most likely to become witches.[124] A suspected witch who was brought before the Essex courts in 1594 was said to be 'a light woman of filthey behaviour and hathe played the bawde'.[125] Older women, such as Joan Flower, were believed to be sexual predators, a notion that the male members of society found repellent. Reginald Scot expressed horror that a mature woman could 'enforce a man, how proper so ever he be, to love an old hag, she giveth unto him to eate (among other meates) his owne doong'. Similar disgust was voiced by Robert Burton, whose *Anatomy of Melancholy* appeared in 1621: 'Yet, whilst she is so old a crone, she cauterwauls and must have a stallion, a champion; she must and will marry again, and betroth herself to some young man.'[126]

Among the assize records for Kent was a case involving an elderly woman who claimed to make powerful love potions.[127] A fifteenth-century book on witchcraft described a particularly shocking case of an old woman who bewitched and seduced four abbots, killing three of them and driving the fourth out of his mind. Upon being arrested and interrogated, she defiantly admitted to her crimes, declaring: '"I have done so and I still am doing so. They won't be able to stop loving me because they have eaten this much of my shit", showing the amount by stretching out her arm.'[128] Given that the church taught that sex was strictly for the purposes of procreation, it is easy to see why sexually active women (such as Joan Flower) who were past childbearing years were viewed with such disgust. It is also easy to see why they were so often accused of witchcraft: since older women were often unable to find partners, they would seek satisfaction with the Devil, who was known for his sexual prowess.

A woman's menstrual cycle was thought to contribute to her 'devilish' inclinations. 'Women are also monethlie filled full of super-fluous humors, and with them the melancholike bloud boileth; whereof spring vapors, and are carried up, and conveied through the nosethrels and mouth, &c.; to the bewitching of whatsoever it meeteth. For they belch up a certeine breath, wherewith they bewitch whomsoever they list.'[129] Menstrual blood was believed to have magical powers: from bewitching a lover and serving as an aphrodisiac, to assisting in conception and even killing a man if he had sex with a woman during her period.

But as many of the accused were elderly women, well past their fertile years, a further explanation for their inherent wickedness had to be provided. Reginald Scot asserted that old women often suffered delusions because of 'the stopping of their monethlie melancholike flux or issue of bloud'. He went on to argue that 'they leave in a looking glasse a certeine froth, by meanes of the grosse vapors proceeding out of their eies. Which commeth so to passe, bicause those vapors or spirits, which so abundantlie come from their eies, cannot pearse and enter into the glasse, which is hard, and without pores, and therefore resisteth: but the beames which are carried in the chariot or conveiance of the spirits, from the eies of one bodie to another, doo pearse the inward parts, and there breed infection, whilest they search and seeke for their proper region.'[130] There may be an element of truth in this otherwise implausible theory. The onset of the menopause can cause a mental or emotional imbalance in women, which in turn can lead to unusual or erratic behaviour. It is therefore possible that those women whose extreme mood swings or shortness of temper were interpreted as a sign of devilish influence were in fact experiencing what we might today call a midlife crisis. But this theory does not satisfactorily explain the sheer volume of cases, or the fact that many of the accused were either too young for the menopause or had already passed it.

If Joan Flower and her daughters conformed to the stereotype of a witch by virtue of their sex, age, poverty and irascible nature, then they also did so because they were part of the same family. That three members of one family were all rumoured to be witches was not unusual. It was widely believed that the powers of witchcraft were passed down from one generation to the next, either as some kind of congenital weakness or a deliberate attempt by the parents to initiate their children. A contemporary of the Flower women, Francesco-Maria Guazzo, claimed: 'The infection of witchcraft is often spread through a sort of contagion to children by their sinful parents, when they try to find favour with their devils . . . And it is one of many sure and certain signs against those accused of witchcraft, that one of their parents was found guilty of the crime.'[131] Jean Bodin opined that 'the witch-mother customarily leads her daughter into perdition', and concluded: 'One can make a rule which will not have many exceptions: that if the mother is a witch, so also is the daughter . . . As far as witches are concerned, this rule is almost infallible, as it has been found from innumerable trials.'[132] Even the sceptic Reginald Scot agreed that most people believed 'witches . . . come by propaga-tion', and the notorious Essex witch-finder John Stearne claimed that witches 'leave' their powers to 'Children, servants, or to some others'.[133] Another authority claimed that it was enough for 'the party to be the Son, or Daughter, or Servant, or Friend neer Neighbour, or old Companion of a Witch' to secure a conviction.[134]

It was not simply a case of genetics. Witches were believed to take an active role in teaching their children and even grandchildren how to practise the dark arts. William Perkins observed that 'witches are wont to communicate their skill to others by tradition, to teach and instruct their children and posteritie, and to initiate them in the grounds and practices of their own trade'.[135] Meanwhile, the influential author Richard Bernard asserted that it was women's inability to hold their tongue which made them 'more ready to bee teachers of Witchcraft to others, and to leave it to children, servants or to some others'.[136] The case of the witches of Warboys involved Mother Samuel and her daughter, both of whom were hanged in 1593. Meanwhile, the women who were implicated in the notorious Pendle witch trials of 1612 included a grandmother, mother and daughter – again, all of whom were executed. Among them was Old Mother Demdike, who was said to have 'brought up her owne children, instructed her grand-children, and tooke great care and paines to bring them to be witches'. Likewise, in the bewitching of Edward Fairfax's daughters, one of the accused, Jennit Dibble, along with 'her mother, two aunts, two sisters, her husband and some of her children, have long been esteemed witches, for that it seemeth hereditary to her family'.[137] Many similar cases can be cited, both in England and throughout Europe.[138]

The fact that revenge lay at the heart of the Belvoir witch contro-versy was typical of other cases. This suggests that contemporaries believed that witches were unlikely to commit random acts of evil. Only if provoked would they visit the full force of their wrath upon the perpetrator. This would have encouraged most people to avoid antagonising anyone within their community who was different from the rest, who did not fit in, or who already had a reputation for malevolence.

In a strikingly similar case to the one that was unfolding at Belvoir Castle, a mother and daughter from Essex were accused of bringing grave misfortunes upon the person and household of Robert Sannever in 1582. Elizabeth Eustace, the daughter, was a servant in Sannever's house, but he reprimanded her for her 'lewde dealynges, and behaviour . . . [and] used some threatning speeches unto her'. Greatly aggrieved, Elizabeth went home and complained about his treatment to her mother, who was said to have bewitched him and his family. The very next day, Sannever suffered what was probably a stroke: he described how 'his mouth was drawne awrye' as he sat by the fire. More catas-trophes soon followed. 'His wife had a most straunge sicknes, and was delivered of childe, which within short time after dyed . . . his beasts did give downe blood in steede of milke . . . his hogges did skippe and leape aboute the yarde in a straunge sort: And some of them dyed.'[139]

Another typical scenario in a witchcraft case was when a poor elderly woman sought alms from a neighbour and was rejected. In a time of economic hardship, and until the Poor Law became fully established in the middle of the seventeenth century, this was an all too familiar scenario. Even though most members of a village commu-nity lived a hard existence, there were gradations of poverty, and everyone would have been very aware of these. There was constant competition between members of the community for status, power and resources. Although there was some sense of responsibility for those who suffered financial ruin, sickness, famine or other catastrophe, the existence of an individual or family in need of charity inevitably created tension, and sometimes led to resentment among those who felt obliged to intervene. Help tended to be grudgingly given, and often only as a form of insurance policy so that if the giver themselves fell on hard times in future, they would be guaranteed assistance.

'The poore old witch, pined with hunger, goeth abroad unto some of her neighbours, and there begge a little milke which is denied,' recounted George Gifford. 'Shee threateneth that she will be even with them. Home she returneth in great fury, cursing and raging.'[140] If any misfortune subsequently befell the person who had refused charity, blame was instantly placed on the old woman. 'Presently he cryeth out of some poor innocent neighbour that he or she hath bewitched him,' observed the seventeenth-century sceptic Thomas Ady. 'For, saith he, such an old man or woman came lately to my door and desired some relief, and I denied it, and, God forgive me, my heart did rise against her . . . and presently my child, my wife, myself, my horse, my cow, my sheep, my sow, my hog, my dog, my cat, or somewhat, was thus and thus handled in such a strange manner, as I dare swear she is a witch, or else how should these things be?'[141] An Elizabethan writer observed that a typical sin of the poor was 'their banning and cursing when they are not served as themselves desire'.[142] The belief in the evil consequences that could ensue if charity was refused was an ancient one. The Bible cautioned: 'He that giveth unto the poor shall not lack: but he that hideth his eyes shall have many a curse'.[143]

The majority of witchcraft cases conformed to this model. They included that of Margery Stanton, who was tried at Chelmsford in 1579. Among the witnesses was Mrs Saunders, who told how she had refused the woman yeast, whereupon her child was 'taken vehemently sick, in a marvellous strange manner'. Other members of the local community testified to similar experiences. As well as causing sickness among the children, Margery was also accused of casting a fatal spell upon a gelding and twenty hogs, and bewitching some cows so that they produced blood rather than milk.[144] That she and hundreds of women like her had been forced to beg in the first place was as a result of very real need. The most outspoken critic of witch beliefs, Reginald Scot, pointed out that these women would go 'from house to house, and from door to door for a pot full of milk, yeast, drink, pottage, or some such relief, without which they could hardly live'.[145] Accusing such women of performing maleficent magic was a way of assuaging the guilt of those who had refused charity. They knew it was their Christian duty to assist the poor, so rather than face the unappealing prospect of divine retribution, they set themselves up as the injured party.

The withdrawal of employment by the Manners family had effectively denied the Flower women the income that they needed to survive, so this scenario also applied to their case. The evidence against them was growing stronger by the day.

6

'This medicine be somewhat doubtful'

From the time of Henry Manners's death in September 1613, life at Belvoir was dominated by the earl and countess's anxiety about their surviving son. Although the contemporary account of the story implies that the boy had been suddenly struck down with a mysterious illness, his health had in fact long been precarious. Before the death of his elder brother, there are no recorded doctors' visits to this sickly child: perhaps, given that he was the 'spare heir', his parents had been more relaxed about his welfare. Now, suddenly, everything possible was done to try to restore him to health.

From 1614 onwards, the family accounts include various payments to physicians who attended the young boy. Not all of them were conventional. One of the earliest to visit Belvoir was the celebrated 'astrological physician' and cleric Dr Richard Napier. By the time of his first consultation with the Manners in October 1614, Napier had a considerable number of clients among the aristocracy and gentry of the Midlands. This was thanks to his brother, a Levant trader who amassed enormous wealth, became a baronet, and won favour with George Villiers, the future Duke of Buckingham, one of the brightest stars of the court and soon to become closely associated with the Manners family. Napier was no less popular among the poorer members of society (to whom he offered reduced rates), and in the same month that he visited Belvoir, he treated more than 50 patients and cast horoscopes for 27.

A shy, studious and fiercely intelligent man, Napier was a true polymath. Physician, astrologer, alchemist and cleric, he mastered a number of contrasting – and contradictory – disciplines, and was widely revered as a result. Like most astrological physicians, he often made his diagnoses based purely on the stars and did not even see his patients. 'It hath been many times experimented and proved,' declared one authority, 'that that which many physicians could not cure or remedy with their greatest and strongest medicines, the astronomer hath brought to pass with one simple herb, by observing the moving of the stars.'[1]

It may have been Napier's reputation for treating the 'falling sickness' (epilepsy) which drew him to the attention of Earl Francis and his wife, for the evidence suggests that their youngest son displayed symptoms consistent with this most feared disease. These were set out in detail in one of the most influential witchcraft tracts of the day: *A Guide to Grand Jury Men* by Richard Bernard. The author described how:

> Some will bite their tongues, and flesh. Some make fearefull and frightfull outcries and shreekings. Some are violently tossed and tumbled from one place to another. Some froth, gnash with their teeth, with their faces deformed, and drawne awry. Some have all parts pestered, and writhen into ougly shapes: as their heads forward, their faces backward, eyes rolling, inordinately twinkling, the mouth distorted into divers formes, grinning, mowing, gaping wide, or close shut. Some have their limbes and divers members suddainely with violence snatched up and carryed aloft, and by their owne weight suffered to fall againe. Some have an inordinate leaping, and hopping of the flesh, through every member of the body, as if some living thing were there.[2]

One can easily imagine how terrifying such violent symptoms must have been for those who witnessed them (not to mention for the sufferers themselves), and why the latter were often thought to be possessed. But although he was a firm believer in the possibility of bewitchment, Bernard counselled his readers not to confuse this with what was a natural affliction. 'For when people come to see such supposed to be possessed by a Divell, or Divels; some are filled with fancyfull imaginations, some are possessed with feare; so, as they at first time, on a sudden, thinke they heare and see more then they doe, and so make very strange relations without truth, if they take not time, & come againe, and againe, to see and consider with judgement, and with mature deliberation such deceivable resemblances.'[3]

There was a bewildering array of suggested remedies for this frightening disease, but the sheer number of them suggests that none were effective. The mid-seventeenth-century manual on medicines, *The Ladies' Dispensatory*, prescribed a host of bizarre and unpalatable natural remedies, ranging from the 'Liver of an Asse rosted', to the blood and 'outward skin' of a weasel, 'Stones found in the belly of the Swallowes first brood, tyed in a peece of Buckskin, worn about the neck', and the 'Gall of a Tortoise put in the nose'.[4]

Whether the earl and countess had tried any of these outlandish treatments is not known. Cecilia would certainly have been aware that, as the mistress of the household, she had a responsibility to ensure the health and well-being of her family. She may well have read the influential manual *The English Hus-wife*, which stated that one of her most important duties was 'the preservation and care of the family touching their health and soundness of body'. Society expected that every woman should therefore 'have a physical kind of knowledge; how to administer many wholesome receipts or medicines for the good of their healths, as well to prevent the first occasion of sickness as to take away the effects and evil of the same when it hath made seizure on the body'. Although the manual's author Gervase Markham admitted that 'the falling sickness be seldom or never to be cured', he advised housewives: 'If the party which is troubled with the same will but morning and evening during the wane of the moon, or when she is in the sign Virgo, eat the berries of the herb asterion, or bear the herbs about him next to his bare skin, it is likely he shall find much ease and fall very seldom, though this medicine be somewhat doubtful.'[5]

If the countess had made any attempts to cure her surviving son, then the fact that she and her husband were forced to call upon the services of expert physicians suggests that they had all been in vain. Napier was the first of many to minister to the young boy. As well as being an expert in the falling sickness, he was also renowned for treating victims of suspected bewitchments. He recorded more than 120 such instances in his casebooks.[6] Among them was that of a patient who, 'taken ill with mopishness', sought help because he 'feared he was bewitched or blasted by an ill planet'.[7] Napier was outspoken in his belief that witchcraft was at the heart of many illnesses – in particular those consistent with the young Lord Ros's symptoms. He remarked that the patients often suffered a similar torment to one who was 'haunted or bewitched', and described how they were beset with 'plucking sensations or convulsions that made them look as if they were being manipulated by invisible creatures'.[8]

It is interesting to note that Napier was also known for treating women disturbed by the deaths of infants. Until recently, it was accepted among historians that because infant mortality was so high during the sixteenth and seventeenth centuries, parents did not develop the same attachment to their children as we do today. They invested little in them, neither recognising their individuality nor taking much trouble over their care. Although this may have been true in some cases, it was certainly not so in the majority. The fact that a tragically high number of children succumbed to sickness and disease did not make their parents immune to grief. Indeed, the overwhelming evidence is that they felt their deaths as keenly as any modern-day mother and father. Richard Napier's casebooks include no fewer than 134 cases of grief so disturbing that it had led a husband or other family member to seek his help in treating the afflicted woman. They included Ellen Craftes, who 'took a fright and grief that a door fell upon her child and slew it. Presently head, heart and stomach ill; eyes dimmed with grief that she cannot see well.'[9] Meanwhile, Ralph Verney's wife was said to be delirious for two days and nights when her baby died of symptoms similar to those suffered by the Manners children. It is possible that it was the earl, concerned as much for his wife's grief over their eldest son as for the afflictions of their youngest, who had sought Napier's services.

The earl and countess no doubt laid out a considerable sum to persuade the renowned physician to visit Belvoir, rather than carry out his diagnosis remotely. Upon being admitted to the young lord's bedchamber, Napier would have carried out his accustomed rituals to diagnose his condition. First, he employed divination to ascertain whether the patient had been the victim of witchcraft. He sometimes conjured the Archangel Raphael, beseeching him to reveal whether a bewitchment had taken place, and whether the patient could be cured. His casebook records that in 1619, for example, he held a seance with the angel, during which Raphael confirmed that five of Napier's patients were bewitched and only two would recover.[10] He may also have given Lord Ros an amulet to protect against evil spirits, and would have written down prayers and charms to bolster its power. If he had considered this to be a particularly extreme case, he might have performed an exorcism. His treatment would also have included casting a horoscope and bleeding the foot of the afflicted boy. Perhaps not surprisingly, none of these outlandish methods produced a positive effect, and the earl and countess very soon sought help from elsewhere.

Dr Ridgley of Newark first appears in the accounts in the same month as Napier, and from then on he became a regular visitor to Belvoir. Unusually, Ridgley was himself descended from an 'old and prominent gentry family', which may have enhanced his credibility as a physician – certainly he was a favourite with the Manners family. A bill for 'apothecarie stuffe and other chardges for my Lorde Roasse, beeinge not well' accompanied the doctor's charges, and the family was apparently concerned enough to summon another doctor, named Sandy, at the same time.[11] In November 1614, Dr Ridgley was paid £7 for spending seven days at Belvoir 'with my Lord Roasse', and shortly afterwards he was summoned back to the castle for a further ten days.[12] He returned in September 1615 when Countess Cecilia bade him attend her son at Garendon Hall, part of the Manners estate and some 20 or so miles from Belvoir, where the physician stayed for six days.[13]

Despite their increasingly frantic concern over their younger son, the earl and countess apparently still refused to heed the rumours circulating that the Flower women were to blame. According to the contemporary ballad inspired by the case, they believed the illnesses which they and their children had suffered to be little more than 'natures troubles' or a punishment from God, 'which crosses patiently they bore, misdoubting no such deed, as from such wicked witches'.[14] This is corroborated by a note in the Belvoir archives dated 16 April 1615 which records that 'goodwyfe Flower' was paid a shilling each for '2 hennes'.[15] It is unlikely that the Mannerses would have been making payments to Joan Flower if they believed that she had bewitched their children. Although life must have been very difficult for Joan and her daughters in the local community during the two years since Margaret's dismissal from the castle, they seemed to be keeping a sensibly low profile.

In August 1616, Dr Ridgley again features in the account books for 'mynistringe phisicq to my Lord Roosse at Belvoir'.[16] This took place just four days before the king paid a visit to Belvoir, on 28 August 1616. James showed a genuine concern for the Manners boy, and it was almost certainly at his suggestion that shortly after his visit the earl and countess decided to consult (by letter) Dr Henry Atkins. A physician of national renown, 'famous for his practice, honesty and learning', and several times president of the Royal College of Physicians, Atkins was already known to the Manners family and had treated them during their visits to London. He had also attended the king's first son, Prince Henry, during his final illness, as well as Sir Robert Cecil and a number of other distinguished families.[17]

In a note written to the Countess of Rutland in December 1616, Atkins gave his opinion about the health of 'the little Lord' and enclosed a prescription.[18] He reassured Cecilia: 'the matter is not great that your Ladyship rigt of because I find not by your letter that the little lord hath any convulsions or fits that take away his sence or his motions but onely a jumping of his mouth by reason of some physicke gathering in his mouth & jawes or throte . . . making him sometime move his mouth some times a little more than ordinary'.[19] These are consistent with the symptoms of epilepsy, which would tally with the 'strange' convulsions both Francis and his elder brother Henry were described as suffering. Atkins also made an intriguing reference to some other symptoms, but excused himself from passing judgement on the basis that 'I for my part am not used to give opinions of things I have not [witnessed?] . . . therefore I pray you pardon me yf I pass that over for I love not to walk in the dark.'[20]

Had the earl and his wife asked Atkins about the possibility that their son had been bewitched? Given that he made only a discreet veiled reference to their request suggests that it was something he did not wish to commit to paper. Atkins seemed to be among the more enlightened of seventeenth-century physicians, and was reluctant to ascribe anything he could not understand or cure to witchcraft. This set him at odds with Francis and Cecilia, who seemed to have abandoned their former rationality.

The increasing desperation of the earl and countess to save their younger son is suggested by the appointment, in 1618, of one of the most controversial of all Jacobean physicians. Dr Francis Anthony was frequently in trouble with the Royal College of Physicians for using an alchemical remedy known as 'essence of gold', which he claimed could be 'helpefully given for the health of Man in most Diseases, but especially available for the strenghning and comforting of the Heart and vitall Spirits the performers of health; as an Universall Medicine'.[21] James I came to Anthony's rescue in his long-running dispute with the Royal College, and as a result his remedy was more readily accepted by the medical establishment. Like the Earl of Rutland, he was apparently willing to explore medical practices on the periphery of acceptability. Two payments for this essence can be found in the Manners accounts, dated January 1618.

Francis and Cecilia's frantic efforts make a lie of the account provided by the contemporary pamphlet that describes the Belvoir witch case. According to its author, the earl and countess interpreted the sickness that had befallen their household as 'gentle corrections from the hand of God' and resolved to 'submit with quietnesse to his mercy, and study nothing more, then to glorifie their Creator in heauen, and beare his crosses on earth'.[22] Its author was here toeing the official religious line, which dictated that God controlled everything that happened on earth. The victim of misfortune was thus expected to draw comfort from the thought that it had happened for a pre-determined (or predestined) reason. Although this reason was known only to God, Christians naturally tried to second-guess his motives. Adversity tended to be interpreted either as punishment for a wicked act, or as a test of faith. Often, those affected desperately cast about to find an explanation. Upon the death of his infant son in 1648, the vicar and diarist Ralph Josselin concluded that he had been punished by God for his vain thoughts and unseasonable playing of chess.[23]

It is possible – likely, even – that, having exhausted the services of the country's best physicians, it was at this point that the earl sought the help of Joan Flower. Desperate as she was to regain the Manners's favour, Joan no doubt readily agreed. But in so doing, she was placing herself at great risk. Although many people still put their faith in cunning folk, with their extensive knowledge of natural remedies, the dividing line between these practitioners and witches had become dangerously blurred. As a result, if a patient sickened or died after being treated, physicians could find themselves accused of having bewitched them. To make matters worse, Joan and her daughters were already rumoured to have cast a spell on the Manners children. If Joan did attend the young lord, then her ministrations worked no effect. His health continued to worsen.

No matter how grave the situation had become at Belvoir, the earl could not neglect his courtly duties. In November 1618, with his only surviving son dangerously ill and the women suspected of bewitching him still at large in the community, he received a summons to attend the king at Newmarket. He stayed there for several weeks, and then moved with the court to Whitehall for the traditional Christmas celebrations. These were legendary. The Master of the Revels and his staff spent many weeks preparing for them, hiring professional companies of actors to perform plays, masterminding glittering court masques, setting up gaming tables, and devising ever more sumptuous banquets, at which the wine flowed so freely that the revelries frequently got out of hand. The Earl of Rutland could hardly have had much stomach for such entertainments. That he was prepared to endure them whilst in the midst of a personal crisis is a testament to how much he wished to court the king's favour. It also suggests that he was a model courtier, adept at concealing his true feelings and motivations beneath a veneer of loyalty and obedience. 'He that thryveth in a courte muste put halfe his honestie under his bonnet,' observed Sir John Harington, a veteran of the institution, 'and manie do we knowe that never parte with that commoditie at all, and sleepe wyth it all in a bag.'[24]

The king himself was hardly more enthusiastic. Now in the fifteenth year of his reign, he had long since abandoned any attempt to ingratiate himself with his English subjects, and had become increasingly short-tempered and intolerant. 'The king . . . seems dissatisfied with his people, stays as little as possible in London, never shows himself in the city, and in entering and leaving always takes the least frequented routes,' observed the Venetian ambassador on a visit to court in 1618. 'In short in all his actions he does not conceal his dislike.' As a more recent authority has noted, he was increasingly apt 'to withdraw himself from a world which obstinately refused to dance to the tunes he piped'.[25]

The onset of old age had not improved the king's humour. Although he was still energetic enough for the hunt – a pastime that continued to take precedence over official business – he was described as 'somewhat heavy in person' and with hair that was 'beginning to turn white'. Sir Anthony Weldon remarked that he was 'more corpulent through his cloathes then in his body, yet fat enough, his cloathes ever being made large and easie.'[26] The Venetian ambassador noted that James 'avoids difficult affairs and listens to troublesome news with impatience'.[27] His only pleasure seemed to derive from his coterie of male favourites. Principal among these was George Villiers, the newly created Marquis of Buckingham, who joined the festivities at Newmarket and then Whitehall.

Charming, handsome and accomplished, Villiers was the very model of an ideal courtier – 'a youth . . . whose personal beauty and spirit' set him apart from other mortals, according to one contemporary.[28] Others described him as 'one of the handsomest men in the whole world', and claimed that 'from the nails of his fingers – nay, from the sole of his foot to the crown of his head, there was no blemish in him'.[29] 'He had a very lovely complexion,' observed Bishop Goodman, 'he was the handsomest bodied man in England; his limbs so well compacted, and his conversation so pleasing, and of so sweet a disposition.'[30] King James himself claimed that his favourite had 'the face of an angel'.[31] But if this was so, then it masked a nature as dark as the Devil's.

Although merely a 'threadbare but ambitious younger son', Villiers had enjoyed a meteoric rise to power. His first appointment as royal cupbearer in 1614, when he was 22 years old, had given him regular, guaranteed access to the king, and he soon became James's closest favourite.[32] They had met at Apethorpe Hall in Northamptonshire during James's summer progress earlier that year, and the king had been instantly captivated by the young man's exquisite good looks. From that time onwards, Villiers became a regular fixture of the court, and it was said that he cemented his place in the king's affections at the Twelfth Night revels that year. Bored with the conceited masque, the king suddenly cried: 'Why don't they dance? What did they make me come here for? Devil take you all! Dance!' Whereat Villiers immediately leapt up, 'cutting a score of lofty and very minute capers, with so much grace and agility that he not only appeased the ire of his angry lord, but rendered himself the admiration and delight of everybody'. In an astonishingly intimate gesture, James rewarded the young man's gallantry by patting his face, kissing and embracing him 'with marks of extraordinary affection' in front of the entire court.[33]

Although his many liaisons with the ladies at court suggest that he was heterosexual, Villiers encouraged the king's affections with flirtatious and suggestive banter, and once assured him that they enjoyed 'more affection than betwene lovers in the best kind man and wife'. In another missive, he passionately declared: 'I naturallie so love your person, and upon so good experience and knowledge adore all your other parts, which are more than ever one man had, that were not onelie all your people but all the world besids sett together on one side, and you alone on the other, I should, to obey and pleas you, displease, nay dispise all them.'[34] These letters aside, there is evidence that strongly suggests there was a sexual nature to their relationship – even if only fleetingly. Among James's many nicknames for his new favourite was 'dog', and a few years after he had first attracted the king's attention, Villiers wrote to him wondering 'whether you loved me now . . . better than at the time I shall never forget at Farnham, where the bed's head could not be found between the master and his dog'.[35]

The difference in their ages (the king was some 26 years his senior) inspired Villiers to give his royal master the cheeky nickname of 'dear Dad'. James, meanwhile, affectionately referred to his new favourite as 'Baby Steenie' (derived from St Stephen, who had angelic features), 'Tom Badger', 'Sweete Hairte', and 'that naughty boy, George Villiers'.[36] He once urged his favourite to hurry to court 'so that the whiteness of his teeth might shine on him' again.[37]

A rapid succession of honours followed for Villiers. Piero Contarini, the Venetian ambassador to England, remarked with some astonishment that Villiers' 'favour with the king increases daily, his Majesty showering upon him every possible mark of honour and greatness'.[38] In 1615, he was knighted and appointed Gentleman of the Bedchamber, and the following year he was made Master of the Horse and Knight of the Garter at the same ceremony at which the Earl of Rutland was honoured. The court gossip John Chamberlain expressed some astonishment that not only should a 'papist' such as Manners be so honoured, but that Villiers should be too, given that he 'is so lately come into the light of the world:

and withal yt was doubted that he had not sufficient likelihoode to
maintain the dignitie of the place according to expresse articles of
the order'.[39]

But that was not the end of it. At the beginning of 1617, Villiers
was created Earl of Buckingham, and a month later he was formally
admitted to the king's Privy Council. Upon the latter occasion, James
made a very personal speech of recommendation for his dear Steenie.
'I, James, am neither a god nor an angel, but a man like any other,'
he began. 'Therefore I act like a man, and confess to loving those dear
to me more than other men. You may be sure that I love the Earl of
Buckingham more than anyone else, and more than you who are here
assembled. I wish to speak in my own behalf and not to have it thought
to be a defect, for Jesus Christ did the same and therefore I cannot be
blamed. Christ had his John, and I have my George.'[40]

Perhaps inevitably, given his dizzying accumulation of titles and
offices, and the unrivalled influence that he exercised over every facet
of court politics and patronage, Villiers had become the subject of
intense jealousy and suspicion among his fellow courtiers. He rapidly
acquired a reputation for corruption and vice which, although
distorted, was not entirely without foundation. He was certainly ruthless and would stop at nothing to get what he wanted. Few men could
oppose him. 'The Marquis of Buckingham, the King's favourite . . .
at present exercises favour and authority over all things,' reported the
Venetian ambassador in early 1619. 'The entire Court obeys his will.'[41]

There was one man in particular whom Buckingham wanted to
bend to his will: Francis Manners, Earl of Rutland. By the dawn of
the new year, 1619, the marquis had already resolved to marry Rutland's
daughter.

Now in her sixteenth year, Katherine had grown into 'a daughter
worthie of all reverence', according to one leading courtier.[42] But she
was also headstrong and had a formidable temper – more than a
match for any potential suitor. The Manners and Villiers families had
long been well acquainted. Their estates lay in close proximity, and
the families were already connected through marriage. That they were
on close terms is suggested by the fact that the 5th Earl of Rutland,
Francis's brother, had bequeathed 'to Mr Villiers all my hounds for
the hare'.[43] The evidence suggests that Katherine had been intended
as Buckingham's bride for some time. A prominent nobleman, Sir

John Holles, shrewdly observed that 'when the times shall be proper for marriage [the Earl] hath a daughter for him'.[44] However, there is also some suggestion that Katherine's father was strongly opposed to an alliance with what he considered to be a 'family of upstarts'.[45]

Villiers was no doubt keenly aware of the advantages of marrying a well-born and well-connected young woman. But there were arguably greater catches at court for a man of his standing and influence – notably the Earl of Exeter's granddaughter, Lady Diana Cecil, whom Villiers was encouraged 'to cast an eye' towards.[46] Neither was Katherine renowned as a great beauty. Although her uncle, Sir Oliver Manners, had referred to her as 'your pretty daughter Kate' in a letter to his brother, contemporary portraits suggest that she was rather plain.[47] She herself later admitted to Villiers: 'You [might] have a finer and handsome . . . wife than your poor Kate is.'[48] Buckingham, on the other hand, had no shortage of admirers thanks to his dashing good looks – and the fact that he was the king's great favourite. One infatuated lady, Frances Shute, mistress of the Earl of Sussex, paid the princely sum of £50 as an annual retainer to a magician in an attempt to win Buckingham's love.[49] Mistress Shute was already well versed in the dark arts, according to a bill brought against her by Sussex's wife, which stated that Frances had 'caused and procured the Earle of Sussex to forsake & abandon the lawful society of his faithful wife . . . And by inchantment, charmes, witchcraftes, sorceries . . . hath procured the forsaking of his wife.'[50]

Katherine, meanwhile, was lacking in intelligence and wit. King James, who would have met her several times when visiting her father at Belvoir, once referred to her as 'that poor fool'.[51] Her later correspondence with Villiers reveals a credulous, even gullible, side to her nature. When he was sent to Spain to help bring about the betrothal of James's son Charles with the infanta, he quipped that the prince had been kept so far away from his intended bride that he needed a telescope to see her. Upon receiving this, Katherine dutifully scoured London for 'some perspective glasses, the best I could get', solemnly adding: 'I am sorry the Prince is kept at such a distance that he needs them to see her.'[52]

Their differences in character and looks aside, what made Villiers' match with Katherine even more improbable was the fact that the Manners family were avowed Catholics and may have been closet papists. They could therefore offer no political advantage to a potential suitor. Why, then, was Buckingham so determined to marry her? Given the close connection between their families, it is possible that he had known her for some time and had either recognised in her the qualities that he wanted in a wife or had become emotionally attached to her. The sources hint that, despite the difference in their religious sympathies, Katherine at least had formed a passionate attachment to Villiers. Or perhaps her suitor wished to achieve as high a standing in provincial society as he enjoyed at court – an ambition that would certainly be realised if he were to marry into one of the greatest families in the Midlands. Moreover, a close alliance with an old landed family such as the Mannerses would help offset the widespread suspicion of Buckingham as a 'new man' at court, grown to greatness too quickly.

But Villiers had more in common with Katherine than contemporaries believed. Far from sharing the abhorrence felt by the rest of the court towards Roman Catholics, he was closely linked to the Catholic community in England. His indomitable mother, who had been created Countess of Buckingham in her own right the previous year, was a professed adherent of the old faith, and both she and her son counted many practising Catholics among their close friends. That Villiers respected and even espoused Katherine's religious beliefs was not an incentive to marriage that he would have wished to make public, but it may have increased her value in his eyes. Nevertheless, it was inconceivable that such a close favourite of the king could marry a Catholic – and Buckingham was not a man to sacrifice political ambition on the sword of principle.

In fact, the most likely reason behind Villiers' enthusiasm for the match was that it had the potential to make him the richest man in the country. Katherine Manners promised an attractive dowry to her future husband, for as well as inheriting the unentailed portions of the extensive Manners estates in Northamptonshire and Yorkshire, she was also heir to the Knyvett property which had passed to her late mother. If she had also been heir to her father's principal estate of Belvoir, then her fortune would have been greater still – irresistible, indeed, for a man with Villiers' aspirations. The fact that she had a half-brother who would inherit the lion's share of the Rutland fortune was a serious bar to their union. But the whole court knew that the boy was of a sickly disposition, so the prospect of Katherine inheriting everything was a tantalising one.

However, any hopes that Villiers had of reaching a speedy agreement with Rutland were dashed when the earl was suddenly called back to Belvoir on business of the gravest nature.

7

'In vengeance strike'

The appearance of a comet early in 1619 was seen by many as an evil portent. When the queen died a short while later, it seemed that their predictions were coming true – particularly as the king himself was ailing. He was too frail to attend his wife's funeral, and it was widely believed that he would soon follow her to the grave. But he rallied, apparently thanks to a bizarre remedy that he himself had devised. 'On Saturday last the King killed a buck in Eltham Park,' it was reported, 'and so soon as it was opened stood in the belly of it and bathed his bare feet and legs with the warm blood; since which time he has been so nimble that he thinketh this the only remedy for the gout.'[1]

There was no such miracle cure for the young Lord Ros, whose condition continued to worsen, despite the ministrations of the country's best doctors. It may have been Joan Flower's failure to heal her son that persuaded Cecilia and her husband to finally heed the 'newes, tales and reports' which their servants and tenants had been whispering ever since the death of the elder Manners boy. Now, 'by degrees', they too came to suspect that their sons had been bewitched by the Flower women.[2] It was said that 'their hearts began to breed dislike, and greatly grew affraid'.[3] In common with the rest of the local community, they had started to believe that they and their children had fallen ill not of natural causes, but of witchcraft.

It is easy to understand the appeal that the rumours about the Flower women held for the earl and countess. If Joan and her daughters had bewitched their young son, then there was always the hope that the curse might be lifted. It transformed the boy's parents from helpless bystanders to active participants, able to hunt down the witches and thus restore their victim. If, on the other hand, the boy was simply suffering from a natural (possibly inherited) disease or condition, then the prospects of his recovery seemed bleak indeed, especially given that his ailment had confounded the best medical minds of the age.

With her husband still at court, Cecilia may have superintended the attempts to cure their son by persecuting the Flower women. Before seeking a cure for bewitchment, it was important to find out the name of the suspected witch. In this case, village gossip had already pointed the finger of blame at Joan and her daughters. A number of options then lay open to the victim or their family and friends. They included 'banging and basting, scratching and clawing, to draw the blood of the witch', 'burning of the thatch of the suspected parties house', making her touch the victim, or simply threatening the accused.[4] Contemporary trial records reveal that other, more obscure methods were also employed. One of the witnesses in an Essex witch trial of 1582 testified that she had taught the victim to 'unwitche her self' by gathering some pigs' dung and bones, telling her to 'holde them in her left hand, and to take in the other hande a knife, and then to cast the said into the fire and to take the said knife and to make three pricks under a table and to pricke the medicine three times, and to make three pricks under a table, and to let the knife sticke there: and after that to take three leves of sage, and as much of herbe John . . . and put them into ale, and drink it last at night and first in the morning'. The witness claimed that this malodorous potion had achieved a marked improvement in her patient.[5]

More traditional methods ranged from burning the victim's hair to plunging a red-hot spit into cream. Alternatively, one could boil, bake or bury a sample of the victim's urine, which would render the witch unable to urinate. Plagued with extreme discomfort, she would be forced to confess her guilt. Also common was the use of witch bottles, which were filled 'with varying quantities of bent nails, cloth, human hair, fingernail clippings and urine' from the victim.[6] At the same time as curing the afflicted, this method was believed to torment the attacker or to bring them back to the scene of the crime. Other methods included burning a sample of the suspect's hair, or making an image of them and pricking it with pins. The father of Elizabeth Chamberlain claimed that she had been bewitched to death by Jane Kent. When his wife looked set to go the same way, he hastened to a doctor in Spitalfields, who advised him to take some of his wife's urine, nails and hair and boil them up in a cooking pot. The man duly did so, and declared that when this unsavoury concoction reached boiling point, he heard Jane Kent at the door and she 'screamed out as if she were murdered, and that the next day she appeared to be much swelled and bloated'.[7] In this way, as one seventeenth-century commentator wryly observed, people 'often become witches, by endeavouring to defend themselves against witchcraft'.[8]

All the 'cures' for witchcraft were united by a common idea: that by causing harm to the witch, the victim would be freed from their malevolent power. Violence towards suspected witches was therefore freely sanctioned. When old Mother Rogers of Sussex was accused of bewitching a child in 1593, a local cunning man advised that she be stabbed in the buttocks. Drawing blood by 'scratching' was a more common practice. 'For some fall upon the Witch and beate her, or clawe her, to fetch blood: that so her spirite may have no power,' observed George Gifford.[9] Joan Flower's friend Anne Baker was beaten by a local man, William Fairbarn, in order to release his son Thomas from her spell. 'They said William Fairbarn did beat her and breake her head,' she testified, 'whereupon the said Thomas Fairbarn, did mend.'[10] But the most effective cure of all was to have the witch prosecuted and put to death. 'The malefic is prevented or cured in the execution of the witch,' declared the mid-seventeenth-century authority John Gaule. Likewise, Jean Bodin counselled that 'with the end of the chief cause, comes the end of the effects'.[11] James I himself agreed that the annihilation of the witch was 'a salutary sacrifice for the patient'.[12]

We do not know which, if any, of the known cures for bewitchment the Countess resorted to in an attempt to save her ailing son. But given how close she was to despair, she must have been willing to try anything. The strength of feeling among her servants and tenants was such that there would have been no shortage of volunteers to carry out the common 'cure' of threatening or harming the suspected witch. Joan Flower and her daughters now found themselves subject to increasing hostility and intimidation on the part of their neighbours.

None of this worked any effect upon the health of young Francis. The accepted wisdom of the day was that if all efforts to 'unwitch' a victim failed, then the only hope was if the suspect was forced to confess and a reconciliation followed. Others insisted that healing would only be achieved if the witch was put to death. In both cases, the law was required to take over. Cecilia needed no further incentive. What happened next is a testament to the injustice possible when the aristocracy accused commoners of witchcraft.

Joan Flower and her daughters were arrested either just after Christmas 1618 or at the beginning of 1619. By now, the process of bringing a suspected witch to trial was well established. In rural communities, a complaint would be made (often by the victim) to the village constable, who in turn would pass it to the local magistrate. The latter would then question both the accused and their accuser. In so doing, he would attempt to draw out information which would be useful at the court of assize. All of this would be written down in quite a formulaic way by the magistrate's clerk in a pre-trial document – or 'information' – against the witch. Finally, the accusation would be put to the defendant, and her response would be recorded by the same clerk as an 'examination'. On the basis of these accounts, the magistrate would commit the suspected witch for trial at the next assizes, and she would pass the period of waiting in gaol. This could be up to six months, depending on when in the court cycle arrest and examination had taken place. At the same time, any person likely to be able to give material evidence in the case would be bound over to appear at the assizes.

According to the author of the Belvoir witch pamphlet, it was apparently thanks to God's intervention that Joan and her daughters were now brought to justice. Rather than their accuser being named directly, he claims that God ensured that their crimes were discovered. We are left to consider whether it was a vengeful neighbour or a member of the Manners family who first raised the alarm. Certainly it was not their alleged victim, Lord Ros, who still lay dangerously ill at Belvoir. Neither was it the Earl of Rutland, who was at the court in Whitehall when the arrest was made. More likely is that his wife Cecilia – increasingly frantic with worry over their ailing son – had taken matters into her own hands.

To bring a suspected witch to justice, one had to either have money enough oneself, or to enjoy the patronage of a local gentleman or aristocrat. Most accusers were drawn from the ranks

of yeoman farmers and their families. It was rare for members of
the gentry to be the prime movers in a case, which is one of the
reasons why the Belvoir trial attracted so much attention. By contrast,
those who were tried for witchcraft were, if not completely destitute,
certainly very poor and always of a lower social grade than their
accusers.

Interestingly, there are no surviving witness statements by whoever
brought the case against the Flower women before the local magistrate. The absence of such statements in a case of this profile suggests
that either the author of the Belvoir witch pamphlet chose not to
include them along with the other evidence cited, or that they were
not taken in the first place. Both scenarios hint at a hasty arrest, the
outcome of which had been predetermined.

That the finger of blame should be pointed at Joan and her daughters after such a prolonged period – at least five years – is typical of
other cases of witchcraft. As one recent authority on the subject put
it: 'an indictment for witchcraft was usually the outcome of a web of
suspicion which was woven over a lengthy period'.[13] Once a suspected
witch had been identified, a process of post-rationalisation would
begin, whereby a whole series of misfortunes that had occurred in
the community over a number of years would be laid at her door.
The arrest of an accused witch therefore rarely followed a single
incident, but was the result of growing tensions and suspicions. The
contemporary legal sources reveal that some women were accused
of witchcraft on several occasions and over a long period of time – 10
years or more in some cases.

Thus, for example, when Amy Duny and Rose Cullender of
Lowestoft were accused of bewitching two young girls to death in
1664, several witnesses came forward to testify that the women were
responsible for various misfortunes over the previous few years. Anne
Sandeswell recalled an incident seven or eight years before, while
Dorothy Durent blamed the witches for her daughter's death five
years earlier and the illness of her infant son in 1657. When Jane
Wenham was tried in the following century, and the judge asked
Elizabeth Field why she had not testified earlier, considering that her
child had allegedly been bewitched to death many years before, she
artlessly replied that she appeared now, 'the opportunity presenting
itself'.[14]

In his *Discourse of the Subtill Practises of Devilles*, George Gifford described the common process by which suspicion of a member of the community could deepen into something altogether more dangerous.

> Some woman doth fal out bitterly with her neighbour: there followeth some great hurt . . . There is a suspicion conceived. Within fewe yeares after shee is in some jarred with an other. Hee is also plagued. This is noted of all. Great fame is spread of the matter. Mother W. is a witch. She hath bewitched goodman B. Two hogges which died strangely: or else hee is taken lame. Wel, mother W doth begin to bee very odious & terrible unto many, her neighbours, dare say nothing but yet in their heartes they wish shee were hanged. Shortly after an other falleth sicke and doth pine, hee can have no stomacke unto his meate, nor hee can not sleepe. The neighbours come to visit him. Well neighbour, sayth one, do ye not suspect some naughty dealing: did yee never anger mother W? Truly neighbour (sayth he) I have not liked the woman a long tyme . . . I thinke verely shee hath bewitched me. Every body sayth now that mother W is a witch in deede . . . Then is mother W apprehended, and sent to prison, she is arraynned and condemned, and being at the gallows, taketh it uppon her death, that shee is not gylty.[16]

There was a strikingly insular nature to accusations of witchcraft in England, most of which were rooted in rural communities, where the presence of an undesirable person could less easily be ignored than in a town or city. A leading authority on the subject has calculated that in 410 of 460 cases in Essex, the witch and their victim came from the same village.[17] The vast majority of the population – as many as 80 per cent – lived in the countryside, and with the exception of London, most urban centres were very small.[18]

Many witchcraft cases concerned not just one village, but sometimes one small section of a village. Reginald Scot argued that a witch's power only extended as far as their neighbours: 'for their furthest fetches that I can comprehend, are but to fetch a pot of milke, &c.: from their neighbors house, halfe a mile distant from them'.[19] The evidence also strongly suggests that almost all of those accused were closely linked to their 'victims' in some way. Most commonly, they had been involved in a dispute. Bringing charges of witchcraft was a means of expressing deep-seated animosity in an acceptable guise.

But the insular nature of communities did not always produce such negative results. There is also evidence that the strength of local ties could help prevent injustice in witchcraft cases. Thus, when the Yorkshire gentleman Edward Fairfax brought charges against the women whom he claimed had bewitched his daughters, they were acquitted after the judges received scores of testimonies that they had never before practised witchcraft. Similarly, when Mary Hickington was imprisoned in York Castle on suspicion of witchcraft in 1651, a petition with 200 signatures was sent to the northern assizes attesting to her good character.

Many of those accused of witchcraft were on the periphery of village life: they were eccentric, unconventional, or just did not fit in. Sometimes, though, as seems likely in the case of the Flower women, the accused were obnoxious characters who were determined to antagonise members of their community with their antisocial behaviour. In short, they were often people one would not have wished to have as neighbours. The witch hunts represented an ideal way of getting rid of them.

Before they were taken to their place of incarceration, it is possible that Joan and her daughters were subjected to one or more common 'tests' used to detect witches. One of the most popular, and feared, was 'swimming' the suspect. The use of ordeal by water – a practice wholeheartedly endorsed by the king in *Daemonologie* – was one of the most notorious ways of 'finding out' a witch. The premise of this brutal method was that water was so pure it would reject anything evil. As John Cotta put it: 'Water is an element which is used in Baptisme, and therefore by the myraculous & extraordinary power of God, doth reject and refuse those who have renounced their vowe and promise thereby, made unto God, of which sort are Witches.'[20] The accused person was duly thrown into a lake or river, often with their hands and feet bound; if they floated they were guilty (and punished accordingly), and if they sank they were innocent.[21]

Two later editions of the Belvoir witch pamphlet include a detailed description of this horrific practice.

The onely assured and absolute perfect way to finde her out, is to take the Witch or party suspected either to some Mildam, Pond, Lake or deepe River, and stripping her to her smocke, tie her armes acrosse, onely let her legs have free liberty; then fastening a rope about her middle which with the helpe of by standers may be ever ready to save her from drowning (in case she sinke) throw her into the water, and if shee swimme aloft and not sincke, then draw her foorthe, and have some honest and discreet women neere, which may presently search her for the secret marke of Witches, as Teates, blood-moales, most warts, and the like, which found, then the second time (binding her right thumbe to her left toe, and her left thumbe to her right toe) throw her into the water againe (with the assistance of the former rope to save her, if shee should chance to sincke) and if then shee swim againe and doe not sincke you may most assuredly resolve she is a Witch.

The author claimed that this method had proved so effective that he could 'receite a world of others in the same nature', adding: 'But the trueth is so manifest that it needeth no flourish to adorne it.'[22] Not everyone was convinced. When an elderly Suffolk vicar was interrogated by Hopkins and his men but refused to confess, they resorted to this ordeal to prove his guilt, as one who was present recorded: 'They swam him at Framlingham, but that was no true Rule to try him by; for they put in honest People at the same time, and they swam as well as he.'[23]

The Belvoir pamphlet describes various other methods used to 'discover' witches. These included 'the pricking of a sharpe knife, naule, or other pointed instrument under the stoole or seate on which the Witch sitteth (for thereon shee is not able to sit or abide)', inviting their victims to scratch or draw blood from the witch, and 'burning any relique or principall ornament belonging to the suspected Witch, which shall no sooner bee on fire; but the Witch will presently come running to behold it'.[24]

Why did the author trouble to include descriptions of these various tortures in his tract about Joan Flower and her daughters? He may have been keen to show off his knowledge of the procedures, but it is more likely that the Flower women suffered the ordeals he described. The hostility towards them amongst the local community would certainly have been strong enough to have ensured ample volunteers to assist in the tasks. But if they did endure such tortures, then they must have remained steadfast about their innocence, because there is no record of a confession at this stage.

Whichever method of arrest was employed for the Flower women, it all happened with bewildering speed. They would not have been allowed to return home first because it was feared that women who had been arrested for witchcraft might take revenge upon their accusers if they saw them again. The case was slightly complicated by the fact that Belvoir Castle was then part of Lincolnshire, whereas Bottesford was in Leicestershire. But it is a testament to the importance of the case that this administrative conundrum did nothing to delay proceedings in any way. It was swiftly decided that Joan and her daughters would be taken to Lincoln, where they would be imprisoned and interrogated at the castle while awaiting their trial.

The records do not tell us whether the women tried to evade capture or refused to go with those charged with arresting them. If they had, then the law dictated that the latter could beat them into submission. The same law stipulated that the conveying of a prisoner to gaol was to be at the prisoner's own expense – or, if they could not afford it, then of the town where they were arrested.[25] Given the poverty of the Flower family, it is unlikely that they met the cost of their journey to Lincoln themselves.

The arrest of Joan Flower and her daughters excited a great deal of interest among their contemporaries. It was unusual for a witchcraft case to involve such a high-profile family as the Manners; most centred upon little more than village squabbles. Although rare, such cases did tend to leave behind more detailed evidence than those in which the victims were much lower down the social scale. A contemporary of the Manners, Edward Fairfax, a Yorkshire landowner, accused six women of bewitching his two daughters, 21-year-old Helen and 7-year-old Elizabeth, in 1621. Meanwhile, in Scotland, a woman named Isobel Gowdie was accused of bewitching the Laird of Park's sons to death in 1662.[26] In the previous century, the notorious case of the Witches of Warboys involved the five daughters of Robert Throckmorton, who were believed to have fallen grievously ill as a result of witchcraft. Interestingly, as soon as the suspected witches were executed, all five girls recovered. This was taken as irrefutable proof that to effect a cure for witchcraft, the perpetrators must be put to death. With the young Lord Ros's life hanging in the balance, there could have been no more powerful incentive for the Manners family to ensure that the full force of the law was visited upon Joan and her daughters.

The Flower women and their captors set out on the 40 or so miles to Lincoln in the depths of winter. After 16 miles, they reached the ancient village of Ancaster, at the foot of the old Roman road, known as Ermine Street, which would convey them in a straight line to the city of Lincoln. This would have been more easily passable in poor weather than the muddier lowland roads along which they had travelled thus far. But for one of the women, it was where the journey would end.

Worn down by the treatment that she and her daughters had already suffered, Joan Flower was also terrified by the prospect of what lay ahead. Despite there being no recorded witch-burnings in England, the fallacy that this was the punishment that they could expect was a well-established part of popular folklore, both in the seventeenth century and today. Joan was said to have confided to a friend 'that her spirits did say that shee should neyther be hanged nor burnt'.[27] She was not alone in believing that burning might be the punishment for her alleged witchcraft. The misconception may have arisen from the rarely exercised power of the church courts to punish all heresy, including witchcraft, by burning. Or perhaps it recalled the notorious mass burnings of Protestants during the reign of 'Bloody' Mary Tudor, which were immortalised by the graphic illustrations in John Foxe's hugely influential *Book of Martyrs*. Most people would also have heard stories of the witch-burnings in Continental Europe and, closer to home, in Scotland.

Fear made Joan desperate. When the party reached Ancaster, she demanded an ordeal that would prove her innocence straight away. According to the contemporary pamphlet, 'Joane Flower the Mother before conviction, (as they say) called for Bread and Butter, and wished it might never goe through her if she were guilty of that whereupon shee was examined.'[28] This method of ordeal had been practised for hundreds of years. The bread was first blessed by a priest to make it pure so that if an evil person attempted to swallow it, their body would reject it immediately. 'Why should not Bread and Wine, being elements in that Sacrament of the Eucharist, be likewise noted and observed to turne backe, or flye away from the throats, mouthes and teeth of Witches?' demanded one advocate of the trial.[29] Legend has it that King Harold's father, Earl Godwine, met his death in 1052 when he choked on a piece of bread in an attempt to prove his innocence of certain crimes.

It is possible that the Reverend Samuel Fleming, chaplain to the Earl of Rutland and rector of Bottesford, was among those who accompanied Joan and her daughters on their journey to Lincoln, for he had been prevailed upon to join in their interrogation. He may therefore have performed the blessing of the bread. Upon being presented with it, Joan broke off a piece and put it into her mouth. 'So mumbling it in her mouth, never spake more wordes after, but fell donne and dyed as she was carried to Lincolne Goale, with a horrible excruciation of soule and body.'[30] Her astonished captors were left gaping in wonder at having apparently witnessed God's vengeance upon a witch.

No satisfactory explanation has been put forward for this extra-ordinary incident. Perhaps Joan – like many others who underwent this ordeal – had believed so strongly in its infallibility that she was seized by panic and terror, and either genuinely choked or had a heart attack. The claim by a nineteenth-century historian that Joan had been 'overpowered by consciousness of the contrariety between these protestations [of innocence] and the guilty design which she had entertained in her mind' is hardly more believable.[31] The less palatable truth is probably that the tale was invented to cover up the fact that the Flower women had been mistreated, and that – as the eldest – Joan had proved fatally susceptible. The rigours of the long journey in the middle of winter must also have taken their toll.

According to the contemporary account of the case, Joan was buried at Ancaster. There is no sign or record of any such burial, but this in itself does not disprove the story. Not all graves were marked, particularly those of poor people, and as a suspected witch Joan would have been denied burial in a churchyard. Her death proves how dispensable such people were: they could literally be made to disappear without trace or recrimination.

With their mother dead and no other defender in the world,

Margaret and Phillipa Flower were forced to endure the rest of the journey to Lincoln, tormented by the thought of what lay ahead.

8

'Unto Lincolne Citty borne'

When the Earl of Rutland learned that the Flower women had been arrested, he hastened to Lincoln with his brother George so that he might help interrogate them in person. He may not yet have known that Joan was already dead. As Justices of the Peace, both men were entitled to join in the examinations. Justices of the Peace were the elite of county society, and were closely linked to the wider political nation. Many of them were qualified lawyers, and some served as members of Parliament for their counties. Their numbers were relatively limited and depended upon the size of the county.[1] As the law's permanent representatives in the localities, the Justices were entrusted with a large amount of judicial and administrative work. The Earl of Rutland and other noble persons who held this post, however, did so more as an honorary appointment, which meant that the bulk of the work fell to a much smaller core of Justices in each county.

Although they set off later, the brothers may have reached Lincoln before Margaret and Phillipa. True, they had a longer distance to travel, but their journey would have been swifter and more comfortable than that of the beleaguered sisters. As the latter came within sight of Lincoln, their eyes would have been drawn to the magnificent cathedral, dominating the city atop the only hill for miles around. They might also have been able to make out the towers of the castle nearby. It was to there that their grim cavalcade now headed, winding its way through the city and up the appropriately named Steep Hill to the cobbled streets of the historic Bailgate area.

Having formerly been one of the principal cities of the kingdom, Lincoln had a long and distinguished history. It had risen to prominence during the Roman period, and traces of its Roman past would have been visible to Margaret and Phillipa as they made their way towards the castle. By the thirteenth century, it was the third largest city in England, and was favoured by a succession of monarchs.

Although it had since declined in importance, James I had graced the city with a visit almost exactly two years before the Flower sisters' arrival, in late March 1617. This had been celebrated with the pomp and pageantry that traditionally accompanied a royal visit, and all the chief noblemen, justices and clerics of the county had turned out in force to greet him. Francis Manners had played a prominent part in the proceedings, as recorded by a contemporary observer:

> The Earl of Rutland, being Lieutenant of the County, did bear the King's Sword, all the said Aldermen, Sheriffs, and other Citizens in their ranks, youngest first, did ride, two and two together, up the High-street, through the Baile unto the Minster-gates at the west end thereof, where the King kneeled down on a cushion, which was there prepared, and prayed a short prayer, and so, under a canopy which was held over him by four or six Prebends in surplices, went into the Quire [of the cathedral], the Mayor still bearing the Sword, the Aldermen and other Citizens in their gowns going before him into the Quire, and there sate by the Bishop's pue hanged about with rich hangings in a Chair all prayer-time.

James later conducted various ceremonies in the cathedral and elsewhere to cure people of the King's Evil.[2] There had followed a number of banquets, entertainments, cock-fighting, hunts and other pastimes designed for the king's pleasure.

But the city of Lincoln had a darker past. It had long been a place of prisons and scaffolds. The focus of statutory punishment had always been the castle that overlooked the city. Originally built by William the Conqueror, it had housed a courthouse and county gaol since Tudor times, and public executions were regularly carried out there in full public view. Margaret and Phillipa Flower entered the castle through the imposing East Gate, with two huge round turrets above the archway and portcullis. They were then conveyed to their place of incarceration, which was almost certainly Cobb Hall, a defensive wall tower in the north-east corner of the bailey which dated back to the thirteenth century. The upper floor was divided into recesses which served as cells, and the prisoners were chained to heavy iron rings, some of which can still be seen today. The lower floor was a dungeon with a similar layout, but it could only be reached by ladder from the trapdoor above. Carvings made by prisoners are also still visible, including an image of a stag being hunted down. Given their notoriety, the Flower sisters were probably chained up in this lower chamber (which became known as the 'witch hole' after their incarceration), where the prospect of escape was even more remote than above.

The two sisters would have endured cramped and insanitary conditions in this grim fortress. Most sixteenth- and seventeenth-century prisons were described as 'mere dens of misery and disease', unfit to 'keep the prisoners free from wind and weather'. Gaol fever – probably a form of dysentery – carried off hundreds of prisoners each year before they had even been brought to trial.[3] A notorious case of it occurred in 1577, when several sick prisoners were tried at the Oxford assizes and proceeded to infect jurors and judges alike, with fatal results.

Prisoners were crammed together in communal cells, with little if any segregation according to sex or offence. These cramped, squalid conditions made them susceptible to disease. As well as gaol fever, plague was particularly virulent in prisons, carrying off many hundreds of inmates at a time. In the Home Counties circuit of the assizes, it has been calculated that some 1,292 prisoners died in gaol between 1558 and 1625.[4] In Essex alone, 21 women accused of witchcraft died in gaol between 1560 and 1603. When the notorious Lancashire witches were holed up in Lancaster Castle in 1612, the octogenarian Elizabeth Southerns soon 'dyed in the castle before she came to her Tryall'.[5]

Living in cold, unhygienic conditions, prisoners were often undernourished or given food more fit for animals. In 1545, a monk appealed for better treatment for prisoners, pointing out that 'their lodging is too bad for hoggys, and as for their meat it is euil enough for doggys'.[6] Their only hope was if they had friends nearby who were prepared to bring them rations, or had the means to bribe their corrupt gaolers; given that most accused witches were 'abandoned wretches, without friends or money', this was rarely an option for them.[7]

Those who survived were commonly mistreated by their gaolers, many of whom also extracted extortionate fees from them in return for paltry 'privileges'. An inquest held in 1630 was highly critical of conditions in the gaol in Colchester Castle, where 'the miseries of the poore prisoners are soe great & lamentable partlie by reason of the crueltie of the Gaoler & partlie by reason of the extreme wantes they suffer that many of them are famished'.[8] Little wonder that the suspected witch Jane Wenham fell down before one of her accusers, 'begging her not to swear against her, using many expressions of fear, least she be sent to gaol'. As the writer of her trial pamphlet noted: 'Under her circumstances, she could expect nothing less than a Course of misery and Hardship worse than death.'[9] Neither could a witch hope for rescue from her satanic master. It was widely believed that, once in custody, a witch lost all her demonic powers. 'If this witch is imprisoned, she is void of hurt, and Satan leaves her,' opined James I in his famous tract on witchcraft. 'For where God beginnes justlie to strike by his lawfull Lieutenantes, it is not in the Devilles power to defraude or bereave him of the office, or effect of his powerful and revenging Scepter.'[10]

Faced with the grim prospect of a miserable, possibly prolonged imprisonment, followed by almost certain death, it may be reasonably expected that a high proportion of suspected witches attempted escape. But the evidence suggests that, although some avoided arrest after a warrant had been issued, escape from prison was exceptionally rare. This perhaps had less to do with the effectiveness of the security measures than the fact that many of the accused were confused and frightened old women who literally had nowhere else to go. In the insular world of sixteenth- and seventeenth-century rural life, there was little migration even between neighbouring communities, let alone further afield. Most people would therefore only have been familiar with their own villages, and as these were effectively closed to them after they had been accused of witchcraft, there must have seemed no other option but to endure the misery of their fate.

The horrors of prison were made even worse for Margaret and Phillipa by the fact that they were incarcerated in the middle of winter, and in a dungeon that was bitterly cold even during the summer months.[11] Neither would they have had much food to sustain them, since their rations were dependent upon the charity of the prison-keepers. Given the notoriety of their crimes, and the fact that they had no friends in the city, it is likely that they went hungry most of the time. As suspected felons, they were not permitted to 'goe at liberty within the prison, nor abroad with their keeper'.[12] Their only comfort – and it was a cold comfort at that – was the prison chaplain, whose job it was to reconcile the accused to their likely fate. But any sympathetic ministrations that he gave would have been far outweighed by the ill treatment, threats and bullying meted out by the gaolers, who often brought pressure to bear on prisoners over a prolonged period in order to extract confessions or the names of other suspects.

The Flower sisters had no hope of bail. This was a privilege denied – in practice, if not in theory – to suspected witches, along with other felons. But it was unlikely that they endured a long wait before their interrogation began. Jean Bodin urged that this must follow as soon as the suspect was incarcerated: 'One must first of all and as soon as possible, begin interrogating the witch. While that is certainly useful for all crimes, for this one it must be done. For it has always been found that as soon as the witch is arrested, she immediately feels that Satan has abandoned her, and terrified she confesses willingly then what force and torture could not extract from her. But if she is left in prison for some time, there is no doubt that Satan will give her instruction.'[13]

In contrast to James I, Bodin urged that, once imprisoned, a suspected witch must never be left alone. 'She speaks to the Devil . . . who dissuades her from telling the truth, or makes her depart from what she has confessed and always promises her that she will not die, which creates many obstacles . . . Others already condemned to death, kill themselves, as we have often seen.'[14] By the time they reached Lincoln Castle, the Flower sisters had already won such notoriety that their gaolers no doubt heeded this advice very carefully for fear that they might escape the grisly fate that looked set to befall them.

Although most women accused of witchcraft received the cursory treatment that an overcrowded justice system could afford, cases involving well-connected families such as the Manners were handled with rather more attention to detail. The author of the trial pamphlet concurs that the Flower women were 'specially arraigned' and the evidence against them 'taken and charily [carefully] preserved'.[15] The account books at Belvoir attest that the Earl of Rutland spared no expense in his determination to see them brought to justice. A payment of £20 was made to the family's treasurer, Francis Jephson, on 16 March 1619 'for charges in prosecuting the witche[s]'. A further £20 was paid to Jephson on 15 July 'upon my Lorde's jorney to the assises at Lyncolne'.[16] One further payment, dated 2 September, was made to Jephson for £17 for unspecified goods or services.[17] In total, the earl

spent almost £6,000 in modern money. His determination may not
have been an act of vengeance but of prevention: if the Flower women
were put to death, then their power over his ailing younger son might
be extinguished.

Francis and George Manners were joined in their examinations by
the other two most distinguished members of the Lincolnshire aristocracy, Lord Willoughby d'Eresby and Sir William Pelham.[18] Lord
Willoughby was a close friend of the earl, and was his deputy in the
lieutenancy of Lincolnshire. Pelham, meanwhile, was also a regular
visitor to Belvoir and had been knighted there by James I in 1612. As
high sheriff of Lincolnshire, he was arguably the most experienced
in the law, having been trained at Gray's Inn following legal studies
at New College, Oxford. As well as their official positions, the men
were connected by blood or marriage and called each other 'brother'
or 'cousin'. It was an extraordinarily close-knit circle, and every
member of it would have been very conscious of the unspoken reason
for their being present at the trial: to bring the Flower women to swift
and brutal justice.

The closed, incestuous world of the local aristocracy and justice
system was not exclusive to Lincolnshire: it was mirrored in every
part of the country and underpinned the entire administration of
local and central government. Anyone who was not part of this privileged world and fell foul of the law could expect little by way of
justice. It was even worse for those who, like the Flower sisters, had
committed crimes against the aristocracy. In cases such as these, the
full power of the English state would be brought down upon their
heads.

The other examiners were hardly less distinguished. They included
Henry Hastings, sheriff of Leicester, who belonged to the distinguished
family of the Earl of Huntingdon. He was of a strong Protestant bias,
and as such took a keen interest in cases of witchcraft. A Justice of
the Peace, Mr Butler, was also among their number. The final member
of the interrogation team stood out from the rest because he was
neither of noble birth nor a member of the judiciary. He was the
Reverend Samuel Fleming, rector of Bottesford since 1581 and official
chaplain to four successive earls of Rutland, including Sir Francis
Manners.

Fleming stood apart from his fellow interrogators because of more than just his birth and profession. He was a writer and intellectual of some renown, and the evidence suggests that he was sceptical about witchcraft, and therefore less motivated than the rest to see the Flower sisters hanged.[19] He was in his early seventies at the time of the trial and emerges from the contemporary records as a gentle and benevolent man, whose generosity towards the poor of the local community can still be seen in Bottesford today.[20] Fleming also differed from his noble patron by dint of his devout Puritan faith.

By the time of Margaret and Phillipa's imprisonment, witchcraft prosecutions had gained the same notoriety as crimes such as murder or treason, which were punishable by death. Among lawyers, witchcraft was known as *crimen exceptum* – which meant that it was not subject to the normal legal procedures. 'It is absolutely necessary to bear in mind that the crime of witchcraft must not be treated in the same way as others,' insisted Jean Bodin.[21] 'Those who let witches escape or who do not carry out their punishment with utmost rigour, can be assured that they will be abandoned by God to the mercy of witches. And the country which tolerates them will be struck by plagues, famines, and wars.' By contrast, he asserted: 'Those who take vengeance against them will be blessed by God, and will bring an end to His wrath. This is why one who is charged and accused of being a witch must never be simply let off and acquitted, unless the calumny of the accuser or informer is clearer than the sun. Since the proof of such wickednesses is so hidden and so difficult, no one would ever be accused or punished out of a million witches if parties were governed, as in an ordinary trial, by a lack of proof.'[22]

Bodin's views were echoed throughout the judicial sphere. Measures of proof could be much flimsier than for other cases, which usually required a confession and two witnesses, while methods of interrogation could be altogether harsher. It was not necessary for a suspected witch to confess to her crimes in order for the authorities to secure a conviction. Indeed, if she denied her guilt, then she was often simply adding perjury to her other sins. Thus, in the notorious case of the Pendle witches in 1612, when Jennet Preston protested her innocence, it was deemed 'a very fearful thing to all that were present, who knew she was guilty'.[23]

Nevertheless, because a confession was accepted as irrefutable proof of guilt, there was a considerable incentive to secure one. Furthermore, once a person had confessed, they became a powerful witness against others. The accused would therefore be subjected to intense pressure and 'sharp speeches' by their interrogators, who all too often goaded them into admitting their crimes by the threat of torture, unending imprisonment or death.[24] The psychological effects of being kept in solitary confinement led many others to confess. The notorious 'Witchfinder General', Matthew Hopkins, recorded with some relish how many of his victims would be 'brought into a sad condition, by understanding of the horribleness of her sin, and the judgements threatened against her; and knowing the Devill's malice and subtile circumventions, is brought to remorse and sorrow for complying with Satan for so long, and disobeying God's sacred Commands, doth then desire to unfold her mind with much bitterness'.[25]

The fact that the trial papers often contain detailed descriptions of curses and spells given by the accused might suggest that they had in fact tried to cause harm by magical means. But these descriptions are so similar as to be almost formulaic. It would have been sufficient for a small number of people to cite such spells and incantations for them to become common knowledge among the legal community. And it is entirely possible that those responsible for interrogating the accused may have planted the idea of these magical arts into the confused, tired and frightened minds of their prisoners in order to secure a conviction. By the time they confessed, most suspected witches had lost the capacity to distinguish truth from fiction; reality from fantasy.

A witch's own confession aside, courts could admit the evidence of those who were not usually permitted to bear testimony: women, 'old silly persons', convicted felons and interested parties.[26] 'One must not . . . insist on the ordinary rules for handling, challenging or admitting witnesses in such a hateful crime as this one,' insisted Jean Bodin.[27] So-called witnesses in witchcraft trials did not even have to have seen the crime. As one cynical contemporary noted, if this had been a requirement, 'it will be then impossible to put any one to death . . . [for] hardly can a man be brought, which upon his owne knowledge, can averre such things'.[28] It was enough to testify to the motives and effects of the alleged witchcraft. The fact that women, in particular, were allowed to act as witnesses was a radical departure from standard legal procedure. Traditionally, as Bodin pointed out, 'according to canon law women in a criminal action are not admissible as witnesses on account of the imbecility and fragility of the sex', and 'one must always have two women to equal the testimony of one man'.[29] That this rule did not apply to witchcraft cases is perhaps an indication of how desperate the authorities were to secure convictions.

The testimonies of children were also considered admissible evidence. An alarming number of children were pressured into giving evidence against their parents. 'Sundry tymes the evidence of children is taken accusing their owne mothers, that they did see them give milke unto little thinges [familiars] which they kept in wooll,' observed George Gifford. 'The children comming to yeares of discretion confesse they were entised to accuse.'[30] In an age when infants were raised on stories of witches, fairies and goblins, it is easy to see how their overexcited imaginations made them swear that they had seen an old woman flying through the night sky on a broomstick, or a devil emerge from the shadows in their room while they were asleep. All too often, children were manipulated by the authorities to confirm outlandish tales of witchcraft. The interrogator in the notorious case of the 14 women who were tried for witchcraft in 1582 persuaded Ursula Kemp's eight-year-old son, Thomas, to confirm that she had four familiars: 'And being asked of what colours they were, [he] saith that Titty is like a little grey cat, Tiffin is like a white lamb, Piggin is black, like a toad, and Jack is black, like a cat. And he saith, he hath seen his mother at times to give them beer to drink, and of a white loaf or cake to eat; and saith that in the night-time the said spirits will come to his mother and suck blood of her upon her arms and other places of her body.'[31]

The most notorious case of a child giving evidence against their family was that of the Pendle witches in 1612. When her elder sister, brother, mother and grandmother and several of her neighbours were accused of witchcraft and brought to trial at Lancaster Castle, nine-year-old Jennet Device was called to the witness stand. Upon seeing her daughter enter the courtroom, Elizabeth Device let out an anguished scream, knowing that the girl's testimony would be enough to send all of the accused to their deaths. But according to the contemporary account of the trial, Jennet was unmoved by her mother's distress and demanded that she be removed from the room. She then stood on a table so that the entire court might see her, and calmly denounced her mother as a witch. Elizabeth and

all of the other members of the Device family who had been implicated, along with most of their neighbours, were hanged the next
day.

Quite what had motivated Jennet to send her family to their deaths
is still a matter for debate. It is possible that relations between them
were not good, but she must have harboured a deep-seated hatred of
them to exact such a revenge. More likely, perhaps, is that she had
been pressured and intimidated by members of the judiciary, who
were intent upon making an example of this Catholic family, and at
the same time winning favour with their Protestant witch hunting
king. Four years later, another mass trial rested upon the testimony
of a child. On that occasion, nine women were sentenced to death at
Leicester on charges of witchcraft which were supported by the uncor-
roborated evidence of one boy.[32]

In other cases, children made their accusations of their own free
will, motivated by a desire to cause mischief. One of the most notorious was Anne Gunter, a 14-year-old girl from Berkshire who in 1604
fell into a series of strange fits. The ministrations of physicians worked
no effect, and in her torment Anne railed against a number of local
women whom she claimed had bewitched her. The story rapidly spread
throughout the local area, and soon her sick chamber became thronged
with people from far and wide, curious to catch a glimpse of the
'hysterical passions and paralytical convulsions' experienced by the
young girl. In her fevered ramblings, she described in extraordinary
detail the familiars of the witches who had brought her to this sorry
state. They included 'a whitish mouse with a man's face and long beard,
called Sweat', 'a black rat with a swine's face and boar's tusk named
Catche', and 'a whitish toad called Vizitt'. Her case attracted the notice
of some of the country's leading scholars and ministers, who all
hastened to see the girl for themselves. Clearly enjoying the attention,
on one occasion when a godly young man was fervently praying at
her bedside, Anne suddenly kicked a lighted candle into his face. On
another, she 'put her head under the bed clothes, as some observers
suspected, to have a quiet laugh'. Determined to silence those who
began to whisper that the whole matter was an elaborate ruse, Anne's
father took her to be examined by King James himself. Bemused by
the whole affair, James referred it to the Archbishop of Canterbury,
who in turn committed Anne to the care of his chaplain, Samuel

Harsnett, who had uncovered a fraudulent witchcraft case some years earlier. Anne and her father were shortly afterwards accused of conspiracy before the Star Chamber. Throwing herself on their mercy, Anne confessed that she had suffered only from a 'natural distemper' and that her father had 'persuaded her to feign strange symptoms'.[33]

Pierre De Lancre, who was actively involved in the hunting down of witches in south-western France, described the familial nature of many of the trials and accusations. He had been told by one member of his local community that 'If the number of witches condemned to the fire is so large, it will be odd if I do not have a share in the cinders.' De Lancre concluded: 'This is why one very often sees a son accuse his father and mother, a brother his sister, a husband his wife, and sometimes the other way round. This family link is why several heads of family, officers, and other people of the better sort finding themselves affected by it, prefer rather to suffer the disability which may exist in this abomination . . . than to see so many executions by gibbet, flame and fire, of people who are so closely related to them.'[34]

Far greater importance was given to the character of the accused than in other, more standard criminal investigations. The demeanour, characteristics, enemies and motives of the suspect were subjected to intense scrutiny. The leading manual for Justices of the Peace, published in 1618, advised that the nature of the accused be examined to determine whether they were 'civill, or hastie, wittie and subtill, a quarreller, pilferer, or bloudie minded, &c.'. Their mode of employment was also looked into, and if they 'liveth idly or vagrant', this was enough grounds to arrest them. Likewise, their way of life was subject to detailed investigation, and if they even so much as dressed in unusual clothes, then they were instantly suspected of being 'of evill fame'. Having thoroughly satisfied themselves of the suspect's character and way of life, the Justices of the Peace were then instructed to investigate the parents to see 'if they were wicked, and given to the same kind of fault'.[35]

Although the investigations made a show of being thorough, in reality they needed to yield very little concrete evidence in order to bring the suspected witch to trial. No impartial observer ever testified that he had witnessed an act of sorcery. Neither did the authorities ever conduct a raid on a suspected witch's house or coven, even though they often did so for other subversive activities. Rather, the evidence for sorcery consisted of the depositions of neighbours who accused them of harm, and the alleged witch's confessions. Both types of evidence were deeply suspect. If the accused was found to have a notorious reputation as a witch, was known to harbour malice towards the victim or to have put a curse on them before ill fortune struck, then the investigators could be satisfied that their efforts would result in a court hearing. Better still if the Devil's mark had been found on the body of the accused, or there were witnesses to attest that a pact with Satan had been forged. In such cases, there was little hope of a reprieve. But even without such 'proof', a conviction could be secured. It was generally acknowledged that 'in the case of Witch-craft many things are very difficult, hidden and infolded in mists and clouds, overshadowing our reason and best understanding'.[36] In short, even if it could not be proved, it could still be punished.

The accused was completely powerless to produce an alibi because it was believed that evil spells could be cast many miles from the intended victim. The 1618 manual advised that 'halfe proofs are to be allowed, and are good causes of suspition'.[37] The law took on a new, dangerously eager credulity, and everything seemed geared towards securing a conviction.

Not everyone was so blinded by the furore of the witch hunts that they could not see the enormous potential for injustice that this system allowed. 'Experience shows that ignorant people . . . will make strong proofs of such presumptions, whereupon sometimes jurors do give their verdict against parties innocent,' lamented William Perkins.[38] Even George Gifford, whose pamphlets helped whip up popular fear and hatred of witches, admitted that 'many times there is innocent blood shed: which is a grevous sin. The jury commit perjury and cruel murther, which uppon blinde surmises of ignorant persons, do give their verduit, for they should see what knowledge of God, the accusers have.' He was aghast at the blatant disregard for the normal procedures of the law, whereby a suspect could be put to death upon the slightest of evidence. 'The Lord doth not allow one witnesse being a man in a cause of death to be sufficient: but these would alow the accusation of one devil if he accuseth xi persons . . . Many Jurers never weigh the force of the evidence which is brought, but as if they had their oth for conjectures or likelihoodes, they are oftentimes very forward to finde guilty, being sicke of the same disease that the accusers be.'[39]

Gifford excused such miscarriages of justice, not on the grounds that the accused could not possibly have committed murder by cursing, spells or other maleficent magic, but because the Devil had misled the victims. 'What vile and monstrous impieties are here committed . . . It is strange to see the madnes of the people, that wil aske the devill who sent him. And then he telleth who is his dame, and to how many she hath sent him, and how many hee hath kylled. If it were the Devill indeede, would they beleeve him: Is it not his desire to bring innocent persons into daunger? Would not hee very gladly have a number of men perjure and forsweare themselves? Doth the Lord will men to goe upon their oth in a matter, at the testimony of a devil?'[40] The situation was little better 30 years later, when Richard Bernard wrote his *Guide to Grand Jury Men*. He lamented how frequently cases were brought to trial which should have been shown to be groundless during the preliminary investigations, 'and so thurst an intricate case upon a jury of simple men, who proceed too often upon relations of meere presumptions, and these sometimes very weake ones too, to take away mens lives.'[41]

But such criticism had no bearing upon the case of Margaret and Phillipa Flower. They had even less hope of justice than most other suspected witches because they were pitted against not just the English legal system, but the wealth and influence of one of the country's most powerful noble families. The Manners had the county, the king and – most people believed – even God on their side. The beleaguered Flower sisters had only themselves. Their chief hope – and it was a faint one at that – was that there would be insufficient evidence against them. But if they could not control what their neighbours and other witnesses might say, they could at least remain steadfast in protesting their innocence.

The latter was easier said than done. With growing scepticism about the validity of witchcraft trials, the importance of securing a confession was greater than ever. And the methods employed to extract such a confession were becoming increasingly sophisticated. Just two years before the arrest of the Flower women, a lengthy treatise was published which set out in great detail the means which should be employed for the detection, examination and conviction of witches. Thomas Cooper's *The Mystery of Witch-craft* was a popular work and, appearing so close to Margaret and Phillipa's arrest, may well have been consulted by the men appointed to luring a confession from them. Cooper urged the presiding magistrate to make careful enquiry concerning the crime, 'and that not upon every corrupt passion, or sleight occasion, but upon weightie Presumptions, probably conjecturing of the Witch'. These 'weightie Presumptions' he defined as being the testimonies of neighbours; the accusation of a fellow witch or witches; 'if after Enmity, quarreling, or threatning, a present mischief do folow'; if the suspect was related to a known witch; whether she had a mark from Satan in 'some privy place'; and finally if the prisoner proved 'contrarie' and 'fearefull' when examined, then this would indicate 'a guiltie conscience'.[42] The author counselled that the following 'proofes' were necessary to secure a conviction: 'The Free confession of the crime by the party suspected, after due examination, being found in divers tales'; if they refused to confess, then the testimony of two witnesses that the accused had made a pact with Satan or 'hath done some knowne practise of Witch-craft' would be more than sufficient. The latter could include anything from entertaining a familiar spirit to calling upon the Devil for help.[43]

Cooper went on to advise that the examination of the suspect 'may either be made by Question from the Magistrate, by certaine wise and crosse Interrogations to this end'. Surprisingly, given that it was in theory illegal, he advised that a conviction might also be obtained 'by Torture, when together with words, some violent meanes are used, by paine, to extort confession, which may have place when the partie is obstinate'.[44] The ordeal that Margaret and Phillipa were about to suffer adds weight to the theory that their interrogators had been influenced by this guidance.

Although torture was illegal in England, the threat of it was often employed, and the practice probably also. The authorities could find ample justification for it if they so wished. The infamous witch hunting manual, *Malleus Maleficarum*, declared that the use of torture was justified because witchcraft constituted 'high treason against God's Majesty'. 'Any person, whatsoever his rank or position, upon such an accusation may be put to the torture, and he who is found guilty, even if he confesses his crime, let him be racked, let him suffer all other tortures prescribed by law in order that he may be punished in proportion to his offences.' Its authors advised the authorities to have a number of different methods of torture at their disposal, but urged them to keep these secret: 'Like a physician who strives to cut out gangrenous limbs and separate the mangy sheep from the healthy, the prudent judge can now surmise that the denounced woman is infected with the sorcery of silence, but no single, unfailing rule or method can be described for wrenching out this silence. Indeed, it would not be safe to give one, because if that method became a common practice and general rule, then, when the sons of darkness foresaw it, they could more easily avoid it as a trap for their damnation or take precautions.'[45]

In Scotland, King James sanctioned – and even encouraged – torture of the most savage kind in order to exact confessions, believing that only the most 'grievous pains and cruel torments' would bring the necessary information to light.[46] According to his dangerously warped logic: 'Experience daily proves how loath they [the accused] are to confess without torture, which witnesseth their guiltiness.'[47] This included pulling off the prisoner's fingernails with a pair of pincers and thrusting needles 'even up to the heads' into what was left of their fingertips.[48] Another horrifying method was the 'torment of the boots', whereby wedges were driven into the prisoner's boots in order to shatter his shins and ankles. A contemporary account describes how one such unfortunate prisoner had his legs 'crushed and beaten together as small as might be, and the bones and flesh so bruised, that the blood and marrow spurted forth in great abundance, whereby they were made unserviceable forever'.

There were similarly horrific accounts from the Continent. One particularly tragic case involved a man named Johannes Junius, burgomaster of Bamberg in Germany. His interrogators subjected him to a horrific cycle of torture, involving thumb-screws, leg-screws and the strappado – whereby his hands were tied behind his back, then he was hoisted up and suspended from the ceiling by a rope, with weights attached to his feet, which would almost certainly cause his arms to dislocate. After his eventual confession, he wrote to his daughter in trembling hand as he awaited death at the stake: 'Innocent have I come to prison, innocent have I been tortured, innocent I must die. For whoever comes into the witch prison must become a witch or be tortured until he invents something out of his head . . . They never leave off with the torture till one confesses something; be he never so good, he must be a witch. Nobody escapes.'[49]

Some torture had strongly sexual undertones. Thanks to the witch hunts, prisons were now filled with large numbers of women, and for the first time men had unrestricted access to them. The legally sanctioned torture that they performed included sadistic experimentation and gratuitous sexual advances. To try to force a confession, a French priest applied hot fat repeatedly to Catherine Boyraionne's eyes, armpits, thighs, stomach and 'dans sa nature' (vagina). The unfortunate woman died in prison, no doubt from her injuries. When the executioner Jehan Minart of Cambrai in northern France prepared a condemned witch for the stake, he examined her mouth and 'parties honteuses' (shameful parts).[50] Cotton Mather, the Puritan minister who played a key role in the notorious Salem witch trials, uncovered and fondled the breasts of a 17-year-old girl whom he claimed was possessed by demons. It was also common for a suspected witch to be stripped to the waist and whipped, her breasts bared to the public. Others were raped during their imprisonment, but stood little chance of justice because their attackers claimed that they had bewitched them.

That the men involved in hunting down and prosecuting suspected witches could thus take sexual pleasure without fear of recrimination may help to explain the bewilderingly rapid spread of the witch craze, and why it took hold for so long. Everyone from gaolers to court officials and even priests could indulge their sadistic fantasies and cause untold suffering and terror among their victims. That they did so under the guise of ridding society of evil is bitterly ironic.

Another favoured method of extracting a confession was the *tormentum insomniae*, or forced sleeplessness. This was particularly popular in England, perhaps because the authorities believed that, with no physical pain involved, it did not constitute real torture. The method involved keeping the suspected witch awake for 40 hours or more until they were so delirious with fatigue that they had no idea what they were admitting to. It proved so effective that one judge claimed that fewer than 2 per cent of all victims failed to submit. 'Watching' was employed to particularly devastating effect by Matthew Hopkins during his reign of terror in Essex. The Puritan cleric John Gaule described this in detail:

Having taken the suspected witch, she is placed in the middle of a room upon a stool or table, cross-legged, or in some other uneasy posture, to which she submits not, she is then bound with cords; there is she watched and kept without meat or sleep for the space of 24 hours for (they say) within that time they shall see her imp come and suck. A little hole is likewise made in the door for the imp to come in at; and lest it might come in some less discernible shape, they that watch are taught to be ever and anon sweeping the room, and if they see any spiders or flies, to kill them. And if they cannot kill them, then they may be sure they are her imps.[51]

One unfortunate victim of this treatment was a vicar from Brandeston in Suffolk who had attempted to protect a convicted witch, and was soon hauled in for the same crime himself. The lord of the manor recorded the dreadful treatment that this unfortunate man, who was then well into his seventies, suffered: 'I have heard it from them that watched with him that they kept him awake several Nights together and ran him backwards and forwards about the Room, until he [was] out of Breath. Then they rested him a little, and then ran him again; and thus they did for several Days and Nights together, till he was weary of his life, and was scarce sensible of what he said or did.'[52] It is easy to imagine how, after undergoing such frightening and exhausting treatment, the half-crazed prisoner would confess to any number of fantastical 'devilish' acts. Those who were tasked with 'watching' them would have been similarly susceptible to fevered imaginings. Once they had been told to expect the appearance of imps and goblins, the slightest noise, movement or shadow within the room could have taken on the ghastly appearance of a witch's familiar.

It has been convincingly argued that the great witch hunt of the sixteenth and seventeenth centuries would not have happened without the use of torture.[53] A witch's 'owne free confession . . . happeneth very rare and seldome', admitted one authority in 1616.[54] It is certainly hard to imagine scores of prisoners willingly confessing to all of the outlandish crimes associated with witchcraft unless torture – or the threat of it – had been employed. King James acknowledged this, but maintained that the suspects' confessions were still an indication of their guilt.[55] It was the prospect of such torture that led thousands of prisoners to effectively sign their own death warrants by fabricating confessions. Among the convicted witches in Lorraine was Mengeatte des Woirelz, who in 1584 explained that she had made false statements because 'tired of being in prison, and of the pain of the torture, joined with the fear of the evil reputation she had been falsely given in the town, she had chosen to die rather than live in such anguish. She had reckoned that in saying what she did to us . . . we would have enough reason to put her to death.' In a similar case 20 years later, Barbelline Chaperey admitted that 'she had confessed more than she had committed or done, but this was because she was under torture, and that she had not reckoned there would be so many people hostile to her, after thinking about which, she had been led to make sure confessions'.[56]

Holed up in their freezing cold, damp and stinking prison, Margaret and Phillipa Flower's resolve not to confess might already have been weakening as they faced their interrogators.

9

'Voluntarie confessions and examinations'

Margaret and Phillipa Flower's interrogation began on 22 January and continued for almost five weeks, culminating on 25 February 1619. Although the Belvoir pamphlet includes a detailed transcription of what was said, it is riddled with inaccuracies and omissions. The first examination of the Flower sisters is dated 'about the 22 of January'. Given that it was the date that their interrogation began, such uncertainty is odd. Moreover, there are no further examinations recorded until 4 February, which is an unusually long gap. The author tells us that other examinations were used at the trial, but these do not appear in his narrative. And there are no examinations of Joan Flower mentioned at all – even though it would have been customary to conduct at least one at the time of her arrest. Does this scantiness of documentation simply suggest carelessness? Considering the extraordinary lengths that were gone to by the earl and his associates to bring the women to trial, this seems unlikely. The conclusion that naturally follows is that certain documents were deliberately excluded.

The Flower sisters were examined separately, but the similarity of their accounts suggests that their interrogators used any damning evidence from one sister to wring a confession out of the other. The French jurist Jean Bodin advised: 'One must also make careful note of inconsistencies and repeat many times at different intervals the same line of questioning.' He also urged that the accused be allowed no respite from the relentless onslaught: 'One must, if possible, pursue the interrogation concerning all the charges without interruption, so that Satan does not dissuade them from telling the truth.'[1]

The initial interrogations were conducted by Sir William Pelham and Mr Butler. Both men were set upon wresting a confession out of the women. Although this was by no means necessary to secure a conviction – English juries regularly delivered guilty verdicts on the basis of hearsay, circumstantial evidence or the testimony of just one

The keep, Belvoir Castle.
Dating back to Norman times,
the castle was largely rebuilt in
the nineteenth century.

Francis Manners,
sixth Earl of Rutland
(1578–1632).

The interior of St Mary's Church, Bottesford. The tomb of Francis Manners and his sons is to the right of the altar.

Detail of the tomb, showing the two Manners boys, who were said to have been done to death 'by wicked practise and sorcerye'.

A seventeenth-century woodcut showing a witch kissing Satan
on the buttocks.

From the same era, a classic illustration of a witch riding a broomstick,
with the devil and another witch riding close behind.

Le Départ pour le Sabbat,
by David Teniers the Younger
(mid-seventeenth century).

The Witches' Sabbath,
by Francisco Goya (1798).

Woodcut from *Newes from Scotland* showing James directing the interrogation of the North Berwick witches (1591).

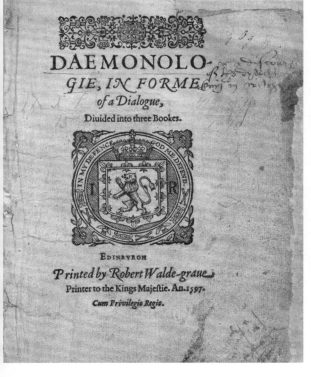

DAEMONOLO-
GIE, IN FORME
of a Dialogue,
Diuided into three Bookes.

IN MY DEFENCE · GOD ME DEFEND
I R

EDINBVRGH
Printed by Robert Walde-graue
Printer to the Kings Maiestie. An.1597.
Cum Priuilegio Regio.

The title page of *Daemonologie*, James's treatise on witchcraft (1597).

James I of England and VI of Scotland, after John De Critz the Elder (c.1606).

George Villiers, Duke of Buckingham, with his wife, Katherine (*née* Manners), their daughter, Mary, and son, George. The family portrait was painted shortly before the Duke's assassination in August 1628.

A seventeenth-century engraving showing the hanging of four witches.

The 'swimming' of a witch, from the title page of *Witches Apprehended* (1613).

THE
WONDERFVL
DISCOVERIE OF THE
Witchcrafts of *Margaret* and *Phillip*
Flower, daughters of *Ioan Flower* neere *Beuer*
Castle: Executed at Lincolne, *March* 11. 1618.

Who were specially arraigned and condemned before Sir
Henry Hobart, and Sir *Edward Bromley*, Iudges of Af-
fife, for confessing themselues actors in the destruction
of *Henry* Lord *Rosse*, with their damnable practises against
others the Children of the Right Honourable
FRANCIS Earle of *Rutland*.

Together with the feuerall Examinations and Confessions of *Anne*
Baker, *Ioan Willimot*, and *Ellen Greene*, Witches in *Leicestershire*.

Printed at London by *G. Eld* for *I. Barnes*, dwelling in the long Walke
neere Chrift-Church. 1 6 1 9.

The title page of the contemporary pamphlet telling the story of
Joan Flower and her daughters (1620).

eyewitness – in a high-profile case such as this, the examiners were determined to leave no room for doubt. They were also determined to convict the sisters not just of witchcraft, but of forming a pact with the Devil. If they succeeded in this, then according to the terms of the 1604 statute, Margaret and Phillipa would be executed.

Initially, both girls held out against the intimidation and threats of their interrogators. Margaret, who was interrogated first, did confess that she had helped her mother bewitch Henry Manners. Some 'foure or five years since', Joan had instructed her to steal a glove or some other item of clothing from Lord Henry. When Margaret asked why, her mother replied: 'To hurt my Lord Rosse.' In so doing, Joan was following one of the most widespread practices of maleficent witchcraft, for it was commonly believed that obtaining and damaging an item of clothing was a sure means of inflicting harm upon its owner. Upon procuring the glove, Joan had dipped it into boiling water and stroked her cat Rutterkin with it, 'after which Henry Lord Rosse fell sicke within a weeke, and was much tormented with the same'.

Margaret went on to confess that the earl's younger son had been bewitched in the same manner some 'two or three yeares since'. She had (apparently by chance) found one of the boy's gloves on a dunghill in the grounds of the castle, and had taken it to her mother, who performed the same spell as before, declaring that the young Francis 'will not mend againe'. This is the only reference to the younger son's illness in their testimonies. It is interesting that the account of Margaret's interrogation should have her insisting that the younger boy would not recover. Events would soon prove this prediction to be suspiciously accurate.

Margaret then went into some detail about how she and her mother conspired to put Lady Katherine to death in the same way as the young boys. At Joan's command, she had stolen a piece of Katherine's handkerchief from the castle. Her mother had plunged this into hot water, then rubbed it on Rutterkin's back, 'bidding him to flye and go'. But the cat had merely 'whined and cryed Mew', for he 'had no power over the Lady Katherine to hurt her'.[2] The latter had therefore escaped the fate that her half-brothers had suffered.

Damning though her testimony was, Margaret had so far only admitted to harming the boys, not to causing Henry's death. The authorities therefore intensified the pressure (perhaps physical as well

as psychological) on both girls. 'If one finds then that the witches do
not confess anything, they must be made to change their clothes and
have all their hair shaved off, and then undergo interrogation,' advised
Bodin. 'And if there is partial proof of any strong presumptions, torture
must be applied.' If an interrogator found the prospect of inflicting
torture unappealing, Bodin recommended that the threat of it was
often enough to achieve the same result, 'since the fear of torment
is itself a torment'. 'One must give the impression of preparing
numerous instruments, and ropes in quantity, as well as assistants for
tormenting them, and keep them for some time in fear,' he wrote. 'It
is also expedient before making the accused go into the torture
chamber to have someone cry out with a dreadful cry, as if he were
in torment, and tell the accused that it is the torture being applied,
dismaying him this way and exacting the truth. I saw a judge who
put on such a dreadful face and terrifying voice, threatening hanging
if they did not tell the truth, and in this way terrified the accused so
much that they confessed immediately, as if they had lost all courage.'
Rebecca Morris, a woman who was arrested and interrogated in 1645,
was recorded as having 'confessed beefore any violence, watching, or
other threts'.[3] Bodin warned, though, that 'this technique works with
timorous people but not with bold ones'.[4] Given the Flower sisters'
reputation for brazenness, they likely fell into the latter category.

Margaret was the first to crack. On 4 February, she confessed to
conspiring with her mother to bring about the death of the Earl of
Rutland's elder son.[5] She told her examiners that 'her selfe, her mother,
and sister were all displeased with him [Rutland], especially with the
Countesse, for turning her out of service'. She had duly gone to
Belvoir and found one of the young lord's gloves on the rushes in the
nursery. Upon bringing this back to her mother, she watched as Joan
'put it into hot water, prickt it often with her knife, then tooke it out
of the water, and rubd it upon Rutterkin [her familiar], bidding him
height and goe, and doe some hurt to Henry Lord Rosse, whereupon
hee fell sick, and shortly after dyed'.[6] According to Margaret's testimony, her mother had thrown the glove on the fire as soon as the
spell was cast.

The interrogators were no doubt triumphant at having wrested a
confession out of Margaret Flower, and they wasted no time in using
it to try to break down Phillipa's resistance. But the elder sister proved

much more stubborn. She consistently refused to admit to murdering Henry Manners; only to causing him to fall sick. She did, though, confess to helping her mother conduct maleficent magic, and told the same tale as her elder sister with regard to the methods used. Her account differed from Margaret's in only two small details: that her mother had rubbed the glove on Rutterkin's back *before* plunging it into hot water, and that she had afterwards buried it in the yard. Interestingly, though, Phillipa made no mention of the bewitching of the younger son, Francis, or of his half-sister, Katherine. This is puzzling, given that otherwise their accounts seem to have been constructed with a painstaking attention to detail. It was with a certain defiance that she insisted that they had done nothing but exact revenge for Margaret's unjust dismissal from his household. To her mind, he and his wife deserved everything they had suffered as a result.

Both Margaret and Phillipa attested that their mother had cast a spell to render the earl and countess infertile, but their accounts differ in detail. Phillipa simply confessed that 'shee heard her mother often curse the Earle and his Lady, and thereupon would boyle feathers and blood together, using many Divellish speeches and strange gestures'.[7] Margaret went into more detail, claiming that her mother had used wool from the mattress that the countess had given her upon being dismissed from the castle, together with a pair of gloves that Joan's lover, Mr Vavasour, had procured for her. She put both items into warm water, mixed them with blood, and then rubbed them on Rutterkin's belly, 'saying the Lord and the Lady should have more Children but it should be long first'.[8] That Margaret should modify the threat of infertility that they had allegedly made towards the earl and his wife is interesting. Perhaps the earl's intense anxiety about this issue compelled him to put pressure on the interrogators to wrest a more reassuring answer from the women.

Damning though these testimonies were, they were insufficient to secure a conviction for the felony of witchcraft – one that would carry the most severe punishment. Even Margaret had confessed to nothing more than 'sympathetic magic'; no mention had yet been made of a pact with the Devil. But it was now that both girls were brought face to face with the Earl of Rutland, who joined the interrogations on 25 February with his brother George and Lord Willoughby. This seems to have worked a dramatic effect upon the terrified young women, who together confessed to conspiring with the Devil and his minions. Their testimonies on this occasion were significantly shorter than before, which suggests that Rutland and his companions had applied intense pressure in order to condemn them. It is likely that it was at this point that torture had been introduced. The fantastical nature of the sisters' confessions – and their uncanny resemblance to those taken in other cases – certainly supports this notion. The earl would have had no fear of reprisals: his royal master had, after all, declared the use of torture to be essential in drawing out the guilt of accused witches. The author of the pamphlet which describes the case was at pains to deny that 'woemen confessed these things by extreamity of torture', but he seems to be protesting too much.[9]

As well as focusing upon the 'facts' of the case, the published testimonies of Margaret and Phillipa have a strong sexual undercurrent. Phillipa apparently confessed to having 'a Spirit sucking on her in the forme of a white Rat, which keepeth her left breast, and hath done for three or foure yeares'. She also admitted that this Spirit had promised to make Thomas Simpson love her 'if she would suffer it to sucke her, which she agreed unto'. As if to lend credence to this tale, the interrogation includes the precise date when the spirit last sucked Phillipa – the night of Tuesday 23 February.[10] Margaret, meanwhile, confessed that she had two spirits sucking on her – one white and the other black-spotted. 'The white sucked under her left breast, and the blacke spotted within the inward parts of her secrets.' In return for this sexual favour, they promised to do everything that she commanded.[11] The message was clear: women such as Margaret and Phillipa used their sexual wiles to wield power and do evil.

When Margaret and Phillipa confessed to being 'sucked' by demons, their interrogators would almost certainly have ordered them to be searched for 'teats' or the Devil's mark to corroborate their story. From as early as 1579, the latter was said to be 'a common token to known all witches by'.[12] The belief was that after a satanic pact had been made, the Devil would suck upon some part of the witch's body, leaving a mark. For as long as this mark – which was insensible when pricked – remained undiscovered, the Devil's influence would prevail over the woman in question. He therefore ensured that the mark was 'placed on a part covered with hair, that it might be more easily concealed: and hence one of the first processes in the examination of a witch was one most shocking to her feelings of modesty, that of shaving her body'.[13] The influential pamphleteer Richard Bernard provided a detailed description of what this mark might look like: 'It's sometimes like a little teate, sometimes but a blewish spot, sometimes red spots like a fleabiting, sometimes the flesh is sunke in and hollow.' He admitted that it might be easily mistaken for a 'naturall mark', and therefore provided a helpful guide to 'pricking' every mark on a suspected witch's body until one was found which did not bleed.[14] It was distinct from – although often confused with – the teat from which the suspect would suckle her familiar.

The person assigned to undertake this brutal task would therefore systematically thrust a long, thick needle (more like a dagger than a pin) into all moles, scars or other marks on a suspected witch's body until one was located which did not elicit a scream of pain. A whole profession grew up around this belief, as 'brodders' or 'jobbers' travelled the country to search out and test the marks found upon the accused, in return for a fee. Midwives were also sometimes called upon, which suggests that the examinations were of a very intimate nature. Interestingly, though, in Scotland the 'witch-pricker' was always male, which reinforces the sexual nature of these examinations.

One of the most notorious witch-prickers was James or John Balfoure, who proudly professed to 'discover persons guiltie of the cryme of witchecraft by remarking the devill's marke upon some part of their persouns and bodeis and thristing of preins in the same, and upon the presumptioun of this knowledge goes athort the countrie abusing simple and ignorant people for his private gayn and commoditie'. He was eventually banned from the profession by the Privy Council.[15] Another man who made a healthy profit from the trade was Alexander Chisholm, who in 1662 was found guilty of having 'most cruellie and barbrouslie tortured the women by waking, hanging them up by the thombes, burning the soles of their feet at the fyre, drawing of others at horse taills and binding of them with widdies about the neck and feet and carying them so alongst on horseback to prison, wherby and by other tortur one of them hath become distracted, another by cruelty is departed this lyfe, and all of them have confest whatever they were pleasit to demand of them'.[16]

These practices were both terrifying and humiliating for the women involved. Often, the examinations would be carried out in front of many witnesses. In 1649, the citizens of Newcastle hired a well-known Scottish pricker to rid their town of witches, promising him 20 shillings for every woman he condemned. Thirty women were duly brought into the town hall and subjected to a horrifying ordeal. 'Presently in sight of all the people, [he] laid her body naked to the waste, with her cloaths over her head, by which fright and shame, all her blood contracted into one part of her body, and then he ran a pin into her thigh, and then suddenly let her coats [skirts] fall, and then demanded whether she had nothing of his in her body but [yet] did not bleed, but she being amazed replied little, then he put his hand up her coats, and pulled out the pin and set her aside as a guilty person, and child of the Devil, and fell to try others whom he made guilty.'[17]

Margaret Moone, one of the witches interrogated by the self-styled 'Witchfinder General', Matthew Hopkins, in 1645, suffered this humiliating and painful ordeal at the hands of a local woman, Frances Mills, who gave evidence in her trial. 'This Informant saith, that being imployed by the Neighbours of Thorpe [Thorpe-le-Soken, an Essex village] aforesaid, to search Margaret Moone, who was suspected for a Witch, she found three long teats or bigges in her secret parts, which seemed to have been lately sucked; and that they were not like Pyles, for this Informant knows well what they are, having been troubled with them herself.' Frances then proceeded to examine Margaret's two daughters, and found that they also had teats in their 'privy parts'.[18]

A similarly offensive examination was suffered by a woman interrogated in Bury St Edmunds in 1664. 'They began at her head, and so stript her naked, and in the lower part of her belly they found a thing like a teat of an inch long, they questioned her about it, and she said that she had got a strain by carrying of water which caused that excrescence. But upon narrower search, they found in her privy parts three more excrescences or teats, but smaller than the former: This Deponent further saith, that in the long teat at the end thereof was a little hole, and it appeared unto them as if it had lately been sucked, and upon the straining of it there issued out white milkie matter.'[19]

The introduction of witch-pricking as part of the interrogation of a suspected witch gave the authorities licence to sexually abuse their prisoners. But the practice was just part of a much broader sexual fantasy surrounding witchcraft. At their basest level, witchcraft pamphlets were a commercial product sold for entertainment. Part of their appeal was as works of true crime designed to shock and frighten the reader. But a still larger appeal derived from their porno-graphic nature. Many tell of sexual intercourse between witches and devils, or with animals, of bewitched men being forced to carry out humiliating tasks by women, and of searching women's genitalia for the Devil's mark. *Newes from Scotland* describes the latter in salacious detail: 'It has lately been found that the Devil does generally mark them [witches] with a private mark, by reason the witches have confessed themselves, that the Devil does lick them with his tongue in some private part of their body, before he does receive them to be his servants, which mark commonly is given them under the hair in some part of their body, whereby it may not easily be found out or seen, although they be searched.'[20]

The *Malleus Maleficarum* dedicates an entire chapter to the nature of sexual intercourse between the Devil or his minions and the women who fall under their spell. The authors describe in almost forensic detail how 'such demons practice the most revolting sexual acts, not for the sake of pleasure but in order to taint the soul and body of those under or on whom they lie'.[21] Likewise, the account of Matthew Hopkins's notorious interrogations includes numerous references to witches' sexual exploits with devils and familiars. One of the accused, the aged Elizabeth Clarke, confessed that two imps 'came into this Examinants bed every night, or every other night, and sucked upon the lower parts of her body'. The same defendant confessed that 'shee had had carnall copulation with the Devill six or seven yeares; and that he would appeare to her three or foure times in a weeke at her bed side, and goe to bed to her, and lye with her halfe a night together in the shape of a proper Gentleman, with a laced band, having the whole proportion of a man, and would say to her, *Besse I must lye with you*, and shee did never deny him'.[22]

All of these erotic, often sadomasochistic tales are told with the clinical precision of a medical textbook. In an increasingly puritanical society, these pamphlets provided a much-needed acceptable outlet for men's baser instincts. The pamphlet about the Belvoir witches is a classic example, and there are sexual references throughout the tale. Evidently wishing to grab his readers' attention straight away, before the Flower women have even been introduced, the author provides a salacious description of how the Devil typically makes a pact with a witch: 'for their better assurance and corroboration of their credulity, they shall have palpable and forcible touches of sucking, pinching, kissing, closing, colling and such like'.[23]

Elizabeth Sawyer, who was tried two years after the Belvoir witches, described how the Devil would suck her 'a little above my fundament' and 'would put his head under my coates, and I did willingly suffer him to doe what hee would . . . He would be sucking of me the continuance of a quarter of an howre, and when hee suckte mee, I then felt no paine at all.'[24] In a later trial, a Scottish witch named Isobel Gowdie confessed that her satanic pact had been sealed by having sex with the Devil: 'He was a large black hairy man, very cold, and I found his semen in me as cold as spring water.'[25]

The latter was a commonly cited fact. In his work on witchcraft, King James agreed that 'in whatsoever way he uses it, that sperm seems intolerably cold to the person abused'.[26] Jean Bodin claimed that the Devil 'ejaculated extremely cold semen', and his compatriot, Jeanne Guillemin, described a case where a woman was seduced by Satan: 'They were a good half-hour together, and he released extremely cold semen.'[27] This rather bizarre detail was rationalised by the Cambridge scholar Henry More, who opined: 'It stands to very good reason that the bodies of Devils being nothing but coagulated Air should be cold, as well as coagulated Water, which is Snow or Ice, and that it should have a more keen or piercing cold, it consisting of more subtile particles, than those of Water, and therefore more fit to insinuate, and more accurately and stingingly to affect and touch the nerves.'[28] Another accused witch, Mary Becket of Suffolk, told how the Devil had appeared to her and told her that he was her husband, and then asked 'to have the use of her body'. When she denied him, he changed tactics, and 'came to her in the shape of handsome yonge gentleman with yelloow hayre and black cloaths & often times lay with her and had the carnall use of her'.[29]

According to some sources, the Devil sometimes deceived the witches whom he had seduced into believing that they had fathered his child. 'To procure some monstrous birth, either through mixture with the seed of the woman, or else (which I rather incline unto) he may by his skill, through Wind or other pestilent humours, so affect the body of the Witch as that it shall swell, and increase, as in a True Generation . . . and then in the time of the breaking open of the wombe may foist in some Infant stollen else where, or delude the eyes of the beholders with some Impe of his owne, in the shape of a child; or with some dead childe taken up and enlivened to the purpose.' The same author claimed that the child might sometimes be that of the Devil, which would always be born after 'a great deale of paine and torment in the bearing and birth: and in the issue, either some Monster or Abortive is brought forth to encrease her sorrow, and procure Horror and Despaire'.[30]

Other works described 'sabbats' (black Sabbaths), when a coven or family of witches would join together – often in a remote place – to worship the Devil. A witch who had made her pact with the Devil would usually attend one of these meetings either immediately afterwards or within a few days. They were sometimes joined by devils and familiars, and sometimes by Satan himself. On these occasions, the sabbats would degenerate into mass orgies between witches and devils. 'The incubus's in the shaps of proper men satisfy the desires of the Witches, and the succubus's serve for whores to the Wizards,' claimed one late-seventeenth-century source.[31] Women were accused of flying to the sabbat on phallic broomsticks, joining in orgiastic dances, copulating indiscriminately with men, women, demons or the Devil himself, and giving birth to demon children.

One of the most lurid descriptions of the sabbats was provided by the French judge Pierre de Lancre, who was a contemporary of the Flower women. According to his account, the witches who attended these gatherings all sought 'to dance indecently, to banquet filthily, to couple diabolically, to sodomize execrably, to blaspheme scandalously, to pursue brutally every horrible, dirty and unnatural desire, to hold as precious toads, vipers, lizards and all sorts of poisons; to love a vile-smelling goat, to caress him lovingly, to press against and copulate with him horribly and shamelessly'.[32] The preface to the Belvoir witch pamphlet agrees that the Devil could 'attend them in some familiar shape of Rat, Cat, Toad, Bird, Cricket, &c.: yea effectuate whatsoever they shall demaund or desire'.[33] Meanwhile, the influential Jean Bodin produced a similarly salacious account:

Marguerite Bremont, wife of Noel Laueret, said that last Monday, after
nightfall, she was with Marion her mother at an assembly [of witches]
. . . Her aforenamed mother had a chimney-broom between her legs
saying – I shall not write the words down – and suddenly they were
both transported to the spot indicated above, where they found Jean
Robert, Jeanne Guillemin, Mary, wife of Simon d'Agneau, and
Guillemette, wife of one named le Gras, who each had a broom.
Present also in that place were six devils, who were in human form,
but very hideous to look at, and then after the dance was finished the
devils laid with them, and had relations with them. Then one of them,
who had led her in dance, took her and made love to her two times,
and remained with her for the space of more than half an hour.[34]

Another popular sexual ritual described by the pamphlets was the
kissing of the Devil's buttocks. The North Berwick witches, who were
tried in the presence of James VI in 1591, testified that at one of their
meetings, the Devil made them 'kiss his buttocks as a sign of obedience
to him'.[35] This so disgusted (or aroused) the Scottish king that he repeated
it in his book about witchcraft, claiming that 'the kissing of his [Satan's]
hinder parts' was a common feature of pacts with the Devil.[36] A later
authority also described this ritual, which he said commonly occurred
at the conclusion of each sabbat: 'Then each one kissing the Posteriors
of the Devil (a sweet bit no doubt) returns upon their aiery Vehicles to
their habitations.'[37] James, meanwhile, went on to describe in detail how
the Devil could 'abuse' men or women in 'abominable' ways, such as
'copulating' or 'stealing out the sperm of a dead body'.[38]

There were various recorded sightings of witches having sex with
devils:

Manie times witches are seene in the fields, and woods, prostituting
themselves uncovered and naked up to the navill, wagging and mooving
their members in everie part, according to the disposition of one being
about that act of concupiscence, and yet nothing seene of the beholders
upon hir; saving that after such a convenient time as is required about
such a peece of worke, a blacke vapour of the length and bignesse of
a man, hath beene seene as it were to depart from hir, and to ascend
that place . . . she hath more pleasure and delight (they say) with
Incubus that waie, than with anie mortall man.[39]

A fifteenth-century manual on witchcraft described the sexual act between a demon and a witch in salacious detail. 'Although the incubus demon always works visibly from the point of view of the sorceress . . . in terms of the bystanders it is frequently the case that the sorceresses were seen lying on their backs in fields or woods, naked above the navel and gesticulating with their forearms and thighs. They keep their limbs in an arrangement suitable for that filthy act, while the incubus demons work with them invisibly in terms of bystanders, although at the end of the act a very black vapour would (very rarely) rise up from the sorceress into the air up to the height of a human.' In this way, copulation with a devil could lead to the propagation of evil. Another account describes how devils could creep into a bed and 'lie down themselves by the side of the sleeping husbands' before having sex with their wives. It warned: 'Husbands have actually seen Incubus devils swiving with their wives, although they have thought that they were not devils but men. And when they had taken up a weapon and tried to run them through, the devil has suddenly disappeared, making himself invisible.'[40] Even 'aged and barren' women were seduced by the Devil or his minions 'for the purpose of causing pleasure', and thus binding them to his cause.[41]

Some authorities claimed that sexual pleasure was greater with a devil than with an ordinary man, which was why so many women fell prey to seduction. Others attested the opposite. A French woman who was accused of witchcraft told her interrogators 'that when Satan copulated with her she had as much pain as a woman in labour'. Another agreed that 'while she was in the act, she felt something burning in her stomach; and nearly all the witches say this intercourse is by no means pleasurable to them, both because of the Devil's ugliness and deformity, and because of the physical pain which it causes them'.[42] The French author and sceptic Cyrano de Bergerac scorned the idea of demonic seduction, and said that the reason one 'encounters ten thousand women for every man' in such tales is that 'a woman has a lighter mind than a man and is consequently bolder in inventing comedies of this kind'.[43] But this did little to diminish the popularity of such tales.

The illustrations that accompanied witchcraft pamphlets often contained barely disguised sexual imagery, such as witches sitting astride phallic broomsticks, or cavorting naked around a cauldron and

playing games of leapfrog. The sixteenth-century German artist Hans
Baldung 'Grien' was particularly renowned for this genre of painting,
and shocked his audience with scenes of a supernatural and erotic
nature.[44]

Towards the end of her interrogation, Margaret seemed to grow
increasingly delirious, worn down perhaps by the interminably long
days and nights of her captivity. In her final confession, she claimed
that four devils had appeared to her one night in Lincoln gaol. 'The
one stood at her beds feete, with a blacke head like an Ape, and spake
unto her, but what, shee cannot well remember, at which shee was
very angry because he would speake no plainer, or let her understand
his meaning: the other three were Rutterkin, Little Robin, and Spirit,
but shee never mistrusted them, nor suspected herselfe til then.'[45] The
last line suggests that Margaret had no conception either that a pet
animal could be an evil spirit or that she herself was a witch until her
examiners suggested it. As in many other trials, the suspect – her mind
addled by fear, discomfort and sheer exhaustion – had been brought
to believe everything of which she stood accused.

That the Flower women's pets should be used as proof of their
evil was typical of other witchcraft trials. These 'familiars' – demons
who took the shape of animals such as dogs, cats, rats, toads or
butterflies – were a peculiarly English contribution to witch lore.
According to the theory, the familiars assisted the witch in her maleficium and were rewarded by being allowed to suck from her special
teat. 'They have their spirites which they keepe at home in a corner,'
related George Gifford, 'some of them twoo, some three, some five:
these they send when they be displeased, and wil them for to plague
a man in his body, or in his cattle.'[46] It was a dog named Tomalin –
'My sweet Tom-boy' – who was said to have lured the witch of
Edmonton to her destruction. Meanwhile, the opening scene of
Macbeth has the three witches crying out to their familiars: 'I come,
Graymalkin . . . Paddock calls . . .'[47]

The seventeenth-century witchcraft trial records are littered with
references to such impious creatures. A deposition taken during the
trial of Margaret Bates in 1645 included a particularly lurid description
of her familiars. She confessed that 'when she was at work she felt a
thinge come upon her legs and go into her secret parts where her

marks weare found, and an other time when she was in the Church yard she felt a thinge nip her againe in those parts & further that she had but two teats and they might be made at once suckinge'.[48] Likewise, during her interrogation the same year, Anne Usher described how 'she felt a thinge like a small cat come over her legs once or twice & that it scratched her mightily after that she felt 2 things like butterflies in her secret parts with witchings, dansings and suckinge & she felt them with her hands and rubbed them and killed them'.[49] Another suspect told how she suckled seven 'imps', but that as she only had five teats, 'when they came to suck they fight like pigs with a sow'.[50] In practice, such creatures were often little more than pets to keep lonely women company in their old age. The affectionate names for them – such as 'Daynty', 'Prettyman' and 'Littleman' – which appear in contemporary trial records support this theory.[51]

By admitting to her conference with familiars and devils, Margaret had sealed her fate. The inclusion of this extraordinary confession in her testimony may have been an attempt by the authorities to remove any lingering doubt that she was a witch. It may also indicate the use of torture in her interrogation. Conference with the Devil is almost never mentioned in witchcraft examinations until torture – or the threat of it – is introduced. Sometimes this was at an early stage of the proceedings, but at others it did not take place until after the accused had already confessed to maleficium, as was the case here.

The tale of Margaret's seeing devils whilst in gaol also evokes James I's own beliefs as set down in *Daemonologie*. He claimed that if the accused proved obstinate in denying their guilt after they had been arrested, the Devil would appear to them and 'fill them more and more with the vain hope of some manner of relief'.[52] There are other parallels between the contemporary account of the trial and James's famous work, notably the description of how the Flower women came to make a pact with the Devil, and the means by which they engineered the deaths of the two young boys. The fact that the Belvoir pamphlet's author refers to *Daemonologie* in the preface is a further testament to how influenced he was by the book. He may also have been under pressure to flatter the king's vanity in this way, thus bolstering the earl's favour with his royal master.

Even if they had not confessed, the likelihood is that Margaret and Phillipa would have met the same fate. Those involved in the seeking out and condemnation of witches at this time reasoned that if a woman did not admit her guilt, this was because 'the devill hath such power over them, that he will not suffer them to confesse'.[53] In short, they were damned if they confessed, and they were damned if they did not.

Having secured a full confession and plenty of fodder to satisfy the judge and jury at the forthcoming assizes (not to mention the scandal-hungry people of Jacobean England), Francis Manners and his fellow examiners concluded their interrogations. Margaret and Phillipa now had to await their trial.

10

'Desperate impenitency'

In late February or early March 1619, the evidence from the examinations of Margaret and Phillipa Flower was presented to the grand jury of Lincolnshire gentlemen. This august collective represented the landed gentry of Lindsey, Kesteven and Holland – the three subdivisions of Lincolnshire – and its role was to determine which prisoners should be put on trial.[1] Given that the Earl of Rutland was lord lieutenant of the county and its most important landowner, and that he arrived in Lincoln the same month, it is likely that he led the meeting. Such juries of necessity comprised local men, as the judge of assize at York in 1620 explained: 'They who live in the countye and have an interest in the country and are sencyble of the mischeyfs which these offences doe breede may present the offenders to the judges.'[2] The accused was never present at these hearings, and the members of the panel were often under pressure from the judges to send the case forward to trial. The grand jury for the Belvoir witch case wasted no time in finding that there was a *billa vera* (true case) for the two sisters to answer at the court of assizes in Lincoln, which was to take place in early March.[3] This court, like the grand jury, was comprised of the local elite, but they were made very aware of their responsibility to carry out national government policies – among them the persecution of suspected witches.

Witchcraft persecutions had been the business of the assizes for some time. This was a twice-yearly court which operated in six 'circuits' across England and had been the country's principal criminal court since the early fourteenth century. It was one of the most effective means of enforcing national authority in the localities. The assize judges (two for each circuit) were appointed by the monarch, who would brief them on their duties, and they would meet in Westminster to divide up the six circuits between them. The assizes was thus a hugely influential instrument of royal policy, and one contemporary referred to 'these halfe-yeerlye circuits whereby the streames of Justice are derived into all the parts of this kingdome, which lyke the streames of paradice doe make this land such a garden of pleasure as now it is'.[4] By the reign of James I, the court had become as much a social as a judicial occasion, drawing members of the gentry from across the county in which the hearings took place.

The court of assize was a much-anticipated event in each of the 50 or so cities that its judges visited, and it occasioned great pomp and ceremony. The entry into Lincolnshire by the judges assigned to the Midland circuit was heralded by trumpeters, and the judges were welcomed into the county by the sheriff's bailiff. When they were within sight of the city of Lincoln, they were given a much grander reception by the sheriff, other local officers and members of the county gentry. This impressive cavalcade, attended by pike- and liverymen in specially made clothing, then progressed into the city amidst great rejoicing, with bells, music and sometimes Latin orations being sung. Once inside the city's walls, the judges were met by the most distinguished local gentry (on this occasion including the Earl of Rutland and his brother), who briefed them on the state of the county. They then progressed to the cathedral for prayers and a sermon by the sheriff's chaplain.[5] Although often very long and tedious for the judges to sit through, these sermons were of real political significance, and would often be published after the event. They were an opportunity to air local grievances against the court or justice system, or to draw attention to the forthcoming business of the assizes. Given that the Belvoir witch case was by far the most notorious of all those that were to be brought before the judges, it is likely that the chaplain used his sermon to pontificate upon the evils of witchcraft.

Regrettably, the records of the Midland circuit assizes have long since been lost. Because it was not a centralised court, its records were not preserved in one place, but rather subject to random dispersal and destruction, whether accidental or deliberate.[6] We therefore have to rely upon the account of the Belvoir witch trial given in the contemporary pamphlet, as well as knowledge of similar trials elsewhere. Where such pamphlets can be compared with surviving court records, factual inconsistencies often emerge. The pamphlets were deliberately sensationalist and their authors could

distort, disregard or fabricate the evidence presented at the trials
in order to make their accounts more appealing to their readers.
There is no reason to suppose that *The Wonderful Discoverie of the
Witchcrafts of Margaret and Phillippa Flower, Daughters of Joan Flower*
was in any way an exception to this general rule. There are inconsistencies – such as in the spelling of names and, more seriously,
the phrasing of the testimonies. Thus, Joan Willimot, an associate
of the Flower women who was interrogated shortly afterwards, is
recorded in the original[pamphlet as saying that a 'Spirit did aske
of her her soule', whereas in a later edition this has changed to a
spirit having 'enquired about her soul', which implies a completely
different meaning.

As befitted a trial of such high profile, the presiding judges were
two of the foremost legal figures in the country. Sir Edward Bromley,
a baron of the Exchequer, had convicted the Pendle witches seven
years earlier and now again sat in judgement. He had a reputation
for thoroughness, albeit one driven by a fierce desire to see witches
brought to justice. In concluding the case of the Pendle witches, he
had been careful to stress the strength of the evidence against them,
thus leaving the jurors and other witnesses in no doubt that justice
had prevailed. He told the accused that they had no 'cause to
complaine: since in the Triall of your lives there hath beene great
care and paines taken, and much time spent: and very few or none
of you, but stand convicted upon your owne voluntarie confessions
and examinations'. He went on to praise the quality of the witnesses
and the thoroughness of their interrogation, claiming that nobody
of their 'nature and condition, ever were Arraigned and Tried with
more solemnitie, had more libertie given to pleade or answere to
everie particular point of evidence'. He therefore concluded that
'extraordinary meanes' had been used to ensure that none of the
proceedings had 'touch[ed] your lives unjustly'.[7] If he had protested
too much, then nobody remarked upon it. Instead, the trial established his reputation as one of the foremost prosecutors of witches
in the country.

His esteemed colleague Sir Henry Hobart was a former Attorney
General, and now Lord Chief Justice of the Common Pleas – an
immensely powerful position which carried national responsibility for
the civil law. Both he and Bromley had been appointed by the king

himself – an indication that James was following the case with great interest.[8] Before they left Westminster, they and the other assize judges would have been summoned by the king, who made it clear that he expected them to apply the law according to his own interpretation of it. 'As Kings borrow their power from God, so Judges from Kings,' he told them. 'And as Kings are to accompt to God, so Judges unto God and Kings.'[9] And the one facet of the law about which the king's views were best known was that relating to witchcraft. But to his credit, while James was fond of quoting the Book of Exodus that 'Thou shalt not suffer a witch to live', he seemed concerned above all to see justice done. *Daemonologie* had included specific instructions in this respect: 'Judges ought to beware to condemne any, but such as they are sure are guiltie, neither should the clattering reporte of a carling [an old woman or witch] serve in so weightie a case. Judges ought indeed to beware whome they condemne: For it is as great a Crime (as Solomon sayeth) *to condemne the innocent, as to let the guiltie escape free.*'

The choice of judge was crucial in a trial such as this. While in theory all four parties – accused, accusers, jury and judge – were given equal participation, in practice everything depended upon the nature and prejudices of the presiding judge. This makes the presence of Sir Edward Bromley, a renowned witch hunter, particularly significant. Both judges would have been aware of – and, the evidence suggests, were heavily influenced by – the publication of a major new handbook for the trial of witches just a year earlier. Michael Dalton's *The Countrey Justice* provided an extraordinarily detailed set of instructions for determining legally acceptable 'proof' in witchcraft cases. This had always been an issue for those involved in the prosecution of suspected witches because the crime, by its very nature, was virtually impossible to prove beyond reasonable doubt, as Dalton himself admitted: 'Now against these witches the Justices of peace may not alwaies expect direct evidence, seeing all their works are the works of darknesse, and no witnesses present with them to accuse them.'[10] Bodin agreed that 'with the deeds of witches . . . the proof is so obscure and the wickednesses so hidden, that out of a thousand there is hardly one punished'. He added, with some regret, that 'one must be very sure of the truth to impose the death sentence'.[11] Both he and Dalton therefore set out to help those involved in the prosecution of witches to chart a course through the increasingly perilous waters of the laws surrounding witchcraft.

According to Dalton, two of the most important signs of guilt were the presence of a 'familiar, or spirit', and a mark on the suspect's body to distinguish where their familiar 'sucketh them'. Other proofs included the testimony of the victim, the examination and confession of the witch's children or servants, and 'their owne voluntarie confession, which exceeds all other evidence'.[12] Bodin added that 'if those whom she threatened have died afterward or fallen into a languor, especially if there are several of them, it is a most powerful presumption'.[13] The interrogators of Margaret and Phillipa Flower had secured every one of these signs during the course of their examinations.

The Justices of the Peace were instructed to acquire a bewildering range of other information from the suspect, such as 'his parents, if they were wicked, and given to the same kind of fault', 'his course of life . . . if a common alehouse-haunter, or ryottous in dyet, play or apparrell', and 'whether he be of evill fame, or report'. The Flower sisters would have given their examiners ample fodder for each of these questions. Even if they had denied their guilt or refused to answer, the simple fact of 'blushing, looking downewards, silence, trembling' was taken as proof of guilt.

Most assize hearings were conducted in buildings which had other uses when the courts were not in session. However, in Lincoln the court of assize had a permanent base in the castle, which also served as the headquarters of the sheriff. A survey carried out by the Duchy of Lancaster mentions the courthouse, which by then was one of the few buildings that survived within the castle walls. The layout of the courtroom followed a more or less standard pattern. The judges would sit in the middle of a raised bench, flanked on either side and on a low bench in front by county magnates. Meanwhile, the custos rotulorum (keeper of the county's records), sheriff, undersheriff and court clerks sat at a low table. Behind them were the jury and the prisoners' dock. Into the rest of the courtroom would be stuffed the throngs of ordinary people who had turned up to witness the proceedings. Criminal trials were one of the most popular spectator sports of the day. There was almost a carnival atmosphere at the assizes, with a constant crush of officials and members of the public, and the

undersheriff desperately trying to maintain order. At the trial of one
Catholic priest in 1582, the courtroom was so crowded that the judges
were 'forced to make room for themselves like ushers'. A similar scene
was witnessed at Warwick in 1669, when a boy fell from a window
and was skewered on the pike of one of the sheriff's men standing
guard below. A few years later, the floor of a courtroom in East
Grinstead collapsed under the weight of spectators.[14] Considering the
high-profile nature of the Belvoir witch case, it is likely that the courtroom in Lincoln was even more crowded than usual on the day of
the trial.

Once the judges and court officials had taken their places, a crier
demanded silence and the formal proceedings began. These included
reading aloud the names of the Justices of the Peace, coroners,
constables and bailiffs, and the prisoners themselves. The jury,
composed of between 13 and 23 'respectable men' (usually middling
yeomen and artisans), was called and sworn.[15] To qualify for jury
service, a man had to be between 21 and 70 years of age, and to
be of property. In an admirable (if rare) attempt to ensure that
justice prevailed, a juryman could not be connected to, or have any
obvious bias against, the accused, and one of the sheriff's duties
was to ensure that he 'returne indifferent juries for the triall of
mens lives'.[16]

Once the jury had been sworn in, one of the judges would then
read a solemn charge 'telling the cause of their coming, giving a
good lesson unto the people', and summarising the cases which
were to be examined.[17] This 'lesson' was a forceful, often intimi-
dating means of conveying the attitudes and priorities of the Crown
and Council in Westminster, thus reinforcing official policy and
making it clear that the king would not tolerate any deviation from
it. Even though James's preoccupation with witchcraft had lessened
by the time the Flower sisters were brought to trial, the fact that
their victim was one of the most influential noblemen both at court
and in the county no doubt prompted the judges to reinforce the
terms of the 1604 Act. The clerk of the court would then call the
prisoners to the bar and tell them to raise their right hand and plead
guilty or not guilty to the charges against them. In cases of felony,
if the accused failed to answer, he was judged 'mute, that is dumme
by contumacie' and condemned to 'peine forte et dure', or being

pressed to death. This horrific procedure was described in a sixteenth-century account of the English justice system as 'one of the cruellest deathes that may be: he is layd upon a table, and an other uppon him, and so much weight of stones or lead laide uppon that table, while as his bodie be crushed, & his life by that violence taken from him'.[18]

As was customary at such courts, there was no defence lawyer for those accused of felony – there was too great a fear that any such intermediary would be bolstered by the power of the Devil. Rather, the truth was expected to emerge from the written testimonies that had been taken before the trial. These testimonies were considered by the grand jury before the trial began. Because the assizes only happened twice a year in each circuit, there was always a great deal of business to get through. Even in winter, the proceedings began at seven o'clock in the morning and continued, by candlelight, until as late as eleven o'clock at night. It was common for seven or eight prisoners (each with entirely different cases) to be dealt with in quick succession, and there could be as many as 40 cases in one day alone. Routine trials lasted just 15 to 20 minutes, and even the more complex ones probably took little more than half an hour from arraignment to verdict. Some prisoners saved the court time by pleading guilty, which meant that their trial was bypassed altogether.

The profusion of different evidence must have been confusing for onlookers and participants alike – not to mention the grand jury which had to consider it all. Added to this was the fact that, in contrast to modern times, the defendant was effectively presumed guilty unless proved otherwise, and even the most circumstantial evidence was enough to secure a conviction. Those indicted for felony (such as the Flower sisters) were denied the assistance of counsel unless a point of law arose from the evidence, so were obliged to defend themselves. As most were not versed in the ways of the law and were at best barely literate, the odds were stacked against them.

Since he was the principal victim in the case, the Earl of Rutland's evidence was heard first and accorded the greatest importance – even more so given his elevated status in society. Interestingly, his reaction to the women before him was rather more muted than that of the other people present. Indeed, he appeared almost penitential when he came to give evidence. The author of *The Wonderful Discoverie* put this down to the natural introspection of a devout man: 'and although the Right Honourable Earle had sufficient greife for the losse of his Children; yet no doubt it was the greater to consider the manner, and how it pleased God to inflict on him such a fashion of visitation'. The use of the plural 'children' is interesting. By the time of the trial, only one of the earl's sons was dead; the fate of the younger still hung in the balance. Katherine, meanwhile, was apparently out of all danger.

The Earl of Rutland showed no desire for revenge against the two women. 'Such was the unparalleld magnanimity, wisedome, and patience of this generous Nobleman, that hee urged nothing against them more then their onne confessions, and so quietly left them to judiciall triall, desiring of God mercy for their soules, and of men charity to censure them in their condemnation.'[19] This is not the behaviour that one might expect of a grief-stricken father when faced with the women who had confessed to his son's murder and the attempted murder of his other two children. Surely if he had truly believed in their guilt, he would have pursued them relentlessly, bringing his considerable influence to bear on the presiding judges and not resting until he saw their bodies swinging from the gallows on the castle wall. Perhaps the earl was playing the jury by this show of meek acceptance of God's will. Or perhaps the author of the Belvoir witch pamphlet was trying to show him as a shining example of true Christian compassion in order to draw a stark contrast with the wickedness of the Flower sisters.[20]

There is no record of any further witnesses being called, after the earl's apparently quiet withdrawal. But since a minimum of two witnesses were required to attest that the accused had entered into league with the Devil or practised witchcraft, there would almost certainly have been more.

A record of another witchcraft trial of the early seventeenth century gives a sense of the type of evidence that witnesses typically gave, as well as of the quick succession with which they appeared in the courtroom. 'There came in eight or ten which gave evidence against her . . . One woman came in and testified uppon her oath that her husband upon his death bed, tooke it upon his death, that he was bewitched . . . The woman tooke her oath also, that she thought in her conscience that the old woman was a witch, and that she killed her husband . . . There came in an other . . . He tooke his oath directly that she was a witch . . . Then came in two or three grave honest men, which testified that she was by common fame accounted a witch.' Flimsy though they seem to modern observers, such testimonies would have carried great weight in a Jacobean court. They were certainly enough to convict the accused in this case, as the author records: 'We found her giltie, for what could we doe lesse, she was condemned and executed: and upon the ladder she made her prayer, and tooke it upon her death shee was innocent and free from all such dealings.'[21]

In the unlikely event that there had been any witnesses called to speak in the Flower sisters' defence, these would have carried little weight. During this period, defence witnesses, unlike those for the prosecution, presented their evidence unsworn. This enabled judges to intimidate them with warnings that they stood in fear of God if they told an untruth. And they further guarded against an unwanted outcome by instructing juries to give little heed to such evidence.

It was probably at this point that Margaret and Phillipa Flower gave their testimonies. Before doing so, the sisters would have been told by the judges that they stood accused of having 'felloniously . . . practised . . . witchcraft against the form of the statute etc. And against the peace of the Crown and the Dignity of the Lord King.'[22] The fact that they had apparently talked so freely of their pact with the Devil might suggest that they pleaded guilty to the charge. However, it was common for defendants to confess their crimes during the examinations that preceded their trial and to still enter a plea of not guilty on the day. Even if the official record of their trial had survived, it is unlikely to have included their plea, so this must rest with conjecture. Besides, it would have made little difference to the outcome of the trial. As one contemporary account of assize trials noted: 'If a man attainted of Felony be brought to the Bar, and asked what cause he can shew why he should not suffer death according to his Judgment, and he will stand mute, he shall be hanged.'[23]

It is unlikely that the sisters were given much time to plead their case. By this stage of the proceedings, most defendants of 'low and

common education' were so overawed and intimidated by the 'awful
Solemnities' of the assizes that they were barely able to utter anything
very comprehensible in their defence.[24] It was all too common for
judges to push home their social and intellectual advantage by bullying
the accused into submission. One critic of the system observed in 1653
that the prospect of acquittal at such trials was extremely remote
because it was virtually impossible to find a Judge who would 'suffer
a Prisoner to speak for himself, nor any one else for him, but he'll
daunt them, vilifie & threaten them with his great menacing words
and big looks, as if the very name of being a prisoner were sufficient
enough to argue him guilty, without any further evidence or testimony;
this practice has cost many an innocent man's life'.[25] When 9 of the
14 women who were brought before the Essex assizes in 1582 refused
to confess, the judge warned that 'they which doe confesse the truth
of their doeings, they shall have much favour; but on the other they
shall bee burnt and hanged.'[26]

It seems, however, that Margaret and Phillipa refused to be intimidated by the august body of men before them. Although Sir Edward
Bromley and Sir Henry Hobart had many years' experience in the
law, they were apparently shocked by the Flower sisters' stubborn
defiance. The trial pamphlet describes how they 'not only wondred
at the wickednesse of these persons, but were amazed at their practises and horrible contracts with the Divell to damne their onn
soules'.[27] Likewise, the persons who were present at the trial were
'amazed' when they heard the lurid details and 'the circumstances
of this divellish contract'.[28] According to The Wonderful Discoverie,
the onlookers were also shocked by Margaret and Phillipa's 'desperate
impenitency, and horrible distraction . . . exclaiming against the
Devill for deluding them, and now breaking promise with them,
when they stood in most need of his help'.[29] The reference to the
sisters' 'desperate impenitency' suggests that they presented little in
their defence.

Given that the accused in cases of this nature had no legal repre-
sentation, few if any reliable witnesses in their defence, and scarcely
any opportunity to present their own evidence, assize trials often
degenerated into an 'altercation' between prisoners, prosecutors and
witnesses.[30] The fact that Margaret and Phillipa Flower were apparently so brazen in their guilt, shocking the packed courtroom with

lurid descriptions of their pact with the Devil, indicates that their trial might well have gone the same way.

There are records of other witchcraft trials collapsing into little more than shouting matches between victims and accused, with members of the public joining in. There was so much noise at the trial of Mary Spencer in 1634 that she was unable to hear the evidence brought against her. There was similar confusion at Anne Bodenham's trial in 1653, when the cacophony was so great that neither she nor the judge could hear each other. 'The crowd of spectators made such a noise that the Judge could not heare the Prisoner, nor the Prisoner the Judge; but the words were handed from one to the other by Mr R. Chandler, and sometimes not truly reported.'[31] In most cases, the people who flocked to witness witchcraft trials were little better than a braying mob, determined to witness the accused being condemned to death. A late seventeenth-century commentator scorned the 'ignorant and foolish rabble' who frequently attended the courts, lamenting: 'It is seldom that a poor old wretch is brought to trial upon that account, but there is, at the heels of her, a popular rage that does little less than demand of her to be put to death.'[32] Sometimes it was the accused themselves who caused the commotion. Anne Ashby, one of the women tried at Maidstone in 1652, 'fell into an extasie before the Bench, and swell'd into a monstous bigness, screching and crying out very dolefully'.[33] Given the highly emotive nature of the Flower sisters' case, involving as it did the bewitching of three innocent children, it is likely that their trial degenerated into similar disorder.

There was no summing-up by the judges when all of the evidence had been heard, because they would already have commented as each individual statement had been made. Instead, they instructed the jury that in reaching a verdict, they must remember God, their consciences and what they had heard. In all of this, the outcome desired by these two formidable representatives of the law would have been made patently clear to everyone present. Assize trials were dominated by the constant and pervasive influence of the judges, who were often the only ones present with any formal legal training. As such, they saw it as their duty to provide the jury with what one authority condescendingly described as 'a great Light and Assistance by his weighing the Evidence before them, and observing where the Question and Knot of the Business lies, and by shewing them his Opinion even in Matter of Fact, which is a great Advantage and Light to Lay-Men'.[34]

The judge could bring such pressure to bear upon the jury that the latter had little choice but to deliver the verdict that was expected of them. If a jury proved particularly stubborn and ignored this pressure, then they would be bullied into submission. Some judges even threatened – or actually used – fines or imprisonment to get their own way. The right to threaten juries, either before or after they reached a decision, was seen as an entirely acceptable convention.

Juries would often retire to consider the evidence of several cases together. On such occasions, they would be given a list of the relevant prisoners 'for their better direction and help of their memory to know who they have in charge'.[35] Sometimes, though, they reached a verdict without retiring. As in modern times, this had to be unanimous: 'all ought to agree, and any one dissenting, no Verdict can be given'.[36] Considering that there was growing scepticism about witchcraft at this time, it was a very real possibility that the jury in the Belvoir witch trial might have included at least one nay-sayer. But the judges would have already made it clear what was expected of the jury, and if they had disagreed with their verdict, they could have had it overturned quite easily. It was not uncommon for a person whom a jury had acquitted to be imprisoned on the orders of a judge who thought otherwise. Sir Edward Bromley had attempted to do just that in the trial of the Lancashire witches, but had been forced to content himself with admonishing those who had been acquitted to 'presume no further of your Innocencie than you have just cause: for although it pleased God out of his Mercie, to spare you at this time, yet without question there are those amongst you, that are as deepe in this action, as any of them that are condemned to die for their offences'. He had concluded by exhorting them to forsake the Devil immediately.[37]

Sir Edward was not to be thwarted a second time. Margaret and Phillipa Flower were pronounced guilty according to the terms of the 1604 witchcraft statute. Satisfied that the two women did 'consult covenant with entertain employ feede or rewarde any evill and wicked Spirit to or for any intent or purpose', the judges passed sentence. 'Thou hast beene endicted of such a felonie and thereof arranged . . . they have found thee guiltie, thou hast nothing to say for they selfe, the Lawe is, thou shalt first returne to the place from whence thou camest, from thence thou shalt goe to the place of execution, there thou shalt hang till thou be dead.'[38] Justice had been done – or had been seen to be done. 'God is not mocked, and so gave them over to judgement, nor man so reformed, but for the Earles sake, they cursed them to that place which they themselves long before had bargained for.'[39]

'By strangling twist'

In most assize cases, even after conviction a felon had several possible avenues of escape. In fact, relatively few felons convicted at this court suffered the death penalty. Judges had a number of ways of mitigating punishment at their discretion. Transportation to places overseas was one such option, as was claiming benefit of clergy – a legal loophole that spared a convict from hanging if they were able to read a certain passage from the Bible. Formerly the preserve of churchmen, the privilege was extended to laymen during the reign of Henry VIII. But it did not extend to those found guilty of witchcraft. The potential for a convicted witch to escape death horrified those who sought their destruction. The authors of the treatises against witchcraft urged those dispensing justice not to flinch from delivering the ultimate punishment. 'Shee is a murtherer both of soules and bodies; and therefore, in this respect, doth also deserve death,' opined the influential pamphleteer Thomas Cooper. 'Therefore, though they should repent, yet die they must, to justifie God, and prevent further ensnaring: that though their body perish, yet the soule may be saved.'[1]

For Margaret and Phillipa Flower, once the sentence had been pronounced, there was little hope of a reprieve. Even if they had been able to produce a reasoned defence, the fact that they were impoverished, insignificant and easily dispensed-with women whose accusers were one of the most powerful and influential families in England afforded them no chance of justice. The sisters could hardly hope for a royal pardon, given the Earl of Rutland's links with court. Their only realistic chance of a reprieve would have been if one or both of them was pregnant. Almost half of the women convicted of felony during the reigns of Elizabeth and James claimed 'benefit of belly'. Such was their desperation to escape punishment that even when it was obvious that they could not possibly be pregnant, some still tried to convince the jurors otherwise. 'Old Mother Samuel', one of the so-called 'Witches of Warboys', caused uproar at her trial when she declared that she was with child. 'Whiche set all the company on a great laughing, and shee her selfe more than any other . . . Her age was neere fourescore, therefore the Judge moved her to leave that answere: but in no case she would be driven from it, till at length, a Jury of women were empaneled, and sworne to search her: who gave up their verdite, that she was not with childe, unlesse (as some saide) it was with the divell.' By contrast, Alice Samuel's daughter Agnes, who also stood accused of sorcery, refused to plead pregnancy, declaring: 'It shall never be sayd, that I was both a Witch and a whore.'[2]

In theory, those women who were discovered to be 'quick' with child gained only a temporary reprieve from the death sentence.[3] But in practice, the overwhelming majority who obtained such a stay of execution were released. Given the Flower sisters' reputation for debauchery, pregnancy was a very real possibility. There is no evidence that they put forward such a plea, but since the original trial papers have been lost, we can never know for certain whether they at least tried to save their lives in this way.

As convicted felons, Margaret and Phillipa Flower were destined to lose not just their lives, but any property or goods that they owned. These were not likely to have amounted to much, but what little they had would have been seized by the local sheriff or undersheriff and forfeited to the king while they were still alive. The law also stipulated that a convicted felon 'shall lose his blood, aswel in regard of his Auncestry, as of his posterity; for his blood is corrupted, so as he hath neither Auncestor, heire, nor posterity'.[4] In short, he was to be wiped off the face of the earth, as if he had never existed. Since neither Margaret nor Phillipa had any children or other known relatives, this was likely to have had little impact upon them. Besides, they had already done enough to secure their place in history.

The Belvoir pamphlet is very specific about the date assigned for the sisters' execution: 11 March 1619. Given that the rest of the chronology it provides is so confused, this suggests that the date was well attested in the contemporary records. It would also fit in with the conclusion of the Lincoln assizes, which had taken place during the first week of March. Executions could be carried out within a matter of hours of the guilty verdict being delivered. The three Essex witches convicted at Chelmsford in July 1589 were returned to prison for just two hours before being led to their place of execution. However, it seems that the Flower sisters were accorded the dubious privilege of a few days' grace.

Most executions at Lincoln Castle during this period took place on a gallows outside the castle walls, opposite the north-west corner of the castle, which afforded an excellent view for those who came along to witness the grisly occasions.[5] All witch-hangings attracted large crowds, and the notoriety of this case must have swelled the numbers even more. The condemned felons were taken to the gallows by cart. As they awaited their fate, a clergyman would mount the same platform and offer spiritual guidance, inviting them to repent of their crimes. Often, it was at this point that the prisoner made a final speech to the waiting crowd. Mary Smith, who was executed in Norfolk a year before the Flower sisters, was said to have 'confessed openly at the place of execution, in the audience of multitudes of people gathered together (as is usual at such times) to be beholders of her death. And made there also profession of her faith, and hope of a better life herafter; and the meanes hereby she trusted to obtaine the same, as before, hath beene specified. And being asked, if she would be contented to have a psalme sung, answered willingly that she desired the same, and appointed it herself, the Lamentation of a sinner.'[6] Another convicted witch, Joan Upney, also satisfied the crowds by giving a performance that was 'very penitent, asking God and the world forgiveness even to the last gasp, for her wicked and detestable life'.[7] Those who proved unwilling to heighten the drama of the occasion for the benefit of the onlookers by pleading God's forgiveness could be put under enormous pressure. Henry Goodcole, the chaplain who attended Elizabeth Sawyer at her execution in 1621, admitted that it was only after 'great labour' that he had 'extorted' a confession from her. Thirty years later, Joan Paterson was so bullied by the attendant cleric that even the hangman told him he ought to be 'ashamed to trouble a dying woman so much'.[8]

The contemporary account of Margaret and Phillipa's final moments hints at a lack of repentance as they were led to their deaths. It tells of 'the terror of all beholders', who looked upon 'such dissolute and abominable Creatures' and no doubt resolved never to fall into such 'devilish' temptations themselves – as, indeed, the author intended his readers likewise to vow. Certainly, they refused to gratify the spectators with any last speeches, either of defiance or penitence. As the women stood on the cart, each with a noose around her neck, waiting for the hangman to fit the rope over the crossbeam of the scaffold and let the horse pull the cart from under them, the chaplain invited them to recite the Lord's Prayer. The fact that the onlookers were so horrified by their 'dissolute' behaviour suggests that they either refused or were unable to comply. If they had stammered over or forgotten the words, then it would have been ascribed not to illiteracy, confusion or sheer terror at being moments away from death, but to the fact that witches were deemed incapable of saying the Lord's Prayer without faltering.

And so the horse was led slowly, agonisingly away and Margaret and Phillipa fell to their choking deaths. The ballad which was composed soon after the trial provides the following cursory and brutal description of their last moments:

> They dyed in shame, by strangling twist,
> And layd by shame in the ground.[9]

The 'strangling twist' implies that the final mercy of a swift death had been denied them. Those who were condemned to hang cherished only the grim hope that their necks would be broken as the ladder was kicked from under them. The painfully slow, suffocating death – taking an average of 15 minutes or more – was the alternative which Margaret and Phillipa suffered.

Their bodies were buried without ceremony or gravestone within an unconsecrated corner of the castle grounds earmarked for convicted felons. It was customary for the prison gaoler to arrange the burial, and he reserved the right to claim their clothes and any possessions they had for himself. If he was so minded (and curious), he might also conduct a final search for the Devil's mark or other supernatural signs on the bodies of the dead women, in order to assure himself that justice had been done. It was noted that once the three women

known as the 'Witches of Warboys' were 'thoroughly dead', the gaoler
stripped them naked and discovered a 'teat to the length of half an
inch' in Alice Samuel's private parts. It was one last indignity inflicted
upon women whose lives had already been blighted by a cruel and
unjust society.

'Infamous persons'

The case of the Belvoir witches had a profound impact upon Jacobean England. It was said to have prompted the Act of Parliament 'against sorcery, and other diabolical practices' passed in James's reign.[1] According to James Howell's *Letters*, compiled in the mid seventeenth century, 'King James, a great while, was loath to believe there were witches; but that which happened to my lord Francis of Rutland's children convinced him.'[2] This was overstating the case: James's conviction had already been formed long before the Flower women had been brought to trial, and by 1619 he was becoming increasingly sceptical about the existence of witchcraft. Nevertheless, the Belvoir trial had been one of the most high-profile and unusual in the history of the European witch craze. In contrast to the thousands of cases rooted in disagreements between members of a local community, it had involved one of the foremost aristocratic families in England, and its tangled web had extended to the heart of the royal court. It may not have been a coincidence that one of the most notorious plays about witchcraft, *Doctor Faustus*, was republished during the year of the Flower sisters' trial, and again in 1620. The Belvoir witch case therefore seemed to have reawakened interest (although not necessarily belief) in a phenomenon that was otherwise rapidly fading from view.

The execution of Margaret and Phillipa Flower also created a heightened awareness of witchcraft in the Bottesford area. The Reverend Charles Odingsells, rector of Langar in the Vale of Belvoir, preached two sermons in 1619 warning his parishioners against any dabbling in magic of any kind. Odingsells was the chaplain of Emanuel Scrope, later Earl of Sunderland, who – like Francis Manners – was a closet Catholic. The prelate was therefore keenly aware of the religious tensions that existed in the local area, and he pointed to witchcraft as a symptom of these. He decried the 'false prophets' who claimed to be able to foretell the future or cure illness by magical means. Their powers, he said, were rooted in evil because Satan 'can by Gods permission, moove and trouble the spirits, the bloud and humors of mans bodie, and so cause strange imaginations and phantasmes in the phantasie; whereby it comes to passe that men and women thinke they see many strange & uncouth things which indeed they see not. For hee [Satan] will so strongly delude the inward phantasie, as that hee will even palpably deceive the outward sense.'

Odingsells went on to instil fear in his parishioners by highlighting how easily the Devil could take other forms in order to lure vulnerable people to his cause: '[Satan] may by Gods permission, either assume a true body, or make of the Ayre and other Elements, fayned, counterfeited bodies, as of Men or Women, of Birds, or Beasts, and other living Creatures, so per fascinum [by witchcraft] hee hides and clokes that thing which is present, and makes another thing seeme to be there, which indeed is not present.' He ended with a somewhat weary admonishment which indicates that he had attempted to dissuade the local people from consulting witches and cunning folk in the past, with little success. 'I have heretofore disswaded you of this Parish of Langar, from running to them that use charmes, and are *good at words* (as they call them here in the Valley). I have forbidden you to resort to such. But how comes it to passe, that you wil not obey? . . . Let none bee found among you that useth witchcraft, or a Regarder of times, or a Marker of flying or Fowles, or a Sorcerer, or a Charmer, or that counselleth with a Spirit, or a Soothsayer.'[3]

But for every person who clung tightly to their magical beliefs, there was at least one who was determined to stamp out witchcraft in all its forms – indeed, the two approaches were by no means contradictory. One contemporary described the terrifying mob mentality which incited thousands of people across the country to hunt down suspected witches and not rest until they saw them dead. 'When men are once so bewitched as to thinke, who can live in safety while witches remaine: they run with madnesse to seeke all meanes to put them to death, and not onely them, but all such as are suspected . . . For they holde that witches should bee put to death, and not onely that, but are inflamed with a wonderfull rage and fury to have it accomplished.'[4]

According to a contemporary of the Flower sisters, there was 'no small multitude [of witches] swarming now in the world'.[5] But in fact, such convictions were becoming increasingly rare. That fact, together with the involvement of the Manners family, would have intensified public interest even further. The sources hint at a level of public unease about the execution of Margaret and Phillipa Flower. Determined to stamp this out, the authorities turned their attention to three other Leicestershire women 'of the like grade in life' whom they accused of conspiring with Joan Flower and her daughters.[6] Anne Baker of Bottesford, Ellen Green of nearby Stathern and Joan Willimot of Goadby were accused of practising black magic to help carry out the Flower women's evil designs against their neighbours. Given that they were arrested so soon after the Flowers, it is possible that Margaret and Phillipa had named them during the course of their confessions. George Gifford admitted that once a suspected witch had been apprehended, her interrogators would put her under intense pressure until she implicated others of her profession: 'They examine witches to know whether their spirites have not told them how many witches be within certaine miles of them, and who they be.'[7] The fact that many suspected witches would, perhaps in hope of a reprieve, name other women who had conspired with them meant that the net often widened at a terrifying rate.

James I himself had emphasised the importance of seeking 'a number of guilty persons' confessions against one that is accused' in order to secure a reliable conviction. The testimony of 'one infamous person' should not, he said, 'be admitted for a sufficient proof . . . For who but witches can be proofs, and so witnesses, of the doings of witches?'[8] Jean Bodin agreed: 'Although accomplices do not constitute necessary proof in other crimes, nonetheless fellow witches denouncing or giving testimony against their accomplices constitute sufficient proof to pass sentence, especially if there are a number of them. For it is quite well known that only witches can testify about being present at the assemblies which they attend at night.'[9] The arrest of Anne Baker, Joan Willimot and Ellen Green was therefore as much about hammering a nail into the Flower sisters' coffin as it was about ensuring that all other suspected witches in the area be apprehended. If the authorities could secure and publish further evidence against the Flower women (the more shocking, the better), then the whisperings of the sceptics could be silenced once and for all.

The three women are depicted on the frontispiece of the Belvoir witches pamphlet and conform exactly to the stereotypical image of a witch. Wearing long skirts and shawls, and with caps on their heads, each of them appears both elderly and poor. Anne Baker and Ellen Green both carry a staff, while Joan Willimot (who was apparently the eldest) rests her crooked frame on crutches. They are all ugly, with long noses and pointed chins, and Joan Willimot (who, like Joan Flower, was a widow) has what appears to be a small beard – perhaps intended as an indication of her age. Anne Baker and Ellen Green have a cat and a dog respectively as their familiars, while Joan Willimot is flanked by a small black dog and an owl on her shoulder. Like the Flower women, all three had a reputation as cunning folk.

Anne, Ellen and Joan were interrogated over a period of 18 days, between 28 February and 17 March 1618. The pamphlet that records their interrogation does not make it clear whether they were taken to Lincoln Castle or questioned in their native Leicestershire. However, the fact that some of the same men who had examined the Flower sisters were employed makes the former seem more likely. Moreover, their first interrogator was Alexander Amcotts, a local Justice of the Peace and member of a Lincolnshire gentry family from Aisthorpe, which was just seven miles north of Lincoln. He was later joined by Samuel Fleming and Sir Henry Hastings. Many different witnesses and victims would be named in the course of their examination – all of whom are recorded in the local parish records – which proves the extent to which fear and suspicion had taken hold in the area.

Joan Willimot was examined first, on 28 February and 1 March 1619. Although she confessed to being a cunning woman, she was careful to insist that she had only ever used her powers for good. She admitted that she had been a close confidante of Joan Flower, and that the latter had complained about the Earl of Rutland's treatment of her daughter Margaret. 'Joane Flower told her that my Lord of Rutland had dealt badly with her and that they had put away her Daughter, swearing to be revenged.'[10] Joan Flower had apparently not been able to exact this revenge against the earl himself, but confided to Joan Willimot that she had 'spied my Lords Sonne [Francis Manners] and striken him to the heart' with a 'white Spirit'. Upon hearing this, Joan Willimot had been so concerned that the previous Friday night, she had sent her familiar (which took the form of a woman whom she called 'Pretty') 'to see how my Lord Rosse did'. Her familiar had reported that the young boy 'should doe well'.[11]

The authorities used this evidence in their interrogation of Anne Baker the following day, over which they took a great of trouble. This may have been because Anne, described as a 'spinster', was thought to be a 'black witch' who had caused harm to her neighbours. She was also the only one of the three to live in Bottesford, and so was most likely to reveal telling details about the Flower family. But Anne's testimony was filled with outlandish claims about spirits and familiars, spells and visions – most of which focused upon her own witchcraft, rather than that of the Flower women. Members of the local community had accused her of murdering two children from different families with similar spells to those employed by Joan Flower, such as burning their hair and nails. Anne strenuously denied this, pleading that she had tried only to cure the children. Neither did she admit to murdering a local woman, Elizabeth Hough, or rendering Anthony Gill incapable of fathering a child.

Only on the second day of questioning, which was conducted by Samuel Fleming alone, did Anne Baker confess to knowing anything relating to the Earl of Rutland's son. According to her testimony, about three years before (in fact it was six), upon returning from a trip to Northamptonshire, the wives of Mr Peate and Mr Dennis – who lived in or near Belvoir Castle – told her that the elder of the earl's sons, Lord Henry, was dead. They also corroborated Margaret and Phillipa Flower's statement that the young lord's glove had been buried in the ground, 'and as that glove did rot and wast, so did the liver of the said Lord rot and wast'.[12] Since Peate was named as one of Joan's lovers, it can be reasonably supposed that his wife's report was motivated by a desire for revenge.

On 17 March, six days after the sisters' execution, Joan and Ellen were interrogated by Sir Henry Hastings and Dr Samuel Fleming. At first, Joan gave them little more than the incoherent ramblings of a confused and no doubt terrified old woman. Perhaps in an attempt to draw a contrast with her own 'good' magic, she spoke of local men and women who were possessed of evil powers. But her interrogators forced her back to what had happened at Belvoir. Eventually she confessed that she had met Joan and Margaret Flower on Blackborrow Hill a week before their arrest. From there they had walked together to Joan Flower's house, where she had seen the latter's two familiars: a rat and an owl. Joan Flower told her confidante that these spirits had assured her she would not be condemned. She then picked up some earth, spat upon it and worked it with her finger before putting it in her purse. Turning to her guest, she told her that although she could not bring harm to the Earl of Rutland, 'yet shee had sped his Sonne, which is dead'.[13]

By contrast, Ellen Green could not be made to prove that justice had been served on the Flower women, for she made no mention of them in her testimony – despite the insistent questioning of her inter-rogators. Instead, she told of her own pact with the Devil, which she had been persuaded to make by Joan Willimot when the two women met in the Wolds – a remote and hilly landscape in the east of the otherwise flat countryside of Lincolnshire. After being 'sucked' by two spirits – a kitten and a 'moldiwarp' (mole) – she claimed that she had begun her evil work by taking revenge upon several members of the local community and bewitching them to death.[14] Ellen was the only one of the three women to confess that she 'gave her soul to the Divell to have the Spirits at her command', and that she used her powers to do evil. Later evidence suggests that she was of unsound mind and genuinely believed that she had magical powers.

Despite confessing to witchcraft, there is no record of any proceed-ings against Anne Baker, Joan Willimot and Ellen Green after their interrogation had been completed. Their role as cunning folk ought to have been enough to condemn them, and in Ellen Green's case she had provided ample testimony of her involvement in malevolent magic to seal her doom. If they had been put on trial, then it would have been in Leicester, rather than Lincoln. This makes it impossible that they were dealt with as part of the Lent assizes, because the judges had already heard cases at Leicester by the time they reached Lincoln in early March.

Another possibility is that once they had given evidence in the Flower case, these women were no longer considered useful and were released. But the fact that they were still being examined several days after the Flower sisters' trial suggests that they may have held interest for the authorities in their own right. The most likely scenario is therefore that they did undergo some formal proceedings against them, but that they escaped condemnation. Given the interest in the

Belvoir witches, if their alleged confidantes had also been put to death, surely this would have been recorded by the contemporary pamphleteers.

The notion that the three women escaped punishment is supported by newly discovered evidence which suggests that Ellen Green was still alive some 15 years after the Flower sisters were hanged. Sir Richard Napier, the renowned physician who treated the Earl of Rutland's younger son, kept a casebook of the treatments that he had ministered during his long career. This still survives in the Bodleian Library today. Among the entries is one written in April 1634 which attests that Napier had treated a woman named Ellen Green, who was 'troubled in her mind, haunted by an ill spirit, whom she saith . . . speaketh to her'.[15] Given that Napier was known to the community of Belvoir thanks to his earlier visit, it is highly likely that his services had been enlisted for Ellen. But a physician of his standing would have commanded a considerable fee, surely far beyond the resources of Ellen herself. Is it possible that Cecilia Manners, or perhaps her stepdaughter Katherine arranged and paid for Napier's intervention? Unless further evidence comes to light, any such notion must remain speculative. But it does present a tempting proposition of the Manners family or some other powerful patron performing a penance for the part they played in bringing about the deaths of the Flower women.

Despite the best efforts of the interrogators in Lincoln, there remained doubt about the validity of the Flower women's conviction. There is even some suggestion in the contemporary records that the Earl of Rutland fell foul of the king as a result of his involvement in the trial. A letter from one Roger Richards to Countess Cecilia, written some 14 or 15 years later, reminded her of the case of those 'dambned witches when I did my best and faythfull service and preserved his Honour from danger of a *premunire*'.[16] It is not clear what service Richards performed, but it is interesting that his master had been at risk of condemnation under the statute of premunire, which forbade any subject to appeal to a foreign or ecclesiastical court if the jurisdiction belonged to the king's courts. Had Francis perceived a risk that the Flower women would not be found guilty and therefore appealed to what he saw as a higher authority? There is a note among the accounts of the Privy Council, dated 4 July 1619, regarding an application for a pass for a gentleman named Ralph Hansbie 'to goe to the

Archdukes' Courte upon speciall busines for the Earl of Rutland'.[17] The archduke was Ferdinand II, Holy Roman Emperor, a fervent Catholic and witch hunter. No further details are given, so the purpose of the mission remains a mystery.

Perhaps in an attempt to downplay the premunire affair, the author of *The Wonderful Discoverie* was at pains to stress that the earl had conformed to the due processes of the law: 'To his eternall praise [he] proceeded yet both religiously and charitably against the Offenders, leaving their prosecution to the law and submitting himselfe, and deplorable case to the providence of God.'[18] Moreover, he apparently withdrew from the examinations before they were concluded, and 'left them [Margaret and Phillippa] to the triall at Law, before the Judges of Assise at Lincolne'.[19] In addition, far from the earl earning the king's disapproval, there is evidence to suggest that James may have been inspired by the Belvoir witch trial, and that it reinvigorated his flagging interest in the persecution of witches. In 1620, a schoolmaster named Peacock was arrested for plotting to influence the king by witchcraft. Alarmed by this threat to his own security, James immediately demanded that Peacock be thrown into the Tower of London and interrogated under torture.[20]

In the immediate aftermath of the Flower sisters' trial, the household at Belvoir struggled to return to some semblance of normality. In July 1619, Cecilia sought refuge in Tunbridge Wells, which would rise in popularity as a spa town during the following century. Judging from the family accounts, she stayed there for some time, because at £100 (equivalent to around £10,000 today), the bill was considerable. But it seems that this visit was more than a means of assuaging her grief. The accounts attest that she went to Tunbridge Wells 'for Barrenness', the waters there being celebrated for relieving that most feared condition among aristocratic wives.[21] Three years later, she was still seeking similar means to fall pregnant. The state papers contain a grant 'to the Countess of Rutland of licence to go to the Spa, with as many servants as she pleases, and 100l. in money'.[22] Spa was a fashionable resort in the Netherlands, famous throughout the world for the healing properties of its spring waters. Many members of the English aristocracy flocked there for either leisure or specific cures. That Cecilia, who was reluctant to stray far from Belvoir, should make such a journey is a testament to her increasing desperation to solve the impending dynastic crisis by falling pregnant.

It would all be in vain: she and her husband were blessed with no more children. The future of their estate lay in the fragile hands of their only surviving son, Francis. But on 5 March 1620, the young boy finally lost his battle. The earl and countess's 'sweet young heir Lord Roos' followed his brother to the grave.

13

'A divilish conspiracy'

The death of Francis Manners's heir played right into the hands of George Villiers, Marquess of Buckingham. Almost a year before, he had stepped up his campaign to marry Katherine Manners. In June 1619, rumours had begun to circulate that a match was imminent between the king's chief favourite and the Earl of Rutland's daughter. Two months later, the Oxford scholar Nathaniel Brent reported to Dudley Carleton, with whom he had spent time in the Hague, that 'the match between Buckingham and the Earl of Rutland's daughter is broken off, because she will not change her religion'. The matter had clearly sparked a great deal of ill feeling between the two families, for Brent added: 'The mother Countesses [Buckingham's mother and the Countess of Rutland] have quarrelled, but are now reconciled.'[1] Cecilia found the idea of her stepdaughter marrying a Protestant utterly distasteful, and it seems that from the time the match was first talked of, she was determined to prevent it. Buckingham himself was no zealot, and if it had been up to him, he would probably have married Katherine regardless of her religion. But his royal master, as head of the Protestant Church of England, would never consent to his favourite marrying a professed Catholic.

The marriage negotiations had also foundered on the issue of money. Although Katherine's dowry was substantial, Buckingham demanded more. This may seem like greed on the part of a man whose annual income amounted to some £18,500 (equivalent to more than £1.7 million today), but the marquess's expenditure was staggeringly high. Partly this was because he had a number of family members to support, but the majority of his lavish spending was necessary to maintain and enhance his standing as the king's favourite. The court was a highly competitive arena filled with wealthy, ambitious men all anxious to outshine each other in their scrabble for royal favour and advancement. Maintaining an extravagant lifestyle, including rich clothes (on which he routinely spent between £1,500 and £3,000 per year) and lavish entertainments, was essential to convey an image of success, and no one was more aware of this than Buckingham. A courtier of his standing might expect to spend between £5,000 and £10,000 a year on entertainments, the hire of footmen and coaches, the renting of a suitable property close to the royal residences, and so on. Added to this was the fact that Villiers had recently acquired the substantial properties of Waddon Chase and Dalby.

Despite the difficulties that the match entailed, Buckingham was determined to bring it to pass. He surrendered the prestigious post of Chief Justice in Eyre, North of Trent, so that this might be granted to his prospective father-in-law. The grant was duly made on 19 November 1619.[2] That Buckingham had surrendered it caused a great stir at court. Tenure of this post was in theory for life, and it was one of the most lucrative available. There was no hint that he had given it up under duress: as the king's chief favourite with a host of titles to his credit, he exercised unparalleled political influence in England. Courtiers soon began to realise that the move was almost certainly a deliberate ploy to win favour with Francis Manners in order to smooth the apparently tortuous path to marrying his daughter.

On 11 January 1620, a commentator at court noted: 'The King departed from London, just when the Nuptials were contracted (as is reported) between the Marquess of Buckingham and the daughter of the Earl of Rutland.'[3] A week later, it was confidently reported that the pair were to marry, and John Chamberlain confirmed this on 22 January in a letter to Dudley Carleton, confiding that Buckingham was 'very forward, and some say contracted to the Lady Katherine Manners . . . Yt is daily expected when the father [Rutland] shalbe sworn of the counsaile.'[4]

The tidings were premature. Even if the Earl of Rutland was now on side, there remained the other, thornier problem that his younger son was still alive. For as long as he was, the full riches of the Manners estate remained beyond Buckingham's grasp. The boy had been in poor health now for at least six years, and as most fatal childhood illnesses were of short duration, there was every chance that he would survive. Was it now that Buckingham hatched a plan to hasten the boy's end himself?

He certainly had the means. He retained the services of the cunning man John Lambe, who made a living from concocting various potions and spells. The pair struck up a close acquaintance in 1619, and Lambe was soon high in the marquess's favour. Many whispered that Buckingham was using witchcraft to maintain the king's affection. As a result, Lambe made a tidy profit from his master and the clients he put his way, and demanded up to £40 or £50 for some individual consultations.[5] He soon gained a reputation for troublemaking, having caused a great deal of marital strife by diagnosing infidelity on the part of husbands and wives. A notorious sexual predator who was implicated in a number of rape cases, he seemed to derive vicarious pleasure from facilitating illicit liaisons for his powerful patron. A contemporary poem had Buckingham declare:

> By Magick charmes
> I wrought the Kings Affection, or his harmes,
> Or that I need Lambes Philters to incite
> Chast Ladies to give my fowle lust delight.[6]

It was common knowledge that Lambe dealt in poisons and belonged to the same fraternity as Simon Foreman, the notorious occultist and herbalist who was implicated in the murder of Sir Thomas Overbury. Buckingham's mother also consulted Lambe on various occasions, and she was ruthless enough to have either concocted a plot herself or assisted her son in carrying it out. In January 1623, the antiquary Simon D'Ewes noted in his diary that a book had been unearthed 'in which was discovered all the villanis, witchcrafts and lasciviousness of the old Countesse'.[7] Sadly, this book has since been lost, but the countess had enough of a reputation for dabbling in the occult for the rumour to have some credence.

Both Villiers and his mother had strong Leicestershire connections, so would not have had much difficulty in finding a means to get at the Manners boy. The countess had spent most of her life in Leicestershire, and she now lived at Goadby. Before his rise to power at court, Villiers had lived there with her, along with his brother. This fact could carry enormous significance, because it was in this same village that Joan Willimot also resided. Given that it was a small, insular community and that Joan was renowned as the local cunning woman, the Villiers family would almost certainly have known her. Is it possible that George and his mother implicated Joan in the scandal at Belvoir as a means of proving the Flower women's guilt beyond doubt? Perhaps it was she, rather than Lambe, who supplied the means of destroying the young Manners boy. Of the three named accomplices, Joan stands out as the most unusual. The fact that, unlike Anne Baker and Ellen Green, she lived a substantial distance (in seventeenth-century terms) from the Flower family makes it unlikely that she would have known them at all. By the time she was interrogated by the authorities, the details of Margaret and Phillipa Flower's confessions would already have been known, so it would have been relatively easy for Buckingham and his mother to bring her in (under either pressure or bribery) to corroborate them. It is telling that of the three testimonies, Joan Willimot's proved the most damning for the Flower women.

The archives at Belvoir offer no clue as to the cause of young Francis's death. Nor do they provide any details about his final hours. But we can at least be certain about where he died. The register of the church of St Martin-in-the-Fields, London, records that the boy's body was removed from that parish to Westminster Abbey on 6 March – the day after his death. This makes it impossible that he died at Belvoir, which was more than a day's ride from London even without a coffin to slow down the entourage. It is more likely that he had died at his parents' London home, Bedford House, which was a short walk from St Martin's and well within the parish boundary.

Perhaps his parents, in a last-ditch attempt to save their younger son, had brought him to the capital because of the superior medical care that was believed to be available there. Or the Marquess of Buckingham may have offered the assistance of his own protégé, Dr Lambe. It is possible, of course, that foul play had not been at work at all, and that the rigours of the journey had been enough to kill the boy even before he was seen by any physician or cunning man.

Even so, the fact that there were just two days between Lord Ros's death and his burial is unusual. Ordinarily, it might lead to doubt about the accuracy of the dates given, but in this respect the sources are reasonably reliable. The reference to the date of his death being 5 March is corroborated by John Chamberlain's letter to Dudley Carleton on 11 March, in which he recorded: 'The younge Lord Rosse the only sonne of the earle of Rutland died this weeke.'[8] Meanwhile, the funeral date (7 March) is recorded in the burial register of Westminster Abbey. It is possible that, because the boy's health had been poor for so long, arrangements for his funeral had been made for some time and could be swiftly executed when the time came. But surely if they had planned it in advance, his parents would have wanted him to be buried with his elder brother in the family vault at Bottesford? Another possibility is that someone had a vested interest in ensuring the boy's body was swiftly interred, before any questions were raised about the cause of his death. But in the absence of further evidence, this must remain speculative.

The funeral was conducted with great ceremony at Westminster Abbey, which was reserved for royalty and only the most prestigious of subjects. The Belvoir accounts include payments for the dean, chapter clerk, organist and 'singinge men', 'coristers', vergers, sextons, bellringers, almsmen and grave makers. There were also eight dozen torches, perhaps to accompany the procession of the coffin from St Martin's to the abbey. In all, it cost some £50. Of this, just 10 shillings was expended on the coffin, which is a poignant reminder of the boy's tender age.[9]

A short while after the funeral, a pamphlet describing the scandalous case of the Belvoir witches was published.[10] By now, the tradition of publicising a witchcraft trial in this way was well established. Such pamphlets had first appeared during Elizabeth's reign, when the growth of cheap print had sparked a surge in their production. Between the publication of the first English pamphlet in 1566 and the repeal of the witchcraft statutes in 1736, as many as 140 such tracts appeared. The print runs were high, particularly for the more notorious cases. The tracts varied in length from 100 pages to just a handful. Most were priced between 2d and 6d, depending upon length, which made them the cheapest publications available. Moreover, even though many people still knew about witchcraft through local folklore and oral tradition, the production of pamphlets on the subject coincided with a significant growth in literacy. Towns generally had higher rates of literacy than the country, and London was the highest of all. Although the rates remained closely linked to status and gender, even some of the lower orders in the capital demonstrated around 70 per cent literacy.[11] The majority of the pamphlets were therefore aimed at the London audience.

But even among communities where most people were illiterate, such tracts could still be influential. Reading aloud was common, and the scandalous nature of the stories contained within the pamphlets would have made them a popular subject with audiences of all classes and abilities. Even after the advent of more rational or 'enlightened' beliefs in the later seventeenth and early eighteenth centuries, witch-craft pamphlets were highly sought after by the educated elite as collectable ephemera. The famous diarist Samuel Pepys bought a copy of the ballad that had been written about the witches of Belvoir Castle.[12] The pamphlet upon which it was based had proved immensely popular, involving as it did one of the most high-profile men at court, and the fact that it ran into several editions suggests that it was a best-seller.

Witchcraft pamphlets often took the form of sensationalist moral-ising tales based only loosely upon the evidence found in trial reports. Although their authors always claimed to be in pursuit of the truth, this tended to take second place to their desire to spin a good yarn. If the actual facts of a case were unsatisfactory, or did not teach a clear enough moral lesson, then they were enhanced, added to or simply changed. And yet many purported to present a verbatim report of everything that had passed at a trial – what was said by the defendant, the witnesses and the judge. Most, however, were based upon pre-trial documents, notably the examinations of the accused and the witnesses. Their accounts of what happened at the assizes are so confused and contradictory that it becomes clear that the authors were often nowhere near the trial itself. But given that the vast majority of assize records have been lost, the pamphlets are often the only contemporary account of the trials that survive.

Filled with hellfire preaching and gruesome, scandalous and lurid details of the case in question, these small works were devastatingly effective in whipping up popular fear, anger and hatred towards the women accused of witchcraft. As part of a state-controlled printing industry, they became one of the most valuable means by which the government could manipulate public opinion. Usually written after the accused had been found guilty and executed, they served to convince the wider public that justice had been done. Moreover, they were often accepted as authoritative by judges and lawyers in other witchcraft trials.

The Wonderful Discoverie of the Witchcrafts of Margaret and Phillippa Flower, Daughters of Joan Flower, neere Bever Castle is a case in point. Written in the shocked and sententious style typical of many demonological works, it presents the Belvoir witch case as a warning to God-fearing people everywhere. 'The wicked (however they may thrive and prosper for a time) yet in the end are sure to bee payed home, either with punishment in this life or the life to come, or both, as a finall reward of monstrous impiety . . . the punishments of the wicked are so many warnings to all irregular sinners to amend their lives, and avoid the judgement to come, by penitency and newnesse of life.'[13] An earlier tract urged the ministers of justice to rid society of 'the most detestable sins of magike and sorcerie'. Its author, Henry Holland, declared that it was 'the duty of al Christian princes, judges and magistrates to bend all the powers of their mindes most religious-lie and carefully, for the discoverie and severe punishment of all the practisioners and favoures of all Sathanicall magick and devilish divinations'.[14] William Perkins agreed that this 'most heinous and detestable sinne' deserved 'the greatest and highest degree of punishment'.[15]

As well as publicising witchcraft prosecutions, the pamphlets helped to standardise them. There is a startling similarity between many of the tales: women who are reviled by their community, pacts with the Devil, familiars who take increasingly fantastical forms, confessions and retribution. The predictable, almost formulaic series of events described in each mirrored the rapid slide from accusation to conviction that most of the women suffered. In the eyes of their accusers, their guilt was already assured. It was simply a matter of weaving the usual lurid details into the accounts of their interrogation and confession to convince the public that another witch had been brought to justice.

The author of the Belvoir pamphlet is anonymous, as is the person who commissioned it. One of the most obvious patrons is the Earl of Rutland himself. The death of his younger son may have driven him to silence the doubts about the justice of the case which had been whispered ever since the trial. The tone of *The Wonderful Discoverie* is certainly very reverential towards him, and he and his family emerge spotless from the sycophantic description of the case. The author's detailed knowledge of the people and events he describes suggests that he was closely connected to the Manners family or their household. He may also have attended the assizes at which the case was tried, or at least gained a detailed account from one who did.

Another indication that Francis Manners could have commissioned the pamphlet is the fact that the author expresses views of witchcraft which are heavily influenced by Continental demonological sources. The earl himself had gained a good grounding in these during his Grand Tour of Europe as a young man. Thus, in the preface, the writer stresses the sexual nature of the relationship between the Devil and witches. Although such lurid details were often included in the record of the trials, this is the only pamphlet in which they are expressed in the preface – and thus appear to be the author's (or patron's) own views, rather than a second-hand report of what was said by the accused.

There was, though, another possible patron of the pamphlet. If Buckingham had been responsible for Lord Ros's death, then he had everything to gain from encouraging the belief that the boy had, like his brother, been struck down by witchcraft. As the king's chief favourite, the marquess could command a host of authors to do his bidding, and had the connections to ensure that the resulting publication was widely distributed. Not only did the pamphlet blacken the characters of the Flower women; it also made a convincing case for the younger Manners son having been bewitched in the same way as his brother. But it also went one step further by implying that the boy was already dead by the time Margaret and Phillipa came to trial. The preface includes a lament for 'the late wofull Tragedy of the destruction of the Right Honourable the Earle of Rutlands Children'. The pamphlet later refers to the earl's visit to Newmarket before Christmas 1618, 'bearing the losse of his *Children* most nobly, and little suspecting they had miscarried by witchcraft'. There is also Margaret's testimony about her mother's prediction that the young lord 'will not mend againe'.[16] At the time that the Flower sisters were brought to trial, young Francis Manners was definitely still alive. This may have been a case of the author falling prey to hindsight: he knew that the boy would die, so wrote his account with that in mind.

But he could hardly have known for certain that Francis and Cecilia would have no more children, and yet he also presents this as a fact rather than a possibility. Why would he risk offending the Earl of Rutland in this way if not at the insistence of an even more powerful patron? Could it have been a psychological ploy on Buckingham's part? Even though Katherine's half-brother was safely out of the way, he still stood to lose everything if the countess conceived another son. He may therefore have tried to make her and her husband believe that this was impossible so that they would stop trying.

The fact that the sequence of events outlined by *The Wonderful Discoverie* is so confused, and that the account as a whole is riddled with contradictory statements, is in itself suspicious. Although the pamphlet was almost certainly commissioned by a leading player in the case – whether the Earl of Rutland or the Marquess of Buckingham – and therefore overwhelmingly condemnatory of the Flower women, the author failed to entirely disguise his own views on the subject. The hesitancy with which he discusses demonology in the preface, anxiously shying away from any 'contentious Arguments . . . because the Scriptures are full of prohibitions to this purpose, and proclaimes death to the presumptuous attempters of the same', suggests both that he himself was sceptical about some of the 'arguments', and that he was anxious not to express an opinion that would offend his patron.[17] But in summing up the works of other authorities, rather than openly expressing his own opinions, it is clear that he had been greatly influenced by the leading sceptic Reginald Scot – although he was careful enough not to mention him, knowing that his works had been condemned by King James himself. This is far removed from the sententious, opinionated prefaces written by other pamphlet authors, who were not answerable to a powerful master.[18] The author of the Belvoir pamphlet is rather braver at the conclusion of his work, for he ends with a curious motto which hints that he himself had his doubts about the Flower women's guilt: 'Utinam tam facile vera invenire possem, quam falsa convincere' ('If only I could find out the truth as easily as I can show up the lies').[19]

The Wonderful Discoverie was printed by George Eld, one of the foremost printing houses in London, whose numerous commissions included the sonnets of William Shakespeare. The pamphlet was produced for John Barnes, a renowned bookseller who published essays, dictionaries and ephemera. Such was the level of popular interest in the case that it also inspired a ballad (printed by Eld the same year) entitled *Damnable Practises Of three Lincoln-shire Witches*. This was sung – appropriately enough – to the tune of 'The Ladies Fall', which often accompanied mournful ballads telling tragic tales, and had the same frontispiece as the pamphlet. It seems to have been intended to promote the latter, for at the end of the song it encourages readers to consult 'a booke printed of these Witches, wherein you shall know all their examinations and confessions at large.'[20] The pamphlet and ballad together ensured that the case rapidly gained notoriety amongst educated, literate circles as well as the lower ranks of the population.

Curiously, the pamphlet was not entered in the Stationers' Register, which had regulated the publication of books in England since the mid sixteenth century. Nevertheless, it sold well, for it went into two further editions – the second published 16 years after it had first appeared. The examination of Phillipa Flower taken on 4 February is omitted from these later editions.[21] It is not clear why. True, there is a slight discrepancy between her statement and that of her sister Margaret with regard to their mother's spell-making. Neither is there any reference to the fact that, according to Phillipa, their mother would 'often curse the Earle and his Lady, and thereupon would boyle feathers and blood together, using many Divellish speeches and strange gestures'. However, these differences in account are hardly significant, and are certainly not enough to sow doubt in the minds of those who read the pamphlet.[22]

At least partly as a result of *The Wonderful Discoverie*, and perhaps partly too the efforts of the Earl of Rutland and his prospective son-in-law, it was soon put about at court that the Manners boy had perished at the hands of the Belvoir witches. Not everyone was convinced. John Chamberlain rather doubtfully reported that he had died 'by witchcraft (as some will have yt) but in all likelihood of the falling sicknes to which he was much subject and a weake child'.[23] His scepticism rapidly took hold elsewhere – particularly among educated circles. Eight years after the execution of the Flower women, a new manual was published for those involved in the interrogation and prosecution of witches. Richard Bernard's *A Guide to Grand Jury Men* rapidly became one of the most influential tracts on witchcraft, and an essential part of any judiciary's library. That it was at least partly inspired by the Belvoir witch trial is evident from the many references to the case throughout the work. For example, the author described the shockingly intimate nature of Margaret and Phillipa Flower's suckling of familiars, and cited the methods used by Joan Flower in explaining the spells most commonly used by witches.[24] Although his aim was to ensure the severest penalties were meted out to those who were found guilty of 'the devilish Art of Witchcraft', there was a new caution that had not been evident in earlier pamphlets of this nature.

Bernard urged judges, magistrates and everyone else involved in bringing a witch to trial to take great pains in ensuring that the guilt of the accused was meticulously proven. In particular, they were to make careful enquiries about the nature of the bewitchment: 'whether it bee not rather from his owne feare, then from any other cause? or whether the affliction bee not from some naturall cause?' They should also make sure that the victim or their family 'hath taken advice of some learned Physicians, and hath also used their best helpes, for remedie, before they enter into consideration of the practices of Witcherie'.[25] This advice might well have been inspired by the example of the Belvoir witch case. Although the Earl of Rutland seemed utterly convinced that his children had been bewitched, nobody could have accused him of blindly following that train of thought without recourse to the expert opinion of physicians. His account books attest to the pains that he had taken in consulting the best medical minds of the day.

The author of the *Guide* went on to cite an example which was so pertinent to the Belvoir case that it is unlikely to have been a coincidence. He claimed that although many diseases were misdiagnosed as being the effects of bewitchment, there was one ailment which was irrefutably the work of maleficent magic. 'In a Convulsion (with which a Noble young man was extraordinarily for a long time tormented) according to the ordinarie causes thereof in nature, it bereaveth the Patient of motion: for his limbes are starke and stiffe: also it depriveth him of sense and understanding. Therefore in a Convulsion to have (as the young man had) an incredible swiftnesse of motion, and withall understanding and sense perfect, it must needs be supernaturall.'[26] The Belvoir trial had gained such notoriety in its time that the 'young man' to whom the author referred was almost certainly Francis Manners. Bernard no doubt also had this case in mind when he later asserted that 'When two or moe [more] in the same family . . . are taken in the like strange fits in most things', it was one of the surest proofs that witchcraft was at work.[27]

Bernard reflected a growing caution in the attitude of the authorities towards witches when he urged those involved in their prosecution that 'To convict any one of witchcraft, is to prove a league made with the Devil. In this only act standeth the very reality of a Witch; without which neither she nor he (howsoever suspected, and great shewes of probability concurring) are not to be condemned for witches.'[28] If this pact could not be proved, 'all the strange fits, apparitions, naming of the suspected in trances, suddaine falling down at the sight of the suspected, the ease which some receive when the suspected are executed, bee no good grounds for to find them guiltie of witchcraft, and to hang them'.[29] This narrowing down of what had been a wide-ranging set of acceptable 'proofs' to just one was a sign of how much the situation had changed in the 20 or so years since James's accession.

If the Belvoir witch pamphlet had not quite achieved its aim of convincing the doubters about the justice of the case, this did little to deter the Marquess of Buckingham. The young boy's death lent new urgency to his plans to marry Katherine, who was now the heiress to her father's fortune (including the lands associated with the barony of Ros), and described as being 'of great wealth'.[30] John Chamberlain was quick to make the connection between the two events, and in the same breath that he reported the boy's demise, he added: 'His death may chaunce bring on the match again twixt the Lord of Buckingam and his sister the Lady Katherine Mannors that was in a manner broken of by reason of his exorbitant demaunds of 20000li redy monie, 4000li land a yeare, and in case her brother shold fayle, of 8000 land.'[31] Buckingham had renewed negotiations for the match with what can only be described as indecent haste. He barely let the funeral pass before he was pressing the bereaved father for an answer.

Within days, the situation had apparently reached stalemate. Affronted by Buckingham's increasingly insistent financial demands, the Earl of Rutland decided that he was not a worthy husband for his daughter. But the real objection lay with Cecilia, who, as a devout Catholic, had no intention of letting her stepdaughter convert to Protestantism, no matter how exalted her potential husband might be. Under pressure from his wife, the earl therefore ordered Katherine to give up all thoughts of marrying Buckingham.

But by now, Katherine was determined to have him at any cost. She therefore paid no heed to her father's instructions, and the pair exchanged harsh words. Rutland was convinced that Buckingham had poisoned her mind against him, as he implied in a letter that he subsequently wrote to the marquess. 'Had I seen any spark of affection in a daughter towards me, but that those words your lordship used might have moved me (and I cannot think but she had some counsel); but when I valued the one with the other, say that your lordship's affection might have altered, I was resolved this was the better course for my daughter's honor, which although she deserves not so great a care from a father whom she so little esteems, yet I must preserve her honor if it were with hazard of my life.'[32]

Eventually, mediators were called in to try to bring both sides to an agreement. They included John Williams, one of the king's chaplains, whom James ordered to assist his favourite. Williams had some acquaintance with the Manners family, as his rectory was not far from Belvoir, so he was well placed to resolve the impasse. According to the chaplain's biographer, he 'brought the Earl about so dexterously with his art and pleasant wit, that his lordship put it into his hands to draw up all contracts and conditions for portion and jointure; which he did to the fair satisfaction of both sides'. The king also commanded Williams to persuade the bride to convert to Protestantism, but this proved a far trickier task. Chamberlain opined that 'some thincke the greatest cause of the breach was her beeing an obstinat papist, and not to be removed'.[33]

In the end, Buckingham's indomitable mother took matters into her own hands. Towards the middle of March 1620, she invited Katherine to supper at her house, where her son was also residing. Katherine spent the night there, and even if her behaviour had been beyond reproach, the fact that she had slept under the same roof as her suitor compromised her reputation – just as her future

mother-in-law had intended. She would now have been seen as soiled
goods by polite society, which effectively ruined her marriage prospects
with anyone other than Buckingham. The Earl of Rutland, who had
specifically instructed his daughter 'to avoid the occasion of ill', was
so outraged that he refused to receive her back at his house until
Buckingham had committed to marry her, and she was forced to seek
refuge with her great-uncle, Lord Thomas Knyvet. Matters reached
such a head that it was said to have been only the timely intervention
of the Prince of Wales which prevented a duel.

Rutland eventually contented himself with the less violent course
of writing to Buckingham. Adopting the condescending tone of a
social superior, he upbraided the marquess for bringing both families
into disrepute. 'For calling our honors in question, pardon me, my
lord, that cannot be any fault of mine; for you would have me think
that a contract, which if you will make it so, be it as secret as you
will, this matter is at an end; therefore the fault is only your lordship's
if the world talk of us both.' He then demanded reassurance that
Buckingham's intentions towards his daughter were honourable: 'The
issue I require, which your lordship desires to know, is, that I may by
some course be assured she is yours, and then you shall find me trac-
table to deal like a loving father; although she is not worthy in respect
of her neglect to me, yet it being once done, her love and due respects
to your lordship shall make me forget that which I confess I now am
too sensible of.'

The earl's anger was understandable, for Buckingham was notoriously licentious and had maintained a number of sexual liaisons with
ladies at court, notably Lucy Percy, the wife of Lord Doncaster. The
chances of his daughter's virtue having remained intact after spending
the night in close confines with such a man must have seemed slim
indeed – particularly as she herself was rumoured to harbour an
intense passion for him. Her father knew this all too well. 'I hope
your lordship will not guess nor imagine of me other than as of one
that, if it be not your fault, you have as great an interest in as in any
man, and she shall not make her yours sooner than I will receive her
again.' He ended the letter with a barely concealed threat that if he
did not receive the necessary reassurance, he would resort to violence:
'To conclude, my lord, this is my resolution: if my conscience may
not be fully satisfied she is yours, take your own courses; I must take

mine, and I hope I shall arm myself with patience, and not with rage.'
And then, as if to temper the threat, he added a rather insincere wish
'to your lordship as much happiness with my daughter as your heart
can desire'.[34]

The court gossips were quick to seize upon the news, and there
was a rash of rumour and counter-rumour. 'The match twixt the Lord
of Buckingam and the Lady Katherine Mannors is either made or
mard,' wrote John Chamberlain on 20 March. 'How matters stand
between them since, I know not . . . This manner of dealing is much
spoken of, and hitherto neither side hath gained by yt, beeing subject
to much construction.'[35] The following day, Sir Francis Nethersole,
secretary to the ambassador of the German states, wrote to Carleton
that 'Buckingham's marriage with the Earl of Rutland's daughter
proceeds untowardly.'[36] On 23 March, the English diplomat Sir Edward
Zouch reported that, desperate to get his hands on the Manners family
fortune, Buckingham had sought the assistance of the king himself
to change Katherine's mind on the issue of religion, but even he failed
to persuade her. In truth, the young woman was driven less by religious zeal than by an obligation to her father and stepmother, who
were determined that she should not stray from the Catholic faith. If
it had been up to Katherine, she would no doubt have willingly
converted months ago.

Although Rutland desperately tried to keep up appearances by
taking part in the traditional Accession Day tournament on 24 March,
he was fooling no one. Sir Edward Zouch reported the unlikely tale
that the earl had asked Buckingham's mother to take charge of his
daughter for a while, in order to get her away from his wife, who
disapproved of the match. 'Lady Buckingham has taken away the
Earl of Rutland's daughter, because though she [Katherine] loves
Buckingham, and he has declared that he will marry no one who
does not attend church, she refuses to go; and the King, who failed
to persuade her, thinks it is through the influence of her mother
and sister [Katherine's aunt, Ann Tresham]; his Majesty is said to be
in the plot. Lady Buckingham says the Earl of Rutland wished her
to take charge of his daughter awhile, and that then her mother
refused to receive her back.'[37]

Buckingham, who resented Rutland's attempt to force him into the marriage, immediately broke off all negotiations. He sent the earl a letter full of righteous indignation, making it clear that he – not Rutland – held all the power, thanks to his confederacy with the king. 'Your mistaking in your fashion of dealing with a free and honest heart, together with your froward carriage towards your own daughter, enforced me the other day to post to Hampton Court, and then cast myself at his Majesty's feet, confessing freely unto him all that ever hath passed in privacy between your lordship and me concerning your daughter's marriage,' he began, 'lest otherwise by this your public miscarriage of the business it might by other means to my disadvantage 'a come to his knowledge. And now that I have obtained my master's pardon for this my first fault, by concealing and going further in any thing than his Majesty was acquainted with, I can delay no longer of declaring unto you how unkindly I take your harsh usage of me and your daughter, which hath wrought this effect in me: that since you esteem so little both of my friendship and her honour, I must now, contrary to my former resolution, leave off the pursuit of that alliance any more, putting it in her free choice to bestow her[self] elsewhere to your best comfort.' He could not resist adding, with a show of wounded pride at the earl's suggestion of impropriety: 'For, whose fortune it shall ever be to have her, I will constantly profess that she never received any blemish in her honour but that which came by your own tongue. It is true, I never thought before to have seen the item that I should need to come within the compass of the law by stealing of a wife against the consent of the parents, considering of the favour that it pleaseth of his Majesty, though undeservedly, to bestow upon me.'[38]

In a studied insult to the earl, Buckingham also sent a mock petition to the king, entreating him that Rutland might be ordered 'to caule whom [call home] his daughter againe or att least I may be secured that in case I should marie her, I may have so much respitt of time given me as I may see some one act of wisdom in the foresayde lord as may put me in hope that of his stocke I may some time begett one able to serve you in some meane imployment'.[39]

Despite this temporary setback, the Dowager Countess of Buckingham's conniving had apparently worked, for the following month it was reported that Lady Katherine had converted to

Protestantism and the marriage plans had therefore resumed. John Williams's seventeenth-century biographer rightly judged, though, that Katherine's capitulation was due to the simple fact that her religious beliefs had not been strong enough to hold out against her emotions: 'She easily perceived that conjugal love would be firmest and sweetest when man and wife served God with one heart.' Her future husband put it rather less romantically when he later attributed his wife's conversion to lechery.[40]

Lady Katherine's conversion was confirmed by her receiving the Anglican Communion at Easter 1620. Even then, Buckingham kept everyone guessing. The whole affair had badly soured his relations with his prospective father-in-law. On 29 April, Chamberlain reported that the marquess had refused to share quarters with Rutland at the St George's Day festivities at Greenwich. 'He left him single to himself and consorted with the earle of Lecester,' he reported, 'and yet the opinion is the match must go on with his daughter, or els he shold do her great wrong as well in other respects, as that she hath condescended so far for his sake and his mothers as to be converted and receve the communion this Easter.'[41]

Chamberlain's prediction proved right. The wedding finally took place on 16 May 1620. It was completely lacking in the ostentation that might have been expected for such a high-profile match. Instead, it was a small, private affair at Lumley House, near Tower Hill, a mansion built in the time of Henry VIII on the site of a former monastery. Only Rutland and the king were present, and the absence of other guests meant that even the usually well-informed Chamberlain could only speak of it as a matter of uncertain report a full 11 days later. Appropriately enough, given all his efforts in bringing about the match, the presiding minister was John Williams, who was presented with the deanery of Westminster for his efforts. The dowry was rather less than Buckingham had hoped, but at £10,000 in cash, and lands worth some £4,000 or £5,000 per year, it was still considerable. Nevertheless, there was some suggestion that he had been forced into going through with the marriage. John Chamberlain confided to Sir Dudley Carleton that 'some doubt this mariage was put upon him sooner than he meant'.[42]

The cynical nature of the alliance did not escape the court wits. Sir Henry Goodere wrote a satirical poem to mark the occasion:

Here Venus stirs no flame nor Cupid guides thy lines,
But modest Hymen shakes his torch and chaste Lucina shines.

With a scarcely veiled reference to the social inequality of the match,
he added that the main hope of those present was that a son

May answer to our hopes and strictly may combine
The happy height of Villiers' race with noble Rutland's line.[43]

'The most hated man then living'

There had been little time for the earl to mourn his surviving son. Just three weeks later, he was among the dignitaries who attended the king's procession to Paul's Cross, an open air pulpit in the grounds of St Paul's Cathedral, on 26 March 1620. Then the controversy of his daughter's marriage to Buckingham was quickly followed by another royal visit to his estate. On 3 August 1620, the king once more made Belvoir Castle part of his summer progress. The Earl of Rutland presided over the entertainments, which included the obligatory banquets, knighting and hunting. With the trial so fresh in everyone's minds, the atmosphere cannot have been as jovial as on previous royal visits, and the fate of the Flower women must surely have formed a topic of conversation between the earl and his sovereign during the week or so that they spent together. No doubt James fully approved of the outcome. The fire might have gone out of his witch hunting fervour, but given that the victim in this case was one of his most important courtiers, he could not flinch from showing his support.

A portrait of the earl was painted at around this time, and still hangs at Belvoir today. It shows him to have been a handsome man, with the clipped pointed beard and elegant ruff fashionable in the late Elizabethan and Jacobean periods. He stares into the distance, and his eyes have a haunted, sorrowful look, as if tormented by a painful memory. He would never recover from the heartbreak of losing both his young sons – and with them his hopes for his estate.

More sorrowful news soon arrived at Belvoir. The Reverend Samuel Fleming, who had served the earls of Rutland as chaplain for more than 30 years, died a few months after the young lord. A godly man to the end, it was said that he had died in the middle of preaching a sermon to his congregation in Cottenham, Cambridgeshire. He was buried not in Bottesford with his brother Abraham and the earls whom he had served, but in the grounds of Cottenham church, in a grave site that is now unknown. One of his bequests hints at a degree of remorse for the death of Joan Flower and her daughters. He left property for the foundation of an almshouse for old women in Bottesford. This can still be seen today, bearing the inscription 'Dr Fleming's Hospital, 1620'.[1]

In contrast to the tragedy in his personal life, the Earl of Rutland's public career was thriving. His daughter Katherine's marriage to George Villiers enhanced his already high standing at court and tied his family more closely to the king – a long-standing and anxiously cherished ambition. Shortly after the wedding, he was the first-named in a list presented to the House of Lords of 'reported recusants and Non-communicants who are in places of trust'. Both he and his wife were described as being 'suspected Popish recusants', but thanks to their new position of influence at court, they escaped reprisals.[2] The following year, the king honoured his favourite's new wife with a visit to her husband's estate at Burley in Rutland. In the same dispatch that he reported the visit, John Chamberlain added that Katherine was 'saide to be with child'.[3]

Despite her earlier reticence on account of their religious differences (or, more specifically, her parents' objections), Katherine seemed quickly to have fallen passionately in love with her husband. 'Never woman was so happy as I am,' she wrote to him three years after their wedding, 'for never was there so kind a husband as you are, and God made me thankful to Him for you . . . I am sure God will bless us both for your sake, and I cannot express the infinite affection I bear you; but for God's sake believe me that there was never woman loved man as I do you.' In another letter she assured him: 'I think ther was never such a man borne as you ar and how much am I bound to god that I must be that hapye womane to injoy you from all outher wemen and the unworthiest of all to have so great a blessing.'[4]

But it was always going to be a turbulent marriage, given the strong will and contradictory opinions of each family. Buckingham himself described it as 'something stormy'.[5] Katherine, like her husband, was possessed of a formidable temper and did not always succeed in playing the passive and dutiful wife that convention dictated. It soon became apparent that Buckingham was not going to return her loyalty and affection, and his womanising continued virtually uninterrupted by the fact that he was now married. The naive Katherine was easily duped for a time. During a prolonged period of absence on diplomatic business, he received a letter from his wife assuring him: 'Everybody tels me how hapy I am in a husband, and how chast you ar; that you will not looke at a woman, and yett how thay woo you.'[6]

But even Katherine could not be fooled forever, particularly as her husband took little trouble to conceal his infidelities. She became intensely jealous of his many mistresses, in particular Lucy Percy, whose affair with the marquess had been unaffected by his marriage. Yet so passionate was her love for him that she always forgave his 'one sin [of] loving women so well', as she herself ruefully admitted. Conscious of her lack of physical charms, she assured him: 'Might you have a finer and handsomer, but never a lovinger wife than your poor Kate is.' She therefore expressed the rather optimistic conviction: 'I am sure you will not commit the like again.'[7] In fact, Buckingham did not have so high an opinion of women as his wife supposed. As one contemporary shrewdly observed: 'He looks upon the whole race of Women as inferior things, and uses them as if the Sex were one, best pleased with all.'[8]

Katherine's relations with her mother-in-law were also volatile. In January 1622, she reaffirmed her conversion to the Protestant faith when, along with her husband and the dowager countess, she dined with the Bishop of London and was confirmed in his chapel.[9] But just a few months later, Buckingham's mother was sent from court because of having 'relapsed into Poperie', though Chamberlain believed the real reason for her dismissal to be 'some pique or harsh usage toward her daughter-in-law'.[10]

None of this was conducive to a smooth pregnancy for Katherine. King James, who, far from being jealous of his favourite's new wife, referred to her affectionately as his daughter, was solicitous of her welfare. He told Buckingham to look after Katherine and 'the sweete litle thing that is in her bellie', and urged that he should 'let her never goe in a coache upon the streete, nor never goe fast in it, lette youre mother keepe all hastie newis from comming to her eares, lette her not eate too much fruite, & hasten her owte of London'.[11] To the king's great angst, Katherine suffered a traumatic labour, which resulted not in the male heir that her husband longed for, but a 'sickly daughter'. Worse still, Katherine fell dangerously ill with smallpox shortly afterwards.

James, who stood as godfather at the hastily arranged christening, was beside himself with worry. It was reported from court that he 'prayed heartily for her [Katherine], and was at Wallingford House, early and late, to inquire after her'.[12] He also made a lavish gift of a 'faire chaine of diamonds' to the Duchess of Lennox 'for her great care and paines in making broaths and caudells and such like for the Lady Marquise in her sicknes'.[13] Much to his relief, and that of her husband, Katherine recovered, and her infant daughter, Mary (known affectionately as 'Little Mall'), became a firm favourite with the king, who constantly cuddled and played with her.[14] Katherine even consulted him on the appropriate moment to wean the little girl, and went into very personal details, confiding: 'I thinke there was never child card [cared] les for the breast then she does.'[15] In the years that followed, she continued to keep her royal master informed of every stage of Mary's development, such as when the girl took her first steps ('I think she will run before she can go') and her love of music ('She will clap her hands together and on her breast, and she can tell the tunes as well as any of us can; and, as they change the tunes, she will change her dancing'). Above all, Katherine assured James, 'she grows every day more like you'.[16]

Despite Buckingham's proclivity for womanising, he seemed to genuinely love his wife, and she returned that love with ever growing passion. 'You could never a had one that could love you better then your poore true loving katte [Kate] doth,' she wrote during one of his missions abroad on royal service, 'poore now in your absencs but els the hapyest and richest woman in the world.'[17] She was rich in more than just her husband's love. Thanks in no small part to her dowry, the Buckinghams enjoyed a luxurious lifestyle, maintaining several homes and an army of servants, and staging lavish entertainments for the king and his courtiers. By 1624, the duchess's housekeeping expenses alone were reckoned at £3,000 per year. Still basking in James's favour, theirs seemed set to be a long and glittering partnership.

Although there were rumours that the king's regard towards Buckingham waned after the latter's marriage, there was little perceivable decline in the marquess's power at court. He became an invaluable ally to his father-in-law, with whom he was now apparently entirely reconciled. Katherine even went so far as to assure her husband: 'I will swear, [he] loves you better, I think, than he does me.'[18] In the spring of 1623, Buckingham brought his influence to bear in having Rutland appointed admiral of the fleet to bring home Prince Charles from Spain, after the collapse of the negotiations for his marriage to the infanta. A court commentator described Rutland's departure in late May, noting that he and his fellow envoys were 'in their best array, and their followers well appointed in fair and rich liveries.'[19] The following month, Villiers himself received another honour at his royal master's hands when he was awarded the dukedom of Buckingham. In June that year, it was rumoured that he would soon be made Lord High Constable of England, and his father-in-law given the post of Lord Admiral.[20]

The Earl of Rutland seemed to be growing ever more indiscreet in his religious beliefs, and his position at court would have become correspondingly more precarious if it had not been for his son-in-law. In March 1624, when Parliament was debating the treaty with Spain, the earl was alone in objecting to a clause relating to religion, and according to one court gossip, it was only Buckingham's timely inter-vention that saved him from 'censure'.[21] Nevertheless, Rutland was still being talked of as one of the most influential men at court. Ben Jonson alluded to him in his *Masque of the Metamorphosed Gipsies*, which was performed for the king at Belvoir on 5 August 1621:

> There's a gentry cove here
> Is the top of the shire,
> Of the Bever-Ken,
> A man among men;
> You need not to fear,
> I've an eye and an ear
> That turns here and there,
> To look to our gear;
> Some say that there be
> One or two, if not three,
> That are greater than he.[22]

There are numerous other references to Rutland's appearance at court during the years that followed, which suggested that he remained at the heart of royal and political affairs. He was still sufficiently in the king's favour to receive two visits from him at Belvoir during the summer progress of 1624. The first took place towards the beginning of the progress in mid July, and the second as the king was making his way back down south in early August. The usual knighthoods were conferred during the latter visit, which lasted a few days, and James left for Newark on 8 August. He would never see Belvoir again.

By now, Buckingham was at the height of his powers. As well as continuing to enjoy favour with the king, he had also shrewdly courted the good graces of James's son and heir, the future Charles I. 'Never was one man so beloved of King, Prince, and people', observed Sir Edward Conway in March 1624.[23] By contrast, in his account of James's court, Sir Anthony Weldon described Buckingham as 'the most hated man then living'.[24] Inevitably, the duke's growing influence had become the source of great resentment and suspicion among the other members of the court. The King of Spain's agent there wrote to his master in some alarm that 'Buckingham desires to be placed above King or Prince, and whilst many dare speak against him, none dare do it against the Duke.' The duke was clearly becoming more arrogant by the day, and 'oftentimes bragged openly in Parliament that he had made the King yield to this and that'. The envoy concluded that Britain was 'not now governed by a monarchy, but by a triumviri, whereof Buckingham was the first and chiefest, the Prince the second, and the King the last'.[25]

Buckingham remained high in favour for the remainder of James's reign. When he fell dangerously ill in May 1624, his royal master was so horror-struck that he immediately hastened to his bedside and spent three hours there, in anxious vigil. On a subsequent visit, he was observed praying on his knees beside the duke's bed, beseeching God to cure his beloved Steenie or else transfer the sickness to him. He proceeded to send regular gifts to his favourite as he convalesced, including 'the eyes, the tongue and the dowsets [testicles] of the deer he killed in Eltham Park'.[26] Perhaps this unsavoury gift had not been appreciated, for when Buckingham suffered a relapse, James resorted to the more tasteful offering of 'excellent melons, pears, sugared beans', strawberries and raspberries. The pair also exchanged a series of impassioned letters, the duke expressing heartfelt gratitude to James as 'my purveyor, my goodfellow, my physician, my make, my friend, my father, my all'.[27]

Similar sentiments were expressed by James in December the same year, when he too was laid low by sickness. In an extraordinarily passionate 'billet' more suited to a spouse than a political associate, he begged Buckingham to hasten to his side, assuring him: 'For God so love me, as I desire only to live in this world for your sake, and that I had rather live banished in any part of the earth with you, than live a sorrowful widow-life without you. And so God bless you, my sweet child and wife, and grant that ye may ever be a comfort to your dear dad and husband.'[28] In another missive to 'my sweete tome [Tom Badger]', he urged his favourite to 'keepe thyselfe verrie warme, especiallie thy heade and thy showlders, putte thy parke of Bewlie [Burley] to an ende, and love me still and still'.[29]

Unlike his beloved favourite, James would not recover. His health had been steadily declining for several years, and in March 1625, whilst on his customary stay at Theobalds House in Hertfordshire, he was stricken with a strange fever. Buckingham was at his side at once, and he and his mother personally ministered to the dying king, rejecting the services of the royal physicians. It was reported that the dowager countess had 'contracted much suspicion to herself and her son, for applying a plaister to the King's wrists without the consent of his Physicians . . . after the applying thereof, the King grew worse'.[30] The duke and his mother had certainly taken an extraordinary risk, and when James's symptoms worsened, there were whispers that he had been poisoned. On 25 March, the king suffered a stroke, which saddened his face muscles and left his jaw hanging loose. This, together with the rising phlegm which constantly threatened to choke him, made it virtually impossible for him to speak. Two days later, the 58-year-old king was dead.

There is a story that almost at James's last breath, Buckingham and his mother had tried to forestall his death by taking part in an extraordinary ritual. As the king lay on his deathbed, racked by pain, his attendants had apparently decided to lessen his suffering by transferring it into the body of an animal. A young pig had duly been brought in for this purpose and dressed in the clothes of a human baby. The Duchess of Buckingham had played the part of midwife to the baby pig, while her husband had been among its godfathers. The animal had been baptised before being chased out of the room. This tale was told in a nineteenth-century account and is not corroborated by any of the contemporary sources. If it was true, then it would be deeply ironic that a monarch who had devoted so much of his life to stamping out all traces of sorcery should have taken part in a blasphemous ritual of witchcraft to prolong his days on earth.

The duke made an impressive show of grief – real or exaggerated – at his late master's demise. Immediately falling ill again himself with 'an impostume that brake in his head', he had to be carried to the funeral in a chair. He subsequently made an impassioned speech in Parliament, defending the treatments that he had given to the king during his final days. 'He spake with tears in his eyes,' remarked one observer, 'expressing much sorrow that he who had been so inifinitely beholden to the King for himself, for his kindred, for all his favours, that he should now be questioned for murdering him.'[31] As well as an attempt to clear his name, this speech may have been for the benefit of the new king, James's son Charles, whose favour Buckingham had been careful to cultivate for some time. If so, then the ploy worked. 'I have lost a good father and you a good master,' Charles wrote, 'but comfort yourself, you have found another that will no less cherish you.'[32] The new king was as good as his word, confirming the duke in all of his former offices and even giving him a golden key to symbolise his right to enter any royal residence at any time he chose.

The Earl of Rutland, who had played a prominent part in the late king's funeral, also appeared to be in the new king's good graces. But this favour was fragile, for the earl's enemies tried their utmost to discredit him. Countess Cecilia wrote with some alarm that her husband had been charged by certain members of Parliament with 'being the cose of the ould Kinge deth and going to coning pepel [cunning people]'.[33] The reference to 'cunning people' is intriguing and – if taken literally – suggests that Francis had encouraged the late king to consult with 'white' witches and sorcerers. As well as revealing the earl's strong belief in witchcraft, this also suggests that even at the end of his life, James had far from abandoned such beliefs himself, despite publicly distancing himself from them after coming to England. The rest of the countess's letter makes it clear just how closely bound were the Catholic religion and belief in witchcraft, for she adds: 'here is gret fere by Catholikes of persecuson'.[34]

Although he enjoyed Charles's favour, the Duke of Buckingham's position at court was increasingly perilous. He had amassed a dangerous body of enemies during his rise to greatness, and they resented his influence and arrogance. Buckingham's sympathy for the French Huguenots prompted him to lead an expedition to France on their behalf in 1627, which failed miserably and only served to bolster his enemies. He set sail for home at the end of the year, and hastened to see his son, George, who was born a few days before his arrival. There was great rejoicing at the long-awaited arrival of a son and heir for Buckingham. His father-in-law was among the first to offer congratulations. Indeed, so keen was Rutland to see his new grandson that he failed to keep an appointment with the king and was obliged to apologise that 'he forgot the day, being occupied with his daughter'.[35]

Meanwhile, allegations that Buckingham had secured royal favour by witchcraft grew ever more insistent. That his former protégé, John Lambe, had helped him to bewitch the late king was an old rumour. More recently, Buckingham and his mother had enlisted the services of Richard Napier, the astrologer physician who had treated the Earl of Rutland's younger son. They hoped that Napier might cure Buckingham's lunatic and adulterous younger brother, Viscount Purbeck. The latter and his unhappy wife had hurled accusations of witchcraft at each other in their sordid and well-publicised marital battles. Buckingham's notorious cunning man, Lambe, was said to have facilitated Lady Purbeck's adulterous affair with Sir Robert Howard. With 'powders and potions' supplied by Lambe it was alleged that 'she did intoxicate her husbands braines'.[36] The cunning man was duly hauled before the High Commission in 1625. By then, he had fallen from favour with Buckingham: indeed, the latter accused him of having used the same 'potions' on him.

Napier proved unwilling to take on the commission, but eventually agreed. His reluctance was justified. Failing to improve Purbeck's condition, the physician blamed it upon Buckingham's mother, whom he hated, and also wrote bitterly of Buckingham that he was 'full of bribery' and not to be trusted.[37] His aversion was at least partially motivated by their religious differences. Napier was a supporter of moderate Protestantism, with its emphasis upon salvation through faith, and wrote a number of refutations of the Catholic faith. When he discovered that Buckingham and his mother were sheltering a Jesuit priest in the 1620s, he was deeply shocked and tried to wean them from this dangerous course, without success. The experience was enough to make Napier suspicious of the nobility and unwilling to accept assignments from them.

Increasingly desperate to hold on to power, Buckingham now retained the services of another cunning man, Pierce Butler, who possessed 'strange faculties'. The tales had reached the ears of the Venetian ambassador, who reported that Butler 'is generally believed to be a magician, and as the duke gives him a handsome salary . . . he can have given him nothing except some secret service'.[38] Buckingham's patronage of witches was seen as analogous with his Catholic faith: both inverted the proper social and religious order. This was enough to condemn him in the eyes of contemporaries – and give sanction to anyone who sought his destruction.

In June 1628, Buckingham's old retainer John Lambe was murdered. By then, Lambe was an object of such popular hatred that he could not venture out of his house for fear of being attacked. But on the afternoon of 13 June, he risked a trip to the theatre. By then in his early eighties, he took the precaution of hiring a group of sailors to protect him. However, they were powerless against the angry mob which hounded him down and savagely beat and stoned him to death. King Charles heard of the riot and was said to have ridden from Whitehall to quell it, but arrived too late to save Lambe.

Just two months later, Buckingham himself was dead. He had already fallen foul of the House of Commons and most of the public, who blamed him for the shortcomings of Charles's foreign policy. The rumours that he had poisoned the late king also resurfaced, and a parliamentary inquiry was held in April 1628, at which evidence was heard from the royal physicians, including the esteemed William Harvey. Although the duke was criticised for ousting the physicians from James's bedside, he was cleared of responsibility for his death. But the tale proved remarkably resilient, and when King Charles himself was facing the prospect of death at the hands of Oliver Cromwell's regime 20 years later, among the indictments against him was included the 'old and almost forgotten charges, that his Majesty hastened the death of his father by poison, or that Buckingham attempted it with his consent'.[39]

It was while planning an expedition in Portsmouth on 23 August that Buckingham was assassinated – stabbed to death by the army officer John Felton. It was not long before people linked his death to that of his former protégé, Lambe. Without Lambe's magical powers to protect him, it was said, the royal favourite's binding spell over the king and the nation was broken: his demise was inevitable. As one contemporary poem neatly put it: 'For want of Lambe the Wolfe is dead.'[40]

The intensity of his widow's grief was matched only by that of the king, who upon hearing the news 'threw himself upon his bed, lamenting with such passion and with abundance of tears the loss he had of an excellent servant'.[41] Thanks to the lasting esteem in which Charles held her late husband, Katherine continued to enjoy favour at court. She used this to good effect, and was instrumental in promoting her father's interests, as a letter she wrote to him in April 1631 suggests. She avowed that she had made his excuses to the king and queen at Greenwich, and that they had forgiven his absence. It may be that Francis had been unable to attend the court due to failing health. Katherine signs the letter 'Your Lordship's most obedient and unfortunat daughter'. It is not clear why she referred to herself as unfortunate – perhaps she still mourned her late husband. It is only in the postscript that she remembers to present her 'humble servis' to her stepmother.[42]

Francis Manners died on 17 December 1632 at an inn in Bishop's Stortford, Hertfordshire. His wife and his brother, Sir George Manners (who was set to succeed him), had been at his side as he gave a curious last speech two days earlier, the notes of which are preserved at Belvoir. He made no mention of the witchcraft controversy that had so blighted his life, but instead set out his last bequests. These were extraordinarily detailed, which suggests that the earl may have known for some time that he was dying and had therefore given the matter careful consideration. The fact that he bequeathed his doctor the extremely generous sum of £50 for attending him 'in this his sicknesse' also suggests a prolonged final illness.

Among the earl's other bequests was 'his best huntinge horsse for the hare or his best buck hunter' for the king, which he desired one of his executors, Lord Savage, to present along with an assurance that 'never Kinge had a more faithfull servant or a more loyall subject then myself nor never subjecte had a more gracious Soveraigne, acknowledginge himselfe infinightly bound to his Majesty for his ever gracious favoures unto him'.[43] Francis also ordered the disbursement of a £2,000 debt to Sir John Ayres, half of which money could be found in 'his iron chest at London' and £500 in his servant Robert Cook's keeping, and begged his executors to supply the remaining £500. This suggests that his finances, like those of so many of his predecessors, were precarious by the time of his death.[44]

Francis begged that 'there might bee no difference' between his wife and his brother George over the execution of his will, but he evidently suspected that there might be because he gave instructions for the resolving of these. He also desired there to be minimal expense upon his funeral. 'For my funerall I wowld have it such as my aunces-tors have had, which will bee no greate charge, for that my toombe is allreddy made, and I wowld have my bodie, so soone as it is embalmed, to bee removed forth of the Inn.' The reference to his tomb makes it clear that the earl had already approved the extraordi-nary inscription, with its reference to his sons' deaths 'by wicked practise & sorcerye'.[45] He had gone to his grave believing that the boys had been bewitched.

So far, there was nothing out of the ordinary in this last speech of a dying earl. What is worthy of note, however, is what Sir Francis said to his wife at the beginning of it: 'Sweete hart give mee your hand, now I pray God blisse you and your children. It greeves me I shall see none of them before I die, but I leave them my blessinge.'[46] There is no record of the earl and his wife having any other children after the death of their two young sons. The clarity and detail of the rest of the speech make it unlikely that Francis's thoughts had become clouded and confused. Is it possible that he had instead begun to lose his reason as his impending death called to mind the tragedy that had been played out at Belvoir some 14 years before?

Francis was right to suspect trouble after his death. The following May, his daughter Katherine complained that 'my uncle has no desire of a good conclusion between us' and that he was trying to force her to give up the lands that her father had left to her. She therefore resolved to take her case to the Court of Wards.[47] A commission was subsequently established to decide upon the matter. Meanwhile, the Belvoir accounts show that Cecilia was still haggling with the new earl over the family jewels a year after her husband's death.[48]

The widowed countess might well have cherished a hope to live in quiet retirement at Belvoir, away from the glittering court that her husband had so frequented. But the tragedy that had plagued Francis right up to his last breath also continued to fascinate society as a whole. In 1635, 16 years after the Flower women's deaths, *The Wonderful Discoverie* was reprinted. It proved one of the most enduringly popular tales of witchcraft ever written.

Neither had the tale been forgotten by Cecilia, who outlived her husband by more than 20 years and died in September 1653. She chose to be buried not with her husband in the family vault at Bottesford church, but with her younger son in St Nicholas's Chapel at Westminster Abbey.[49] The controversy surrounding his death had apparently haunted her until she too drew her last breath.

Epilogue

'Wicked practise & sorcerye'

Although the case of Joan, Margaret and Phillipa Flower is emblematic of the treatment suffered by thousands of others accused of witchcraft, it had come at a time of growing scepticism. By 1619, even King James had seemed thoroughly bored with both the theory and persecution of witchcraft. As one commentator put it, he 'came off very much from these notions in his elder Years'.[1] He even went so far as to personally examine the evidence in a number of trials in order 'not to hound them [witches] down but to detect impostors'. In the same year that Margaret and Phillipa Flower were executed, six women from Leicestershire who had been convicted of bewitching a local man were pardoned as a result of James's personal intervention.[2] He had also sent some suspected witches to the medical faculty at Cambridge for psychiatric study. There had been no royal proclamations or other acts against witches for some time, and James seemed to be more preoccupied with other affairs of state. As one historian put it, he was by this time 'more passionate about deer-hunting than ever he had been about witch hunting'. By nature given to intense but short-term attachments to both people and causes, he 'appeared to have lost sight of demonology'.[3]

A further indication of James's increasingly moderate views on witchcraft was the publication of his *Meditation on the Lord's Prayer* in 1619. In this, he made no attempt to use the 'deliver us from evil' phrase as the basis for a discussion of Satan's powers. Instead, he wrote, this phrase referred solely to the evil of temptation, which was referred to in the previous line of the prayer. He asserted: 'The Greek hath it, from the evil one; and these words put us in mind what need we have of continual prayer to God, to be preserved from that old traiterous and restless enemy.' But he concluded that the Latin phrase '*a malo*' could mean 'any evil thing or the evil one – whether by means of Satan or otherwise'.[4]

The king's attitude reflected a more widespread scepticism about witchcraft in his kingdom. The assize records for the Home Counties in the same year as the Flower sisters' trial reveal that no women were convicted of witchcraft, and in 1620 one woman was acquitted of the crime.[5] Instances of witchcraft had traditionally been higher in the Home Counties than elsewhere in England, so the Flower women's conviction was highly unusual for this period.

Although there were still staunch supporters of the witch hunts, their voices were increasingly drowned out by those of the sceptics. The fact that the author of the Belvoir witch pamphlet felt at pains to attack those who 'bring in question the integrity of Justice' rather than 'such horrible offendors' is telling.[6] He was also careful to stress: 'My meaning is not to make any contentious arguments about the discourses, distinction or definition of Witchcraft, the power of Divells, the nature of Spirits, the force of Charmes, the secrets of Incantation, and such like.'[7] A similar note of caution crept into the formerly strident pamphlets as their authors wrestled with the task of appealing to cynics and believers alike. In describing the case of Elizabeth Sawyer in 1621, Henry Goodcole insisted: 'It is none of my intent here to discusse, or dispute of Witches or Witchcraft.'[8] 'How uncertaine are among all people differing judgements?' opined the prominent witch hunter John Cotta. 'Some judge no Witches at all, others more than too many.'[9]

The growing scepticism in England was reflected by the almost complete absence of any pamphlets on the subject during the 1620s. Towards the end of James's reign, two proclamations were issued against the printing of pamphlets that offended the state, notably 'Popish and Puritanical Bookes and Pamphlets'. Publishers were more reticent about propounding beliefs which were increasingly controversial and had lost a great deal of popularity among the educated and ruling elite. The absence of such tracts both reflected and helped to accelerate the decline of interest in the subject.

At the same time as interest in witchcraft declined, those who had suffered at the hands of accusers began to demand justice. The records of the Star Chamber – one of the most prestigious courts in the land, comprising privy councillors as well as common-law judges – include an increasing number of complaints brought by those whose lives had been blighted by witch hunters. Agnes Fenn, the elderly Norfolk widow, decided to avenge the horrific treatment that she had suffered at the hands of her accusers, and brought a case against them in the Star Chamber. Two weeks later, she learned that several of the defendants had responded, but had wholly denied the charges. They suffered no further reprisals.[10]

The pamphlet describing the Belvoir witch controversy was one of the last to be published in England until the breakdown of state control that preceded the Civil War. The reign of Charles I saw virtually no such pamphlets published. This was partly due to the fact that the new king was a good deal more sceptical about the existence of witches than his father had been, and there was a marked decline in such trials as a result.

By the 1630s, it seemed that witch hunting would soon be a thing of the past in England. A notable example of the authorities' growing reluctance to prosecute suspected witches came in 1633, when Edmund Robinson, an 11-year-old boy from Pendle in Lancashire, almost sparked a repeat of the notorious trials of more than 20 years before when he claimed to have been taken to a sabbat by several local women. As the accusations rapidly mounted, the officiating judge became alarmed and called to central government for assistance. The boy was subsequently taken to London, and the suspected witches were examined by a medical team headed by the eminent William Harvey. The latter found no evidence of witches' marks, and Robinson confessed that he had made up the tale to cover up the fact that he had been late getting the cattle home.

The situation in England was mirrored on the Continent. The Thirty Years War, which began in 1618 and raged across central Europe, with Germany particularly hard hit, accelerated the decline of the witch hunts. When the fighting reached a particular place, it became imperative for the inhabitants to unite in order to defend themselves against the common enemy. Dividing communities with accusations of witchcraft was not just counterproductive: it could spell death for the inhabitants of the area. Together with the growing scepticism about the validity of witchcraft beliefs, this led to a rapid decline in the number of trials and executions.

But just as it seemed that the witch craze was to be consigned to history, it came back with renewed vigour during the English Civil War of the mid seventeenth century. Charles I had always believed that the witch hunts were inextricably bound up with the Puritan cause, and this was borne out by the increased persecution of witches during Oliver Cromwell's regime. The persecutions had a new edge of brutality. One account tells of a group of Parliamentarian soldiers who encountered an old woman sailing on the River Kennett. Assuming she was a witch, they immediately began firing at her, but the woman apparently mocked their assault by chewing the bullets. Determined to annihilate her, the soldiers then slashed her face before shooting her dead at point-blank range.[11]

An even more shocking expression of this new brutality was the massive wave of witch hunting in East Anglia in 1645–7, during the brief and brutal ascendancy of the Witchfinder General, Matthew Hopkins. A petty gentleman living in Manningtree, Essex, Hopkins claimed to have become greatly troubled by the presence of witches during the winter of 1644–5. He initiated a series of investigations and extracted his first confession – from an elderly and disabled widow named Elizabeth Clarke – in March 1645. This set the pattern for a rush of similar interrogations and convictions, which spread with terrifying speed across Essex and into Suffolk, Norfolk and Huntingdonshire. A total of 184 women were tried in the two years of Hopkins's activity, at least 100 of whom were executed. This was by far the greatest witch panic ever seen in England, and was comparable to the worst excesses of the Continental trials. The renewed fervour for witch hunting continued after Hopkins's sudden disappearance (and probably death) in 1647. Two years later, 19 witches were executed together at Chelmsford – the largest group execution ever to take place in England.

The restoration of the monarchy in 1660 did not immediately bring an end to the witch trials, although their numbers gradually dwindled. Neither – as has often been supposed – did the advances in science and so-called 'rational' beliefs of the Enlightenment sound the death knell of the witch craze. Certainly, the more educated members of society were increasingly attributing extraordinary occurrences to natural causes. Even Shakespeare, whose life spanned the height of the witch craze in England, penned the following lines for one of his characters: 'They say miracles are past; and we have our philosophical persons to make modern and familiar, things supernatural and causeless.'[12]

As the seventeenth century progressed, advances in medical science began to solve some of the mysteries of death and disease that had formerly been blamed upon maleficent magic. William Harvey famously dissected a toad alleged to be a witch's familiar, and finding it had no special powers, he convinced many doubters that witchcraft was based upon the shakiest of foundations. The new emphasis upon the need for evidence seriously undermined witchcraft persecutions, the vast majority of which were based solely upon hearsay, rumour and suspicion. Leading scientists were eager to challenge old opinions and traditions, of which magic was one of the foremost. Belief in witchcraft thus rapidly became unfashionable among the educated elite, who scorned the credulous and naive attitude of those who sought the services of their local cunning man or astrologer, or accused a member of their community of practising maleficent magic. Sorcery was dismissed as 'at bottom no other than artful poisonings', and astrology as a 'superstitious foppery' and 'almost ridiculous'.[13] It mattered little that there was still no viable alternative explanation for the misfortunes and disasters that had formerly been ascribed to witchcraft. Even as late as the twentieth century, the psychoanalyst Ernest Jones observed: 'The average man of today does not hesitate to reject the same evidence of witchcraft that was so convincing to the man of three centuries ago, though he usually knows no more about the true explanation than the latter did.'[14]

There was also an emerging belief in an orderly universe, governed by God and nature, rather than the caprices of the Devil. According to this world view, the confessions of suspected witches who claimed to have made pacts with Satan or killed people by maleficent magic were completely unfeasible. 'It is . . . simply impossible for either the Devil or witches to change or alter the course that God hath set in nature,' claimed the English clergyman John Webster.[15] By 1677, one contemporary could confidently assert: 'We live in an age and a place, wherein all stories of witchcrafts, or other magical feats are by many, even of the wise, suspected: and by too many that would pass for wits derided and exploded.'[16]

With advances in science came greater knowledge of the human body, and thus of the treatment of disease. By the end of the seventeenth century, flourishing overseas trade had brought a wealth of new drugs into England, including quinine, which was used to treat malaria, and guaiacum for syphilis. There was also a new emphasis upon self-help in preventing the spread of disease, such as increased hygiene and quarantine during bouts of plague. Other advances gradually made people feel more in control of their environments, notably industrialisation and the growth of urban centres. Improvements in communications, in particular the rise of printed news-sheets, helped to locate lost property or persons. Meanwhile, the emergence of deposit banking gave greater security to men of property, and the growth of insurance at the end of the seventeenth century provided considerable peace of mind for the victims of theft, fire, sickness or other misfortunes.

Crucially, there was also growing scepticism among the judiciary, both in England and on the Continent. In 1697, the former Secretary of State for Scotland observed that although belief in witches had not diminished among his profession, 'the Parlements of France and other judicatories who are persuaded of the being of witches never try them now, because of the experience they have had that it is impossible to distinguish possession from nature in disorder; and they choose rather to let the guilty escape than to punish the innocent'.[17]

But while belief in witchcraft may have become unfashionable among the elite, it continued among the lower orders for many years to come. Superstitious practices and beliefs were too deeply rooted to be eradicated overnight. Even so, there was no resurgence of the hysteria that had flared up at various times between the mid sixteenth and mid seventeenth centuries. The year 1685 saw the last known execution for witchcraft in England, when a woman named Alice Molland went to the gallows.

By contrast, America – which had hitherto remained in the background as far as the witch hunts were concerned – experienced a late and spectacularly dramatic explosion of witchcraft, just as Europe was beginning to leave that whole sorry part of its history behind. Ever since the foundation of Virginia by Elizabeth I, America had been strongly influenced by English culture and religion. This influence became stronger still when James I established the first permanent English colony there, and it was not long before a contingent of Puritan ministers, planters and tradesmen was drafted over. Their evangelising zeal was matched by their determination to stamp out any hint of heretical practices – above all, witchcraft and sorcery. This was not achieved overnight, but as the seventeenth century progressed, their ideas began to take hold, and before long the colony was gripped with the same horror of witches as James I's subjects in England had experienced.

Perhaps no single witch hunt has attracted so much attention as the trials which took place in Salem, New England, in 1692. This extraordinary case began with the young daughter and niece of the local minister being seized by violent fits. To the horror of their elders, the contagion soon spread to other girls in the local community. There could be only one explanation: they must have been bewitched. Before long, there was a rash of accusations against members of the community, and a staggering 150 people were arrested and imprisoned – among them a four-year-old child. A total of 19 people were hanged and at least five more died in prison.

The Salem trials have since been ascribed to mass hysteria, sparked by the fevered imaginations of the impressionable young girls involved. They gained notoriety both in their day and for the centuries that followed, and have inspired a host of popular culture – notably Arthur Miller's 1952 play, *The Crucible*, which was later translated to the screen. The image of witchcraft and witch hunting that this projected became hugely pervasive in the English-speaking world, and remains so today.

In England, the last conviction for witchcraft (which was subsequently overturned) was in 1712. The accused was Jane Wenham, a Hertfordshire woman who was said to have communed with the Devil and flown through the air as a witch. Sir John Powell, who presided over the case, famously summed up the growing scepticism about witchcraft by remarking: 'There is no law against flying.' The last recorded witch trial in an English civil court took place five years later, when a number of women were brought before the assizes at Leicester. One of their victims claimed to have 'vomited up a great quantity of gravell and dirt and thatch of a house', while another 'young maiden voided downwards by the help of a midwife, and with as much pain as if it had been a child birth a great number of stones of a large size'.[18] Despite the fact that the stones were produced as evidence, the jury was not persuaded and the charges were thrown out.

Many of the most outspoken sceptics were clergymen. In 1715, the Dean of Peterborough preached that 'Witchcraft . . . is all but impudent Pretence and Delusion only; a perfect Cheat and Imposition upon the credulous Part of Mankind.'[19] Three years later, the East Anglian cleric Francis Hutchinson published a major intellectual attack on witchcraft beliefs in his *Historical Essay Concerning Witchcraft*. Then in 1736, George II's Parliament passed an Act which repealed the English and Scottish witchcraft statutes. Significantly, this prescribed punishment for anyone who should 'pretend' to practise any kind of witchcraft or sorcery. By the middle of the century, the controversial English cleric Conyers Middleton was able to declare that 'the belief in witches is now utterly extinct'.[20]

This was overstating the case. In fact, witch hunting would never die out altogether. Between the Restoration in 1660 and Hutchinson's essay in 1718, almost 30 books were published in defence of witchcraft beliefs. As late as 1722, Richard Boulton wrote two long and carefully reasoned treatises vindicating the existence of witchcraft, and of the many persecutions of preceding centuries.[21] He confidently asserted that 'the Being of Witches is undeniable from their ill Practices, and the Mischief they do'. Interestingly, among the cases he cited was that of Joan Flower and her daughters, and he included an abridged version of the Belvoir pamphlet in his first volume.[22] Boulton was a rare example of a member of the educated classes who still believed in witchcraft. But such beliefs remained mostly the preserve of poorer people and were prevalent in village communities for many years to come. Well into the nineteenth century people set store by magical beliefs, rituals and traditions which stretched back hundreds of years.

Moreover, the practice of witchcraft lasted far longer than the theory. 'A cunning-man, or a cunning-woman, as they are termed, is to be found near every town,' remarked Robert Southey in 1807, 'and though the laws are occasionally put in force against them, still it is a gainful trade.'[23] The unofficial hunting-down of suspected witches in local communities remained a feature of English rural life until the late nineteenth century. In 1863, an alleged male witch was drowned in a pond in Headingham, Essex. In 1894, the husband, relatives and friends of a young woman from southern Ireland named Bridget Cleary beat and burned her to death on suspicion that the real Bridget had been abducted by fairies and a witch put in her place. In 1945 the body of an elderly farm labourer was found near the village of Meon Hill in Warwickshire. His throat had been cut and his corpse was pinned to the earth with a pitchfork. The murder remains unsolved, but the man was reputed locally to be a wizard.

Cases of witchcraft can still be found in modern times. An account of a strange occurrence concerning an old woman from Cambridgeshire who died in 1926 could just as well have been written during the seventeenth century. 'One day a black man called, produced a book, and asked her to sign her name in it. The woman signed the book, and the mysterious stranger then told her she would be the mistress of five imps who would carry out her orders. Shortly afterwards the woman was seen out accompanied by a rat, cat, a toad, a ferret, and a mouse. Everybody believed she was a witch, and many people visited her to obtain cures.'[24] A much more valid comparison for historical witchcraft can be found in certain parts of modern-day Africa, where ancient magical rituals and beliefs are still prevalent.

During the 1940s, a form of spirituality known as Wicca emerged. Drawing upon the ritual magic of the ancient world, it began as a secret sect influenced by Freemasonry, complete with initiation and passwords. Gradually it came to encompass the traditions of witchcraft during the early modern period, as well as the practices of so-called white witches and cunning folk. Today, the distinction between Wicca, witchcraft and paganism is so blurred as to be almost non-existent. The beliefs may be frowned upon – mocked, even – by most people, but to their adherents they represent the continuation of an ancient and vital tradition. In stark contrast to the history that they claim to preserve, however, modern-day proponents of witchcraft celebrate it as a symbol of femininity; of the secret powers of nature and of woman. They are proud to call themselves witches, whereas their earlier counterparts shrank from being given this name by others because it carried with it the threat of death. The number of practising 'witches' (or Wiccans) has increased significantly since the late 1960s, especially in Britain and America, and it has been estimated that there are as many as 300,000 in these two countries alone.[25]

The stereotypical image of a witch, spawned hundreds of years ago, as an evil old hag with a wart on her nose, a conical hat and black robe, a broomstick and a cackling laugh lives on in our consciousness today. She appears in countless fairy tales, films and other fictional creations – from the Wicked Witch of the West in *The Wizard of Oz* to Roald Dahl's *The Witches*. She also enjoys her heyday every year on All Hallows' Eve. The fact that Halloween has become an increasingly popular – and lucrative – date in the annual cycle of feasts and celebrations suggests that the witch will continue to fascinate and terrify people for many years to come.

The Belvoir witchcraft case, meanwhile, rapidly became a part of local folklore. Its place in the national consciousness was secured by at least 10 reprints of the contemporary pamphlet. The story has been published in some form during every century since the Flower sisters' execution. It was included in *The Kingdom of Darkness*, a collection of tales of 'Daemons, Spectres, Witches, Apparitions, Possessions, Disturbances . . . Delusions, Miscevous Feats, and Malicious Impostures of the Devil', which was compiled by Nathaniel Crouch and published in 1688. Two centuries later, the character of Joan Flower appeared in *A Cavalier Stronghold*, a romantic play set in the seventeenth-century Vale of Belvoir and written by Mrs Chaworth Musters.

Interestingly, the guilt of Joan, Margaret and Phillipa Flower has rarely been called into question. The account provided by the contemporary pamphlet seemed to be unquestioningly accepted by all of the subsequent authorities. The author of a late seventeenth-century collection of witchcraft tales confidently asserted that the Earl of Rutland's children 'were bewitched and one murthered by the devilish malice of Joan Flower and her two daughters'.[26] A century later, the celebrated historian and antiquarian John Nichols maintained that 'there could be no doubt of their intentional guilt. In short, they believed themselves witches.'[27] Even though later historians dismissed such superstitious notions, they nevertheless believed that the Flower women were responsible for the boys' deaths. In his nineteenth-century account of Belvoir Castle, the Reverend Eller asserted: 'That these women were guilty of the murder of the two noble children; and attempted the lives of the Earl and Countess, and their daughter Catharine, can be little doubted: by the means probably of some vegetable poison.'[28] He places the blame for Joan's wickedness upon 'the distaste of her neighbours', who goaded her into becoming the evil character that they believed she was: in effect, she lived down to their expectations.[29]

As late as 1873, an article appeared in the *Pall Mall Gazette*, reporting a visit by the Prince of Wales (the future Edward VII) to Belvoir Castle. Perhaps frustrated that the occasion was 'unmarked by any sensational incident', the journalist instead filled his account with a description of the infamous Belvoir witch case. He concluded: 'There was no doubt of the guilt of these wretched women, for they both confessed their crimes before execution.' That, apparently, was proof enough even for a more enlightened nineteenth-century mind. The journalist noted that while the fate of the Flower women is well attested, nobody knows what happened to their familiar, Rutterkin. 'Perhaps he was shot by one of the gamekeepers attached to the establishment,' he mused.[30]

The story continues to fascinate today. Hilda Lewis's popular novel *The Witch and the Priest*, first published in 1956, reignited interest in the story. The Belvoir witches also inspired an opera, named after Joan Flower's cat Rutterkin, which was performed in the Vale of Belvoir in 1972 and 1995. In 2008, a petition was presented to the then justice secretary, Jack Straw, calling for the pardon of those who had been executed as witches in Britain. The plight of the Flower women was highlighted as one of the most serious miscarriages of justice.[31]

Over the centuries, various embellishments have been added to this already extraordinary story. But the basic premise for the case remains chiselled in marble above the magnificent tomb of the 6th Earl of Rutland. It was the deaths of his beloved sons – two tiny figures shown kneeling by the tomb – that lay at the heart of a conspiracy far more 'wicked' than the supposed crimes of Joan, Margaret and Phillipa Flower.

Notes and Sources

Abbreviations

APC   *Acts of the Privy Council of England, 1617–1623* (London, 1929–1932)

CSPD   Green M.A.E. (ed.), *Calendar of State Papers, Domestic Series, Elizabeth and James I,* (London, 1858–72)

CSPV   Hinds, A.B. (ed.), *Calendar of State Papers and Manuscripts, Relating to English Affairs. Existing in the Archives and Collections of Venice.* Vols. XV–XVI (London, 1909–10)

HMC   Historical Manuscripts Commission

Preface

1. Dare, p.27.
2. Ibid., p.29.

Introduction: 'The works of darknesse'

1. Gifford, *Discourse*, sig. B2.
2. Perkins, sig. A2v.
3. *The Wonderful Discoverie*, pp.3–4.
4. William West, *Simboleography* (1594), cited in Hart, pp.20–1. A juggler was someone who cured diseases with spells or charms.
5. Holland, in Sharpe, J. (ed.), *English Witchcraft 1560–1736*, Vol. I: *Early English Demonological Works* (London, 2003), p.51.
6. Bernard, p.155.
7. Briggs, p.85.
8. Ewen, C.L., *Witch Hunting and Witch Trials. The Indictments for Witchcraft from the Records of 1373 Assizes held for the Home Circuit, AD 1559–1736* (London, 1929), p.295.

Chapter 1: 'Naturally inclin'd to Superstition'

1. In the early seventeenth century, Belvoir Castle itself fell within the boundaries of Lincolnshire, whereas Bottesford was in Leicestershire.

2. W. Burton.

3. Hutton, p.115.

4. Thomas, p.631.

5. Scot, II.x; Macfarlane, *Witchcraft*, p.632.

6. Honeybone, *Wicked Practise*, p.30.

7. Thomas, p.6.

8. Sharpe, *Witchcraft in Early Modern England*, p.35. Keith Thomas's estimations are broadly similar. He claims that the population of England and Wales grew from 2.5 million in 1500 to 5.5 million in 1700 (Thomas, p.3).

9. Gifford, *Discourse*, sig. C2.

10. Scot, p.86.

11. Kramer, H., and Sprenger, J., *Malleus Maleficarum* (1486), trans. M. Summers (New York, 1978), p.2.

12. Bruce, pp.140–1.

13. Cotta, p.98.

14. Edmund Spenser, *The Faerie Queene* (1590); Hart, p.25.

15. Scot, p.1.

16. Gifford, *Discourse*, sig. H3; ibid., sig. A2.

17. Bernard, pp.11, 22–3.

18. *The Wonderful Discoverie*, p.21.

19. Ibid., p.14.

20. Thomas, p.242.

21. Ibid., p.243.

22. Bate and Thornton, p.206.

23. People believed that the pouch contained an amulet, but when Reynolds was captured and searched, it was found to contain nothing more than a piece of green cheese.

24. Thomas, pp.31, 34.

25. Ibid., p.33.

26. Honeybone, *Wicked Practise*, p.89.

27. Thomas, pp.58, 60.

28. Ibid., p.84.

Chapter 2: 'A continuall Pallace of entertainment'

1. The 1st Earl of Rutland, Thomas Manners, had been appointed such by Henry VIII in 1525. The title lasted in this form until after the death of John Manners, the 8th earl, whose son and namesake was appointed Duke of Rutland in 1703. *Burke's Peerage*, Vol. III, pp.3447–8.

2. Roger, meanwhile, was thrown into the Tower and George was imprisoned at Ludgate. HMC, *Rutland*, Vol. I, pp.366–9; HMC, *Longleat*, Vol. V, pp.277–82; *CSPD 1580–1625*, p.409.

3. HMC, *Salisbury*, Vol. XI, pp.34–5.

4. Roger was fined £30,000, and Francis and George 4,000 marks each. Sir Robert Cecil (who had strong family ties to the brothers) obtained a remission of the latter fine shortly afterwards, so Francis and his younger brother escaped lightly from the affair – certainly a good deal more so than most of the other rebels. HMC, *Rutland*, Vol. I, pp.366–7, 374, 376; Vol. IV, p.210; HMC, *Salisbury*, Vol. XI, p.214; McClure, Vol. I, pp.122–3.

5. HMC, *Rutland*, Vol. I, p.367.

6. Broughton, p.2v.

7. HMC, *Rutland*, Vol. I, p.374.

8. Katherine was christened in August 1603. HMC, *Rutland*, Vol. IV, p.446.

9. Goodman, Vol. I, p.97.

10. I am indebted to Fiona Torrens-Spence for sharing her research on Cecilia for her forthcoming biography of Katherine Manners.

11. Henderson and McManus, p.86.

12. Ibid., p.87

13. Fraser, p.27.

14. HMC, *Rutland*, Vol. I, p.413.

15. Holmes, *Seventeenth Century Lincolnshire*, p.40.

16. HMC, *Rutland*, Vol. I, p.413. Sir Francis's elder brother, Roger, made a generous settlement so that the match might go ahead. Cecily was to receive 1,000 marks per year for the maintenance of herself and any sons that she bore.

17. Ibid., Vol. I, p.414.

18. Best, pp.5–8.

19. Nichols, *Progresses*, Vol. I, p.91.

20. McClure, Vol. I, p.474.

21. *CSPD 1611–1618*, pp.386–7. The conferring of the title to Cecil had been the cause of resentment on the part of Manners and his followers at court. This flared up in July 1613, when Cecil carried the sword at the head of a royal procession, 'wherto some noble men tooke exceptions'. McClure, Vol. I, p.607. However, the matter was resolved when William Cecil died childless in 1618. The original baronial title passed back to the Manners family and Francis became the 17th Baron de Ros. His eldest son was known as 'Lord Ros'.

22. *CSPD 1619–1623*, p.580.

23. For examples of Francis's involvement in court masques, see McClure, Vol. I, pp.487, 498.

24. Nichols, *Progresses*, Vol. II, p.362.

25. Prior, p.195.

26. Broughton, p.2v.

27. W. Burton, p.43.

28. Stone, *Crisis*, p.565. The funeral of his uncle, Edward, 3rd Earl of Rutland, had been even more lavish. It was said that between 3,000 and 4,000 people were fed on the leftovers from the funeral feast.

29. HMC, *Rutland*, Vol. IV, pp.474–94; Dare, p.27.

30. Broughton, p.2v.

31. *The Wonderful Discoverie*, pp.7–8; Chambers, p.356; *Damnable Practises*.

32. Broughton, p.2v.

33. Ibid.

34. *The Wonderful Discoverie*, pp.7–8; Chambers, p.356.

35. *Damnable Practises*; T. Wright, Vol. II, p.120.

36. HMC, *Rutland*, Vol. IV, pp.462–4, 467, 471, 498.

37. Ibid., Vol. IV, p.467.

38. Ibid., Vol. IV, pp.465, 473.

39. See, for example, ibid., Vol. IV, pp.508, 518.

40. Ibid., Vol. II, p.334; Vol. IV, p.493.

41. Ibid., Vol. IV, pp.493, 505, 516.

42. Ibid., Vol. IV, pp.465, 472, 516.

43. Ibid., Vol. IV, pp.507, 512, 516.

44. Ibid., Vol. IV, p.504.

45. Ibid., Vol. IV, pp.511, 513.

46. Ibid., Vol. IV, p.491.

47. Ibid., Vol. IV, p.467.

48. Ibid., Vol. IV, pp.460, 503.

Chapter 3: A Storm at Sea

1. T. Wright, Vol. I, p.161.

2. Harington, Vol. I, pp.369–70.

3. Weldon, pp.178–9.

4. Goodman, Vol. I, p.3.

5. Stewart, pp.107–8.

6. Ibid., p.111.

7. Ibid.

8. Ibid., p.112.

9. Ibid.

10. Ibid., p.125.

11. Ibid., p.126.

12. Tyson, p.12.

13. T. Wright, Vol. I, p.181.

14. *Newes from Scotland*, in Tyson, p.190.

15. T. Wright, Vol. I, p.185.

16. *Newes from Scotland*, in Tyson, p.193.

17. *Newes from Scotland*, in ibid., p.195.

18. T. Wright, Vol. I, p.189; Crouch, p.130.

19. Larner, C., 'James VI and I and Witchcraft', in A.G. Smith, pp.84–5.

20. *Newes from Scotland*, in Tyson, pp.192–5; T. Wright, Vol. I, p.189.

21. Tyson, p.209.

22. Stewart, p.127.

23. *Newes from Scotland*.

24. Larner, *Witchcraft and Religion*, p.14.

25. T. Wright, Vol. I (London, 1851), p.179

26. Ibid., p.161.

27. Tyson, p.56.

28. Ibid., pp.129–30.

29. Ibid., p.181.

30. Ibid., p.138.

31. Ibid., p.182.

32. Ibid., pp.179–80.

33. *The Wonderful Discoverie*, p.5.

34. Scott and Pearl, p.176.

35. Gifford, *Dialogue*, f.A3r.

36. 1 Samuel 28:3–25.

37. Gifford, *Discourse*, sig. B2v.

38. Exodus 12:18; Leviticus 20:27. See also Deuteronomy 18:10–11.

39. Although it was arguably the most influential papal bull against witchcraft, it was not the first: that had been issued by Pope Alexander IV in 1258.

40. Papal bull, *Summis desiderantes affectibus* (1484), issued by Pope Innocent VIII. Cited in Institoris and Sprenger, Vol. II, Appendix, pp.613–15; Hart, pp.12–15.

41. Thomas, p.682.

42. Institoris and Sprenger, Vol. II, p.19.

43. MacCurdy, p.87.

44. I Samuel 15:23.

45. Institoris and Sprenger, Vol. II, pp.429–610.

46. J. Weyer, *De Praestigiis Daemonum et Incantationibus ac Venifiicis* (1563), cited in Monter, *European Witchcraft* , p.39.

47. Henningsen, pp.36–9. Among those implicated were 1,384 children aged between 7 and 14 years.

48. Ady, p.103.

49. HMC, *Rutland*, Vol. I, pp.146–7, 294–6.

50. Hart, p.106; Sharpe, *Instruments of Darkness*, p.125; Thomas, p.535; Ewen, C.L., *Witch Hunting and Witch Trials. The Indictments for Witchcraft from the records of 1373 Assizes held for the Home Circuit, AD 1559–1736* (1929), p.112.

51. Ewen, *Witch Hunting*, p.29.

52. Institoris and Sprenger, Vol. II, pp.20, 23–4, 501.

53. It is notoriously difficult to ascertain the exact number of people tried and executed for witchcraft, due to the loss or absence of many contemporary judicial records. This has led to intense speculation amongst historians, with estimates ranging from 50,000 to 9 million executions. There is now a broad consensus that around 100,000 suspected witches were tried and 40,000 executed. A useful summary is provided by Levack in *The witch hunt*.

54. Maxwell-Stuart, *Witch hunters*, pp.51–2.

55. Larner, C, 'Witch Beliefs', pp.33–4.

56. Scott and Pearl, pp.197–8.

57. Thomas, p.676.

58. Ibid., p.633.

59. Briggs, p.24.

60. Levack, *The witch hunt*, p.97.

61. Nichols, *Progresses,* Vol. I, p.129.

62. Harington, Vol. I.

63. Stewart, pp.171–2.

64. Weldon, p.186.

65. Ibid., p.178.

66. Ibid.

67. Ibid., p.179.

68. Williamson, p.19.

69. Stewart, p.177.

70. Goodman, Vol. I, p.224; Weldon, p.178.

71. Goodman, Vol. I, p.168.

72. Weldon, pp.181–2.

73. Stewart, pp.278–9.

74. Ibid., p.175.

75. Nichols, *Progresses*, Vol. I, p.491.

76. T. Wright, Vol. I, p.179.

77. Ewen, *Witch Hunting*, p.4.

78. Ibid., p.10.

79. *Henry VI, Part 2*. Shakespeare retained her real name for the character.

80. Peters, p.31.

81. Sermon of Bishop John Jewell of Salisbury (1560), cited in Sharpe, *Instruments of Darkness*, p.89.

82. Ibid.

83. Statute 5 Elizabeth I, cap.16, 'An Act Against Conjurations, Inchantments and Witchcrafts'. Macfarlane, *Witchcraft*, pp.13–16.

84. Gifford, *Dialogue*, p.8.

85. Macfarlane, *Witchcraft*, pp.97–8.

86. Ewen, *Witch Hunting*, p.30.

87. *The Witches of Northamptonshire*, quoted in Elbourne, *Bewitching the Mind*, p.62.

88. Durston, p.423.

89. Ibid., p.425.

90. *CSPD Addenda 1566–79*, p.551; Thomas, p.693.

91. Scot, pp.1, 3.

92. Hart, p.21.

93. Thomas Hobbes, *Leviathan* (1651); Hart, p.24.

94. R. Burton, p.33.

95. J. Weyer, *De Praestigiis Daemonum et Incantationibus ac Venifiicis* (1563), cited in Monter, *European Witchcraft*, pp.38–40.

96. James I: 1603/4 Act of Parliament against conjuration and witchcraft and dealing with evil and wicked spirits.

97. Ibid.

98. Macfarlane, *Witchcraft*, p.69.

99. Fairfax, pp.26–7.

100. Jonson, pp.945–6, 948.

101. Nichols, *Progresses*, Vol. II, pp.215–44.

102. *Macbeth* IV, i.

103. Wrightson, p.208.

104. Nichols, *Progresses*, Vol. I, p.578.

105. Ibid.,Vol. I, p.584.

106. Dalton, p.317.

107. Harington, Vol. I, pp.371–4.

108. Brown, F.B. (ed.), *Calendar of State Papers and Manuscripts, Relating to English Affairs. Existing in the Archives and Collections of Venice*, Vol. X (London, 1900), p.333.

109. Perkins, pp.248–9.

110. Cooper, p.8.

111. Henningsen, p.39.

112. Perkins, p.1; Thomas, p.542.

113. Nichols, *Progresses*, Vol. II, p.458.

114. Ibid., Vol. II, p.458.

115. HMC, *Rutland*, Vol. IV, pp.474–94.

116. Tyson, p.170.

117. Broughton, p.2v.

118. HMC, *Rutland*, Vol. I, pp.xviii–xix.

119. Sir Charles and Lady Manners were also listed as 'convicted, suspected or sought for' recusancy in 1620. *CSPD 1619–1623*, p.208.

120. McClure, Vol. I, p.625.

Chapter 4: 'Witches three'

1. *Damnable Practises; The Wonderful Discoverie*, p.8; T. Wright, Vol. I, p.120.

2. *The Wonderful Discoverie*, p.8.

3. *Damnable Practises*.

4. HMC, *Rutland*, Vol. IV, pp.385, 452.

5. Ibid., Vol. II, p.411; Vol. IV, p.471.

6. Ibid., Vol. IV, p.505.

7. *Damnable Practises; The Wonderful Discoverie*, p.9.

8. *The Wonderful Discoverie*, p.9.

9. Eller, p.66.

10. *Damnable Practises*.

11. Thurston, p.73.

12. Married women were far from immune from suspicion, however. The surviving assize records show that a significant proportion of those tried for witchcraft had husbands still living. Macfarlane, *Witchcraft*, p.164.

13. *King Lear*, V, iii, Larner, C., 'Crimen Exceptum? The Crime of Witchcraft in Europe', in Levack, *Witch Hunting*, p.101.

14. Fraser, p.109.

15. *The Wonderful Discoverie*, p.9.

16. Ibid.

17. Harsnett, p.136.

18. Fraser, p.113.

19. The term is derived from the three wise men, or Magi, who attended the infant Jesus. It is thus easy to see the link with the word 'magic'.

20. R. Burton, p.210.

21. Thomas, p.17.

22. Perkins, p.153.

23. Gifford, *Discourse*, sig. H1v.

24. Bernard, p.132.

25. Gifford, *Dialogue*, sig. B; Macfarlane, *Witchcraft*, p.120.

26. Gifford, *Dialogue*, sig. M3v; Macfarlane, *Witchcraft*, pp.129–30.

27. Thomas, p.211.

28. Ibid., p.212.

29. Ibid.

30. Ibid., p.213.

31. Ehrenreich and English, p.15; Perkins, sig. H; Macfarlane, *Witchcraft*, p.128.

32. Parkinson, pp.20–1.

33. Gifford, *Discourse*, sig. C2v.

34. Gifford, *Dialogue*; Macfarlane, *Witchcraft*, p.128.

35. Bernard, p.139.

36. Thomas, p.215.

37. Ibid., p.800.

38. Ibid., p.254.

39. Macfarlane, *Witchcraft*, p.125.

40. Weyer, p.117.

41. Gifford, *Discourse*, sig. G1v.

42. *The Wonderful Discoverie*, p.4.

43. Ibid.; Gibson, *Reading Witchcraft*, p.178.

44. Gifford, *Discourse*, sig. H2.

45. Thomas, p.277.

46. Ewen, *Robert Ratcliffe*, pp.2–5.

47. Thomas, p.643.

48. Ibid., p.287.
49. Weyer, p.117.
50. Gifford, *Discourse*, sig. H1v.
51. Thomas, pp.291–2; R. Burton, p.6; Holland, sig.B1.
52. Gibson, *Reading Witchcraft*, p.178.
53. Gifford, *Discourse*, sig. H2v.
54. Ehrenreich and English, p.56.
55. Gifford, *Discourse*, sigs. H1v, I.
56. Ady, p.159.
57. Thomas, p.654.
58. *A True and Exact Relation*, p.1; Macfarlane, *Witchcraft*, p.123.

Chapter 5: 'Busie-bodies and flatterers'

1. *The Wonderful Discoverie*.
2. Briggs, p.232.
3. *The Wonderful Discoverie*, p.9.
4. *CSPD 1623–1625*, p.557.
5. *The Wonderful Discoverie*, p.8.
6. Crouch, p.141.
7. *The Wonderful Discoverie*, p.8.
8. Ibid., p.9.
9. T. Wright, Vol. I, p.120.
10. *The Wonderful Discoverie*, p.9.
11. Ibid., p.21.
12. Interestingly, that village would soon be the centre of another witchcraft controversy. In July 1616, nine women had been executed there for bewitching the grandson of the lord of the manor of Bosworth.
13. *The Wonderful Discoverie*, p.22.
14. Scot, p.4.
15. *Damnable Practises*; Crouch, p.141.
16. *The Wonderful Discoverie*, p.9.
17. *Damnable Practises*.
18. *The Wonderful Discoverie*, p.22.
19. Ibid., pp.6–7.
20. Ibid., p.8.
21. Ibid., p.22.
22. Chambers, p.356.
23. *The Wonderful Discoverie*, pp.9–10.

24. Scot, p.5.
25. Perkins, p.202.
26. *The Wonderful Discoverie*, p.4.
27. Bernard, p.156; Stearne, p.20.
28. Isaiah 8:19.
29. Macfarlane, *Witchcraft*, p.72.
30. *The Witches of Northamptonshire*, sigs. B2–B2v.
31. Thomas, p.606.
32. *The Wonderful Discoverie*, p.8.
33. Perkins, p.141.
34. *The Wonderful Discoverie*, p.10; *Damnable Practises*.
35. *Damnable Practises*.
36. Harsnett, sig. A2, pp.136–7.
37. Gifford, *Discourse*, sig. G2v–G3.
38. *Damnable Practises*; *The Wonderful Discoverie*, p.10.
39. *The Wonderful Discoverie*, p.4.
40. Scot, p.4.
41. Thomas, p.599.
42. Harner, M.J., 'The Role of Hallucinogenic Plants in European Witchcraft', in Levack, *Witch Hunting*, p.252.
43. See plates X–XX.
44. *The Witch of Edmonton* (1621), II, i.
45. Another account claims that he died soon after falling ill. Crouch, p.144.
46. HMC, *Rutland*, Vol. IV, p.497.
47. *Damnable Practises*; *The Wonderful Discoverie*, p.11.
48. *The Wonderful Discoverie*, p.10.
49. Rosen, p.44.
50. *Damnable Practises*; *The Wonderful Discoverie*, p.11.
51. *Damnable Practises*.
52. Gaule, p.85.
53. Thomas, p.640.
54. Guazzo, *Compendium Maleficarum* (1626); Hart, pp.51–4.
55. Thomas, p.640.
56. Cotta, pp.76–7.
57. Scot, p.5.
58. Potts; Briggs, p.74.
59. Ewen, *Witch Hunting*, p.293.
60. Ibid., pp.294–5.

61. Baroja, J.C., *The World of Witches* (Chicago & London, 1964), cited in Monter, *European Witchcraft*, p.156.
62. Macfarlane, *Witchcraft*, pp.82–3.
63. Briggs, p.39.
64. Monter, *European Witchcraft*, pp.75–81.
65. Scott and Pearl, p.182.
66. Papal bull, *Summis desiderantes affectibus* (1484), issued by Pope Innocent VIII; Hart, p.14.
67. Briggs, p.79.
68. Institoris and Sprenger, Vol. II, pp.138–45.
69. Macfarlane, *Witchcraft*, pp.183–4.
70. Ibid., p.162.
71. Scot, p.4.
72. Harsnett, p.136.
73. Peters, p.23.
74. Quoted in Levack, *The witch hunt*, p.129.
75. Briggs, p.20.
76. Hutchinson, p.138.
77. Ewen, *Witchcraft in the Star Chamber*, pp.18–19.
78. Gaule, p.5.
79. Scott and Pearl, p.155.
80. *The Wonderful Discoverie*, p.5.
81. Gifford, *Discourse*, sig. F4v, G1v.
82. Filmer, sig. B4.
83. Perkins, p.44.
84. Gifford, *Discourse*, sig. H3v.
85. Bernard, p.185.
86. Ibid., p.134.
87. Remy, p.159; Levack, *The witch hunt*, p.134.
88. *The Witches of Northamptonshire*, quoted in Elbourne, *Bewitching the Mind*, p.62.
89. Bernard, p.155.
90. Fraser, p.112.
91. Gifford, *Discourse*, sig. G1v.
92. Harington, Vol. I, pp.368–9.
93. Thomas, p.677.
94. *The Witch of Edmonton* (1621), 2, i, 1–15a.
95. Potts.

96. Perkins, p.191.

97. Scot, p.4.

98. There was a high degree of variation between different countries, however. For example, as many as half of convicted witches in France were men, and 25 per cent in Germany. Briggs, p.261.

99. Larner, *Enemies of God*, pp.1–3.

100. Pearson, J., 'Wicca, Paganism and history: contemporary witchcraft and the Lancashire Witches', in Poole.

101. Institoris and Sprenger; Barstow, *Witchcraze*, p.172.

102. Papal bull, *Summis desiderantes affectibus* (1484), issued by Pope Innocent VIII; Hart, pp.12–15.

103. See for example Leviticus 14:31; 20:27; Isaiah 8:19.

104. Stearne, p.10; 1 Samuel 28:7; Chronicles 10:10, 13, 14; Exodus 25:28.

105. Institoris and Sprenger, Vol. II, pp.114–15. Extracts cited are Ecclesiasticus 25:22–6, Matthew 19:10.

106. Institoris and Sprenger, Vol. II, p.115.

107. Scot, p.63.

108. The Home Circuit assize records show that between 1600 and 1702, there were 1,207 calls for witnesses at witch trials, of which 576 (48 per cent) involved women. Sharpe, J., 'Women, witchcraft and the legal process', in Kermode and Walker, p.112.

109. Sharpe, *Instruments of Darkness*, pp.178–80.

110. Perkins, pp.168–9.

111. Stearne, p.11; A. Roberts, p.42.

112. Swetnam, cited in Henderson and McManus, p.193.

113. Tyson, p.128.

114. Scot, p.158.

115. Swetnam, cited in Henderson and McManus, p.194.

116. Stearne, p.11; A. Roberts, p.43.

117. A. Roberts, p.43.

118. Bernard, p.93.

119. Institoris and Sprenger; Barstow, *Witchcraze*.

120. Institoris and Sprenger, Vol. II, pp.117, 122.

121. Bodin, J., *De la démonomanie des sorciers* (1580), f.225r; Briggs, p.259.

122. *The Wonderful Discoverie*, p.9. Interestingly, despite their reputation for promiscuity, there is no hint in the contemporary records of any unwanted pregnancies. While Joan was past childbearing years, her daughters may have just been lucky in this respect – or more virtuous

than the gossips claimed. Another explanation is that their mother had taught them about birth control or had given them certain herbal concoctions known to prevent conception. Whether it was for avoiding pregnancy or carrying out an abortion, this was considered the greatest sexual sin of all. It was impeding the course of nature – and of God's creation – and those who practised it ran the risk of being accused of witchcraft.

123. Tyson, p.107.
124. Macfarlane, *Witchcraft*, p.158.
125. Ibid., p.159.
126. Quoted in Levack, *The witch hunt*, p.130.
127. Scot, p.12; Barstow, *Witchcraze*, p.29.
128. Institoris and Sprenger, Vol. II, p.131. This distasteful analogy was commonly used in colloquial German to express a lustful yearning.
129. Scot, p.158.
130. Ibid., p.282; Macfarlane, *Witchcraft*, p.163.
131. Guazzo, *Compendium Maleficarum* (1626); Hart, p.30.
132. Scott and Pearl, pp.187, 199.
133. Scot, p.12; Stearne, pp.12, 29, 33.
134. Perkins,; Filmer, sig. B4v.
135. Perkins, p.193; Potts, pp.16–17.
136. Bernard, p.93.
137. Sharpe, *Witchcraft in Early Modern England*, p.110.
138. See for example Barstow, *Witchcraze*.
139. [W.W.], sigs. C7–C7v.
140. Gifford, *Discourse*, sig. G3.
141. Ady, p.114.
142. Thomas, p.608.
143. Proverbs, 28:27.
144. Thomas, p.662.
145. Scot, iii; Thomas, p.663.

Chapter 6: 'This medicine be somewhat doubtful'

1. Thomas, pp.375–6.
2. Bernard, pp.14–16.
3. Ibid., p.39.
4. Sowerby, pp.5–6.
5. Markham, pp.14–15.

6. Thomas, p.534.

7. Bodleian Library, Ashmolean Manuscripts 412, f.235v; Thomas, p.757.

8. Honeybone, *Wicked Practise*, p.93.

9. Fraser, p.80.

10. MacDonald, p.210.

11. HMC, *Rutland*, Vol. IV, p.501.

12. Ibid., Vol. IV, p.502.

13. Ibid.,Vol. IV, p.507.

14. *Damnable Practises*.

15. HMC, *Rutland*, Vol. V, pp.385, 452, 471, 505.

16. Ibid., Vol. IV, p.510.

17. Nichols, *Progresses*, Vol. II, pp.471, 478. It is interesting to note that in attending the late Prince Henry during his final illness, Dr Atkins had raised no suspicion of bewitchment, even though it would have deflected any criticism that he had failed to save the kingdom's heir. Perhaps the prince's symptoms – which were described as being a 'continuall headache, lazinesse, and indisposition' – did not conform to those commonly associated with bewitchment.

18. HMC, *Rutland*, Vol. I, p.449.

19. Ibid.

20. Ibid.

21. Honeybone, *Wicked Practise*, p.93.

22. *The Wonderful Discoverie*, p.10

23. Macfarlane, *Diary of Ralph Josselin*, pp.113–14.

24. Harington, Vol. I, p.343.

25. McElwee, *Wisest Fool*, p.201.

26. Weldon, p.177.

27. *CSPV*, Vol. XV, p.420.

28. Ibid., p.468.

29. Williamson, pp.13, 28.

30. Goodman, Vol. I, pp.225–6.

31. Stewart, p.280.

32. McElwee, *Wisest Fool*, p.213.

33. *CSPV*, Vol. XV, pp.113–14; Stewart, p.280.

34. Stewart, p.330; British Museum Harleian MS 6987, f.234.

35. Somerset, p.51.

36. Stewart, p.330; McElwee, *Wisest Fool*, p.214.

37. Williamson, p.12.

38. *CSPV*, Vol. XV, p.335.

39. McClure, Vol. I, p.625.

40. Stewart, pp.281–2.

41. *CSPV*, Vol. XV, pp.459, 468.

42. *CSPD 1623–1625*, p.28.

43. Lockyer, p.26.

44. Ibid.

45. Williamson, pp.84–5.

46. Lockyer, p.58.

47. HMC, *Rutland*, Vol. I, p.416.

48. British Museum Harleian MS 6987, f.119.

49. Ewen, *Robert Ratcliffe*, p.4.

50. Ibid., pp.4-5. Although the Privy Council ordered that Frances Shute be arrested and brought before the Archbishop of Canterbury, she was never taken. Perhaps thanks to Villiers's intervention, she was pardoned by the king and went on to marry the Earl of Sussex the day after his wife's death in December 1623.

51. Williamson, p.84.

52. Akrigg, p.222.

Chapter 7: 'In vengeance strike'

1. Stewart, p.301.

2. *The Wonderful Discoverie*, p.9.

3. *Damnable Practises.*

4. Macfarlane, *Witchcraft*, p.109.

5. *A True and Just Recorde of the Information, Examination and Confession of all the Witches, taken at S. Oses in the countie of Essex* (1582), sigs. A7–A7v, cited in Macfarlane, *Witchcraft*, p.109.

6. Honeybone, *Wicked Practise*, p.33.

7. Briggs, p.183.

8. Thomas, p.649.

9. Gifford, *Discourse*, sig. H3.

10. *The Wonderful Discoverie*, p.224.

11. Scott and Pearl, p.218.

12. Thomas, p.650.

13. Sharpe, *Crime*, p.110.

14. Holmes, 'Women, witnesses and witches', pp.55–6.

15. Gifford, *Discourse*, sigs. G4–G4v; Macfarlane, *Witchcraft*, pp.111–12.

16. Gifford, *Discourse*, sig. G4–G4v.
17. Macfarlane, A., 'Witchcraft Prosecutions in Essex, 1560–1680: A Sociological Analysis', PhD Thesis (Oxford, 1967), p.223.
18. There were few towns with populations of more than 10,000. Even as late as 1700, Norwich – which was the second largest city in the country – had only 30,000 inhabitants. London was the only large urban centre, with a population of 500,000 by the same date.
19. Scot, p.374; Macfarlane, *Witchcraft*, p.168.
20. Cotta, p.108.
21. A detailed guide to 'swimming' a witch was provided in the 1613 pamphlet *Witches Apprehended, Examined and Executed*. Another explanation for the effectiveness of the trial was put forward by James in *Daemonology*: that those who renounced the sacred water of baptism would be themselves rejected by water. Tyson, p.39.
22. *The Wonderful Discoverie*, Epilogue.
23. Briggs, p.54.
24. *The Wonderful Discoverie*, Epilogue.
25. Dalton, pp.308, 310.
26. Hart, pp.50–1.
27. *The Wonderful Discoverie*, p.19.
28. Ibid., p.11.
29. Cotta, p.108.
30. *The Wonderful Discoverie*, p.11.
31. Chambers, p.356.

Chapter 8: 'Unto Lincolne Citty borne'

1. In populous Kent, there was an average of 76 Justices during the late Elizabethan period, whereas Rutland (which was tiny by comparison) had only 12.
2. Nichols, *Progresses*, Vol. III, pp.262–3.
3. Introduction by Rev. Montague Summers to Scot, p.xx; Cockburn, *History of the English Assizes*, p.107.
4. Sharpe, *Crime*, p.47. No fewer than 20 deaths were recorded in Guildford Castle gaol in 1598 alone. Ewen, *Witch Hunting*, p.27.
5. Durston, p.334.
6. Ewen, *Witch Hunting*, p.27.
7. Durston, p.333.
8. Ewen, *Witch Hunting*, p.27.

9. Durston, pp.333–4.

10. James VI, p.51.

11. The dungeons at the base of Cobb Hall can still be visited today.

12. Dalton, p.312.

13. Scott and Pearl, p.177.

14. Ibid., p.178.

15. *The Wonderful Discoverie*, title page and p.24.

16. HMC, *Rutland*, Vol. IV, p.514. Putting an 'e' on the end of a word was a common way of pluralising it.

17. Ibid., Vol. IV, p.514.

18. This Lord Willoughby d'Eresby was Robert Bertie, who succeeded to the barony in 1601.

19. His brother, Abraham, had written a popular pamphlet about the notorious legend of the Black Dog of Bungay. Although eagerly devoured by the credulous Elizabethan readership, Abraham had intended it as a morality tale, aimed at inspiring his readers to lead a more godly life. He may also have been involved in editing the most influential work by a witchcraft sceptic, Reginald Scot's *The Discoverie of Witchcraft*. I am indebted to Dr Clare Stubbs for sharing her extensive research on Abraham.

20. As well as leaving various endowments to the poor and female members of his parish, Fleming also ordered – during his lifetime – the construction of a bridge so that the people of Bottesford might safely cross the fast-flowing stream near the entrance to the church. He himself had almost drowned when attempting to navigate his way across some time before.

21. Scott and Pearl, p.188.

22. Ibid., p.218.

23. Potts, sig. P2v.

24. Bernard, pp.239–40.

25. Hopkins, p.59; Macfarlane, *Witchcraft*, p.20.

26. Bernard, pp.228–38.

27. Scott and Pearl, p.188.

28. Perkins, pp.214–15.

29. Scott and Pearl, p.186.

30. Gifford, *Discourse*, sig. G4v.

31. Briggs, p.235.

32. Cockburn, *History of the English Assizes*, p.120.

33. Ewen, *Witchcraft in the Star Chamber*, pp.28–36.

34. Maxwell-Stuart, *Witch hunters*.

35. Dalton, p.266; Macfarlane, *Witchcraft*, p.16.

36. Cotta, p.101.

37. Dalton, pp.275, 277; Macfarlane, *Witchcraft*, p.16.

38. Perkins, p.210.

39. Gifford, *Discourse*, sig. I.

40. Ibid., sig. G4v.

41. Bernard, p.25.

42. Cooper, pp.274–6.

43. Ibid., pp.277–8.

44. Ibid., p.276.

45. Institoris and Sprenger, Vol. II.

46. *Newes from Scotland*, in Tyson, p.202.

47. Tyson, p.107.

48. *Newes from Scotland*, in ibid., p.201.

49. Monter, *European Witchcraft*, p.85.

50. Barstow, *Witchcraze*, p.131.

51. Gaule, pp.78–9; Ewen, *Witch Hunting*, p.66.

52. Briggs, p.54.

53. Levack, *The witch-hunt*, p.73.

54. Cotta, p.77.

55. Tyson, p.30; Thomas, p.599.

56. Briggs, p.43.

Chapter 9: 'Voluntarie confessions and examinations'

1. Scott and Pearl, p.178.

2. *The Wonderful Discoverie*, p.23.

3. Ewen, *Witch Hunting*, p.308.

4. Scott and Pearl, pp.179, 192.

5. The contemporary ballad describing the case inaccurately states that it was Phillipa, not Margaret, who was first to confess. *Damnable Practises*.

6. *The Wonderful Discoverie*, pp.22, 24.

7. Ibid., p.21.

8. Ibid., p.22.

9. Ibid., p.7.

10. Ibid., p.23.

11. Ibid.

12. Thomas, p.530.

13. T. Wright, Vol. I, p.182.

14. Bernard, pp.218–20. James I provided a detailed explanation in his book about witchcraft of how a woman was marked by the Devil. He claimed that Satan 'gives them his mark upon some secret place of their body, which remains sore unhealed until his next meeting with them, and thereafter insensible, howsoever it be nipped or pricked in any way, as is daily proved; to give them a proof hereby, that as in that doing he could hurt and heal them, so all their ill and well doings thereafter must depend upon him. And besides that, the intolerable distress that they feel in that place where he has marked them serves to waken them, and not to let them rest until their next meeting again; fearing lest otherwise they might either forget him, being as new apprentices and not well enough founded yet in that fiendly folly: or else, remembering of that horrible promise they made him at their last meeting, they might balk at the same, and press to call it back.' Tyson, pp.112–13.

15. Ewen, *Witch Hunting*, p.70.

16. Ibid.

17. Barstow, *Witchcraze*, p.130. The woman described here was released after a second examination. The pricker was eventually hanged, but not before he had sent 220 women to their deaths – earning 20 shillings for each conviction.

18. *A true and exact Relation*, p.24.

19. *A Tryal of Witches at Bury St Edmunds* (1664), p.16; Ewen, *Witch Hunting*, pp.61–2.

20. *Newes from Scotland*, in Tyson, p.192.

21. Institoris and Sprenger, Vol. II, p.84.

22. *A true and exact Relation*, pp.2, 6.

23. Colling meant to kiss and embrace around the neck. *The Wonderful Discoverie*, p.5.

24. Goodcole.

25. Trial account of Isobel Gowdie, Scotland (1662); Hart, p.32.

26. Tyson, pp.163–4.

27. Scott and Pearl, p.130.

28. Almond, p.103.

29. Ewen, *Witch Hunting*, p.306.

30. Cooper, pp.121-3.
31. *A Pleasant Treatise of Witches*, p.6.
32. McGowan, M.M., 'Pierre de Lancre's Tableau de L'Inconstance des Mauvais Anges et Demons: the Sabbat Sensationalized', in Anglo, pp.182-201.
33. *The Wonderful Discoverie*, pp.23-4.
34. Scott and Pearl, p.130.
35. *Newes from Scotland*; Hart, p.41.
36. Tyson, p.117.
37. *A Pleasant Treatise of Witches*, p.7.
38. Tyson, pp.163-4.
39. Scot, pp.43-4.
40. Andreski, S., 'The Syphilitic Shock', in Levack, *Witch Hunting*, p.286.
41. Institoris and Sprenger, Vol. II, pp.262, 265. An incubus is a sexual spirit in the form of a male, and a succubus is in the form of a female. Many demonologists believed that these spirits could change from male to female form depending upon the sex of the person they were trying to seduce.
42. Almond, p.102.
43. Monter, *European Witchcraft*, p.117.
44. See, for example, *Witches' Sabbath* (1510).
45. *The Wonderful Discoverie*, pp.23-4.
46. Gifford, *Discourse*, sig. G3.
47. Shakespeare, *Macbeth*, I, i.
48. Ewen, *Witch Hunting*, p.305.
49. Ibid., p.306.
50. Ibid.
51. Thomas, p.626.
52. Tyson, p.139.
53. Gifford, *Dialogue*, p.102.

Chapter 10: 'Desperate impenitency'

1. Those serving as grand jurymen had to pay substantial sums for the privilege. By the beginning of the eighteenth century, it cost £80 per year, compared to £10 to be a petty juryman. Durston, p.350.
2. Honeybone, *Wicked Practise*, p.176.
3. The pamphlet dates the Flower women's arrest and trial to 1618, rather than 1619, although this may just be because it is using the old-style calendar. But the examination of Joan Willimot is dated 'the 16. yeare

of the raigne of our Soveraigne Lord, James, over England King &c. and over Scotland the 52', which does tally with the 1618 date. Meanwhile, Nichols's *History and Antiquities*, Vol. II, Part 1, p.49, cites it as 1620. However, Reverend Samuel Fleming, who played a key part in the trial, died that year but we do not know exactly when. The witches' own testimonies are of no help because none of the specific dates or days they provide fit with any of the possible years in which the events could have taken place. Marion Gibson provides a useful analysis of the chronological problem surrounding the Belvoir witch case in *Early Modern Witches*, pp.276–9. See also: Cockburn, *Calendar of Assize Records*, p.80.

4. 'Preamble to the charge given to the Grand Jury by Serjeant Davis at York Assizes Lent 1620', in Cockburn, *History of the English Assizes*, Appendix 5, p.311.

5. For an excellent account of the history and proceedings of the assizes, see: Cockburn, *History of the English Assizes*.

6. The papers from Margaret and Phillipa's trial probably survived until 1800, when the Midland circuit clerk declared that he saw no point in keeping the 'cart load' of records received from his predecessor and proposed to destroy everything when it was 60 years old. He evidently did so, for when most surviving assize records were transferred to the National Archives in 1911, the earliest document from the Midland circuit was dated 1818. A fragmentary series of indictments from this circuit covering the period 1652–88 was later recovered from private custody. Cockburn, *Calendar of Assize Records*, p.10.

7. Durston, p.404.

8. Bromley and Hobart had served as judges of the Midlands assizes since 1618. Cockburn, *History of the English Assizes*, p.270.

9. Honeybone, *Wicked Practise*, p.178.

10. Dalton, p.251.

11. Scott and Pearl, pp.195, 209.

12. Dalton, p.251.

13. Scott and Pearl, p.210.

14. Cockburn, *History of the English Assizes*, p.110.

15. Ibid., p.67; Cockburn, *Calendar of Assize Records*, pp.44–50. There were usually 17 or 19 members of the jury.

16. Durston, p.383.

17. Cockburn, *History of the English Assizes*, p.67.

18. T. Smith, p.78.
19. *The Wonderful Discoverie*, pp.24–5.
20. 'There is no murmuring or repining against God, but quietly to tolerate his inflicting, whensoever they chance, of which this worthy Earle is a memorable example of all men and Ages.' *The Wonderful Discoverie*, p.26.
21. Gifford, *Dialogue*, L3–L3v; Macfarlane, *Witchcraft*, pp.18–19.
22. Potts, S1 verso, R3 recto.
23. T.W., p.59.
24. Sharpe, *Crime*, p.33.
25. Durston, p.363.
26. [W.W.], sig. B6v; Macfarlane, *Witchcraft*, pp.19–20.
27. *The Wonderful Discoverie*, p.24.
28. Ibid., pp.24–5.
29. Ibid., p.25.
30. Cockburn, *Calendar of Assize Records*, p.106.
31. Durston, p.390.
32. Thomas, p.547.
33. Durston, p.390.
34. Ibid., p.362.
35. T.W., p.15; Macfarlane, *Witchcraft*, p.24.
36. Durston, p.385.
37. Ibid., p.349.
38. James I: 1603/4 Act of Parliament against conjuration and witchcraft and dealing with evil and wicked spirits; T. Smith, p.83.
39. *The Wonderful Discoverie*, p.25.

Chapter 11: 'By strangling twist'

1. Cooper, pp.313–14.
2. *The most strange and admirable Discoverie*, sigs. O2v, O3.
3. Cockburn, *Calendar of Assize Records*, pp.121–3.
4. Dalton, p.266.
5. A public house, appropriately named 'The Strugglers', stands close to the site today.
6. Durston, p.430.
7. Ibid.
8. Ibid., p.431.
9. *Damnable Practises*.

Chapter 12: 'Infamous persons'

1. Nichols, *History and Antiquities,* Vol. II, Part I, p.49n.
2. Quoted in ibid.
3. *Two Sermons,* pp.10, 12, 13, 14, 17, 20, 28, 35, 40–1, 50–1.
4. Gifford, *Discourse,* sig. H4v.I.
5. A. Roberts, dedicatory pages.
6. Chambers, Vol. I , p.356.
7. Gifford, *Discourse,* sig. I.
8. Tyson, p.181.
9. Scott and Pearl, p.188.
10. *The Wonderful Discoverie,* p.16.
11. Ibid., pp.16–18.
12. Ibid., pp.15–16.
13. Ibid., pp.18–19.
14. Ibid., pp.19–21.
15. Bodleian Library, Ashmolean Manuscripts 412, f.119.
16. HMC, *Rutland,* Vol. IV, p.225.
17. *APC, 1619–1621,* p.3.
18. *The Wonderful Discoverie,* p.7.
19. Ibid., p.11.
20. Sharpe, *Instruments of Darkness,* p.49.
21. HMC, *Rutland,* Vol. IV, pp.514, 516.
22. *CSPD 1619–1623,* p.412.

Chapter 13: 'A divilish conspiracy'

1. *CSPD 1619–1623,* p.71.
2. *CSPD 1619–1623,* pp.94, 97.
3. Nichols, *Progresses,* Vol. III, p.585.
4. McClure, Vol. II, p.284.
5. Thomas, p.297.
6. Bellaney, p.61.
7. Ibid., p.63.
8. McClure, Vol. II, p.293.
9. HMC, *Rutland,* Vol. IV, p.519. Ironically, this was less than the earl spent on ensuring that the Flower women were brought to justice.
10. The publication date is cited as 1619, but this was due to the fact that the old-style dates were still being used. In fact the pamphlet was published in 1620. This is consistent with the dates cited in the pamphlet

itself, which are all in old style – notably the trial, which it gives as 1618, rather than 1619 when it actually occurred.

11. Bayman, pp.26–7.

12. Pepys' is the only surviving copy of the original ballad, and it is thanks to his presenting it to Magdalene College, Cambridge, along with the rest of his ballad collection, that it has endured for posterity. See Gibson, *Early Modern Witches*, p.7.

13. *The Wonderful Discoverie*, pp.25–6.

14. Holland, in *English Witchcraft*, Vol. I, p.89.

15. Perkins, pp.181–2, 184.

16. *The Wonderful Discoverie*, pp.7, 11, 22.

17. Ibid., sig. B.

18. See, for example, *The Witches of Northamptonshire*.

19. *The Wonderful Discoverie*, p.26.

20. *Damnable Practises*; Gibson, M., *Early English Trial Pamphlets* (London, 2003), p.275.

21. There are various other minor discrepancies with the original version of the pamphlet.

22. *The Wonderful Discoverie*, p.21.

23. McClure, Vol. II, p.293.

24. Bernard, pp.92, 111, 113, 129, 136, 157–62, 178–81, 189, 206, 225, 233.

25. Ibid., pp.24–5.

26. Ibid., p.27.

27. Ibid., p.170.

28. Ibid., p.216.

29. Ibid., pp.216–17.

30. *CSPV*, Vol. XVI, p.169.

31. McClure, Vol. II, p.293; *CSPD 1619–1623*, p.129.

32. Goodman, Vol. II, p.190.

33. McClure, Vol. II, p.293.

34. Goodman, Vol. II, pp.190–1.

35. McClure, Vol. II, pp.296–7.

36. *CSPD 1619–1623*, p.132.

37. Ibid., pp.113, 133.

38. Goodman, Vol. II, pp.191–2.

39. British Museum Harleian MS 6987, f.69. See also Akrigg, pp.220–1; Williamson, p.240; Lockyer, p.60.

40. Lockyer, p.60.

41. McClure, Vol. II, pp.301–2; *CSPD 1619–1623*, p.140.

42. McClure, Vol. II, p.306.

43. Beaumont, J., *Epithalamium to my Lord of Buckingham and his Lady*.

Chapter 14: 'The most hated man then living'

1. Samuel's sister, Hester, was responsible for carrying out his last wishes. She married her brother's curate soon after his death, and died in 1622.

2. Honeybone, *Wicked Practise*, p.133.

3. McClure, Vol. II, p.401.

4. Lockyer, pp.60–1; Akrigg, p.221.

5. Lockyer, p.60.

6. British Museum Harleian MS 6987, f.119; Akrigg, p.222.

7. Goodman, Vol. II, p.310; Lockyer, p.60.

8. Akrigg, p.221.

9. *CSPD 1619–1623*, pp.300, 333.

10. McClure, Vol. II, p.451; *CSPD 1619–1623*, p.449.

11. British Museum Harleian MS 6987, f.178.

12. *CSPD 1619–1623*, p.366. Buckingham had purchased Wallingford House shortly before Katherine's lying-in. It stood in a prime position, next to the palace of Whitehall and overlooking St James's Park.

13. McClure, Vol. II, p.434.

14. The duchess gave birth to the longed-for son in 1625; he was named after the new king, Charles, but died in infancy. In January 1628, Katherine gave birth to another son, George, who became the 2nd Duke of Buckingham upon his father's death just four months later. A third son, Francis, who was said to have inherited his father's striking good looks, was born in April 1629.

15. British Museum Harleian MS 6987, f.231.

16. Williamson, pp.142, 245.

17. Lockyer, p.152.

18. Goodman, Vol. II, p.312.

19. Nichols, *Progresses*, Vol. IV, p.855.

20. McClure, Vol. II, pp.502–3. The rumour proved accurate for Buckingham, but not for Rutland.

21. *CSPD 1623–1625*, pp.196, 198.

22. Ben Jonson, *A Masque of the Metamorphosed Gipsies* (1621), cited in Nichols, *Progresses*, Vol. IV, p.678. The other 'three' whom Jonson implied were greater than Rutland were the king, the prince and Buckingham.

23. *CSPD 1623–1625*, pp.197–8.

24. Weldon, p.162.

25. *CSPD 1623–1625*, p.231; Stewart, pp.334–5.

26. Stewart, p.337.

27. Ibid., p.338.

28. Ibid., p.341.

29. British Museum MS Harleian MS 6987, f.101.

30. Nichols, *Progresses*, Vol. IV, p.1033.

31. Goodman, p.409.

32. Stewart, p.348.

33. HMC, *Rutland*, Vol. IV, p.221.

34. Ibid.

35. Williamson, p.192. The child, christened George after his father, would be like him in almost every respect. Pleasure-seeking and ambitious in equal measure, he became a firm favourite of the future Charles II, and was rewarded for his loyalty towards him during the long years of exile before the Restoration in 1660. But his profligate lifestyle won him many enemies, and he even fell foul of the king. 'He was true to nothing,' wrote one observer. 'He at length ruined both body and mind, fortune and reputation equally.' Williamson, p.88n.

36. Bellaney, p.59.

37. MacDonald, pp.20–1.

38. *CSPV*, Vol. XIX, pp.604–5, 605n; Bellaney, p.62.

39. Stewart, p.349.

40. Bellaney, p.69.

41. Lockyer, p.454.

42. HMC, *Rutland*, Vol. I, p.490.

43. The earl's executor was possibly Sir Thomas Savage. The Savages were evidently well acquainted with the Manners, and Sir Thomas's wife had been at Spa at the same time as Cecilia, during the summer of 1622. *CSPD 1619–1623*, p.420.

44. Although Francis Manners had been less extravagant than other members of his family, his clothes were valued at the not inconsiderable sum of £500 upon his death.

45. Proof that the monument was built during the earl's lifetime is that at its base is an inscription, apparently added later than the rambling, self-congratulatory prose of the main epitaph. This simply reads: 'Francis Earl of Rutland was buried Feb. 20, 1632.' Eller, p.376. The first

mention of a tomb in the family accounts is dated 8 January 1614 (1615), when a footman was sent from Belvoir to bring Dr Fleming from his parish at Bottesford to discuss the making of the tomb with the earl. This could have been prompted by the death of the earl's elder son, Henry, in September 1613. HMC, *Rutland*, Vol. IV, p.504.

46. HMC, *Rutland*, Vol. I, p.492.

47. Ibid., Vol. I, pp.493–4.

48. Ibid., Vol. II, p.344.

49. Eller notes that she was buried on 11 September 1653 in St Nicholas Chapel, Westminster Abbey, without any monument for herself or her son Francis. Eller, p.67. Their tomb was probably close to that of their relation, Lady Elizabeth Ros.

Epilogue: 'Wicked practise & sorcerye'

1. Hutchinson, p.180.

2. Elbourne, *Bewitching the Mind*, p.56. These women had been implicated in the case of the Husbands Bosworth bewitching, which had already resulted in the execution of nine local women (see p.83).

3. Gaskill, *Witchfinders*; Larner, quoted in Elbourne, *Bewitching the Mind*, p.56.

4. Larner, C., 'James VI and I and Witchcraft', in A.G. Smith, p.89.

5. Cockburn, *Calendar of Assize Records*, Appendix VI, pp.190–7, 230. The Home Counties are Essex, Hertfordshire, Kent, Surrey and Sussex.

6. *The Wonderful Discoverie*, p.7.

7. Ibid., p.3.

8. Goodcole.

9. Cotta, p.A2v.

10. Ewen, *Witchcraft in the Star Chamber*, pp.18–19.

11. *A Most Certain, Strange, and true Discovery*.

12. Shakespeare, *All's Well That Ends Well*, II, iii.

13. Brinley, p.69.

14. Thomas, p.774.

15. Webster, p.68.

16. Thomas, p.693.

17. Fourteenth Report of the Historical Manuscripts Commission, Appendix, Part iii, p.132; Thomas, p.686.

18. Ewen, *Witch Hunting*, pp.314–16.

19. Kennett, p.9.

20. Thomas, p.694.

21. Boulton, *Compleat History*; Boulton, *Possibility and Reality*.

22. Boulton, *Compleat History*, Vol. I, pp.11, 177–95.

23. Thomas, p.295.

24. Ewen, *Witch Hunting*, p.115.

25. Levack, *The witch hunt*, p.231.

26. Crouch, p.141.

27. Nichols, *History and Antiquities*, Vol.II, Part I, p.49n.

28. Eller, p.65.

29. Ibid.

30. *The Pall Mall Gazette* (London), Monday 10 March 1873.

31. Earlier that year, the Swiss government officially pardoned Anna Goeldi, who was beheaded in 1782 and is commonly regarded as the last person to be legally executed as a witch in Europe.

Bibliography

Primary Sources

1. General

Acts of the Privy Council of England, 1617–1623 (London, 1929–32)

Arber, E. (ed.), *A Transcript of the Registers of the Company of Stationers in London; 1554–1640*, Vols. III and IV (London, 1876–7)

A true and exact Relation of the several Informations, Examinations, and Confessions of the late Witches, arraigned and executed in the County of Essex (London, 1645)

Broughton, R., *The Ecclesiasticall Historie of Great Britaine* (London, 1633)

Bruce, J. (ed.), *The Works of Roger Hutchinson* (Cambridge, 1842)

Burton, R., *The Anatomy of Melancholy* (London, 1827)

Burton, W., *Description of Leicestershire* (1622)

Cockburn, J.S. (ed.), *Calendar of Assize Records* (London, 1975–85)

Day, W.G. (ed.), *The Pepys Ballads* (Cambridge, 1987)

English Witchcraft 1560–1736 (London, 2003): Vol. I: Sharpe, J. (ed.), *Early English Demonological Works*; Vol. II: Gibson, M. (ed.), *Early English Trial Pamphlets*; Vol. III: Gaskill, M. (ed.), *The Matthew Hopkins Trials*; Vol. IV: Elmer, P. (ed.), *The Post-Restoration Synthesis and its Oponents*; Vol. V: Elmer, P. (ed.), *The Later English Trial Pamphlets*; Vol. VI: Sharpe, J. (ed.), *The Final Debate*

Gaule, J., *Select Cases of Conscience touching Witches and Witchcrafts* (1646)

Goodman, G.G., *The Court of King James the First*, 2 vols. (London, 1839)

Green, A.E. (ed.), *Witches and Witch Hunters* (Wakefield, 1972)

Green, M.A.E. (ed.), *Calendar of State Papers, Domestic Series, of the Reign of James I. 1611–1625* (London, 1858)

Green, M.A.E. (ed.), *Calendar of State Papers, Domestic Series, Elizabeth and James I. Addenda, 1580–1625* (London, 1872)

Harington, J., *Nugae Antiquae*, 2 vols. (London, 1804)

Harsnett, S., *A Declaration of egregious Popish Impostures, to with-draw the harts of her Maiesties Subiects from their allegeance, and from the truth of Christian Religion professed in England, under the pretence of casting out devils* (London, 1603)

Hinds, A.B. (ed.), *Calendar of State Papers and Manuscripts, Relating to English Affairs. Existing in the Archives and Collections of Venice*, Vols. XV–XVI (London, 1909–10)

Historical Manuscripts Commission, *Calendar of the Manuscripts of the Most Honourable The Marquess of Bath, Preserved at Longleat, Wiltshire*, Vol. V (1980)

Historical Manuscripts Commission, *Calendar of the Manuscripts of the Most Honourable The Marquis of Salisbury, Preserved at Hatfield House, Hertfordshire*, Vols. XI–XXIV (London, 1906–76)

Historical Manuscripts Commission, *Report on the Manuscripts of the Duke of Buccleuch & Queensberry, Preserved at Montagu House, Whitehall*, Vol. III (London, 1926)

Historical Manuscripts Commission, *The Manuscripts of his Grace the Duke of Rutland, KG, Preserved at Belvoir Castle*, 4 vols. (London, 1888–1905)

Jonson, B., *The Workes of Beniamin Jonson* (London, 1616)

Kennett, W., *A sermon upon the Witchcraft of the present Rebellion* (London, 1716)

Latham, R., and Matthews, W. (eds.), *The Diary of Samuel Pepys* (London, 1985)

McClure, N.E., *The Letters of John Chamberlain*, 2 vols. (Philadelphia, 1939)

Macfarlane, A. (ed.), *The Diary of Ralph Josselin, 1616–1683* (Oxford University Press, 1976)

Markham, G., *The English Hus-wife, Contayning, The inward and outward vertues which ought to be in a compleat woman* (1615). Ed. Best, M.R. (Montreal, 1986)

Pollard, A.W., and Redgrave, G.R., *A Short-title Catalogue of Books Printed in England, Scotland, & Ireland 1475–1640* (London, 1926)

Smith, T., *De Republica Anglorum. The maner of Governement or policie of the Realme of England* (London, 1583)

Sowerby, L., *The Ladies' Dispensatory* (1652). Ed. Balaban, C., Erlen, J., and Siderits, R. (New York & London, 2003)

T.W., *The Office of the Clerk of Assize* (London, 1694)

Weldon, Sir A., *The Court and Character of King James* (London, 1650)

2. Witchcraft Tracts

A Discourse proving by Scripture & Reason And the Best Authours, Ancient and Modern, That there Are Witches (London, 1686)

Ady, T., *A Candle in the Dark: or, a Treatise Concerning the Nature of Witches &*

Witchcraft: being Advice to Judges, Sheriffes, Justices of the Peace, and Grand Jury-men, what to do, before they passe Sentence on such as are Arraigned for their Lives, as Witches (London, 1656)

A Most Certain, Strange, and true Discovery of a Witch. Being taken by some of the Parliament Forces, as she was standing on a small planck-board and sayling on it over the River of Newbury (London, 1643)

A Pleasant Treatise of Witches. Their Imps, and Meetings, Persons bewitched . . . with the difference between Good and Bad Angels, and a true Relation of a good Genius (London, 1673)

A Tryal of Witches at Bury St Edmunds (1664)

Bayman, A., 'Large hands, wide eares, and piercing sights': the 'Discoveries' of the Elizabethan and Jacobean Witch Pamphlets, in *Literature & History*, 3rd Series, Vol. VI, Part I (Spring 2007)

Bernard, R., *A Guide to Grand Iury Men: Divided Into Two Bookes* (London, 1627)

Brinley, J., *A Discovery of the Impostures of Witches and Astrologers* (London, 1680)

Boulton, R., *A Compleat History of Magick, Sorcery and Witchcraft*, 2 vols. (London, 1715)

Boulton, R., *The Possibility and Reality of Magick, Sorcery, and Witchcraft, demonstrated. Or, a Vindication of a Compleat History of Magick, Sorcery and Witchcraft, in Answer to Dr Hutchinson's Historical Essay* (London, 1722)

Cooper, T., *The Mystery of Witch-Craft. Discovering The Truth, Nature, Occasions, Growth and Power thereof* (London, 1617)

Cotta, J., *The Triall of Witch-craft, Shewing the True and Right Methode of the Discovery: with A Confusation of erroneous ways* (London, 1616)

Crouch, N., *The Kingdom of Darkness* (London, 1688)

Dalton, M., *The Countrey Justice, Containing the practise of the Justices of the Peace out of their Sessions* (London, 1622)

Damnable Practises Of three Lincoln-shire Witches, Joane Flower, and her two Daughters, Margret and Phillip Flower, against Henry Lord Rosse, with others the Children of the Right Honourable the Earle of Rutland, at Beaver Castle, who for the same were executed at Lincolne the 11 March last (London, 1619) 1619/20

Fairfax, E., 'Daemonologia: A Discourse of Witchcraft, As it was acted in the Family of Mr Edward Fairfax, of Fuystone, in the County of York, in the Year 1621', in *Miscellanies of the Philobiblon Society*, Vol. V (London, 1858–9)

Filmer, R., *An Advertisement to the Jurymen of England, Touching Witches. Together with a Difference between an English and Hebrew Witch* (London, 1653)

Fleming, A., *A Straunge and Terrible Wunder* (London, 1820)

Gifford, G., *A Dialogue concerning Witches and Witchcrafts, in which it is layed open how craftily the Divell deceiveth not onely the Witches but many Other, and so leadeth them awrie into manie great Errours* (2nd edn, 1603; reprinted London, 1842)

Gifford, G., *A Discourse of the subtill Practises of Devilles by Witches and Sorcerers* (London, 1587)

Goodcole, H., *The wonderfull discoverie of Elizabeth Sawyer a Witch, late of Edmonton, her conviction and condemnation and Death* (London, 1621)

Holland, H., *A Treatise against Witchcraft: or, a Dialogue, wherein the greatest doubts concerning that sinne, are briefly answered* (Cambridge, 1590)

Hopkins, M., *The Discovery of Witches: In Answer to severall Queries, lately Delivered to the Judges of Assize for the County of Norfolk* (London, 1647)

Hutchinson, F., *A Historical Essay Concerning Witchcraft* (London, 1718)

Institoris, H., and Sprenger, J., *Malleus Maleficarum* (1486). Ed. and trans. Mackay, C.S., Vol. II (Cambridge, 2006)

James VI, *Daemonologie, in Forme of a Dialogue, Divided into three Bookes* (Edinburgh, 1597)

Mayer, J., *A Patterne for Women: Setting forth the most Christian life, & most comfortable death of Mrs Lucy late wife to the worshipfull Roger Thornton Esquire, of Little Wratting in Suffolke* (London, 1619)

Moore, M., *Wonderfull News from the North: or, a true Relation of the sad and grievous Torments, inflicted upon the Bodies of three Children of Mr George Muschamp, late of the County of Northumberland, by Witchcraft* (1650)

Newes from Scotland. Declaring the damnable life of Doctor Fian a notable Sorcerer, who was burned at Edenbrough in Januarie last (London, 1591)

Parkinson, R. (ed.), *The Life of Adam Martindale, Written by Himself*, Cheetham Society publications, Vol. IV (1845)

Perkins, W., *A Discourse of the Damned Art of Witchcraft; so farre forth as it is revealed in the Scriptures, and manifest by true Experience* (Cambridge, 1608)

Potts, T., *The Wonderfull Discoverie of Witches in the Countie of Lancaster. With the arraignment and Triall of nineteen notorious Witches, at the Assizes and generall Gaole Deliverie, holden at the Castle of Lancaster, upon Munday, the seventeenth of August last, 1612* (London, 1613)

Remy, N., *Demonolatory*. Trans. Ashwin, E.A., and ed. Summers, M. (London, 1930)

Roberts, A., *A Treatise of Witchcraft, Wherein sundry Propositions are laid downe, plainely discovering the wickednesse of that damnable Art* (London, 1616)

Scot, R., *The Discoverie of Witchcraft* (first printed 1584; reprinted New York, 1972)

Scott, R.A., and Pearl, J.L. (trans. and ed.), *Jean Bodin, On the Demon-Mania of Witches* (Toronto, 1995)

Stearne, J., *A Confirmation and Discovery of Witchcraft* (London, 1648)

Swetnam, J., *The Araignment of Lewde, idle, froward, and unconstant women: Or the vanitie of them, choose you whether. With a Commendacion of wise, vertuous and honest Women* (London, 1615)

Taylor, J., *A Juniper Lecture. With the description of all sorts of women, good and bad* (London, 1639)

The Apprehension and confession of three notorious Witches. Arreigned and by Justice condemned and executed at Chelmes-ford, in the Countye of Essex, the 5. day of Julye, last past. 1589 (London, 1589)

The Lawes against Witches, and Coniuration. And Some brief Notes and Observations for the Discovery of Witches (London, 1645)

The most strange and admirable Discoverie of the three Witches at Warboys, arraigned, convicted and executed at the last Assizes at Huntingdon, for the bewitching of five daughters of Robert Throckmorton Esquire, and divers other persons (London, 1593)

The Witches of Northamptonshire. Agnes Browne. Joane Vaughan. Arthur Bill. Hellen Jenkenson. Mary Barber. Witches. Who Were All Executed at Northampton the 22. of July last. 1612 (London, 1612)

The Wonderful Discoverie of the Witchcrafts of Margaret and Phillip[pa] Flower, daughters of Joan Flower, neere Bever Castle: executed at Lincolne, March 11.1618. Who were specially arraigned & condemned before Sir Henry Hobart, and Sir Edward Bromley, Judges of Assize, for confessing themselves actors in the destruction of Henry, Lord Rosse, with their damnable practises against others the Children of the Right Honourable Francis Earle of Rutland. Together with the severall Examinations and Confessions of Anne Baker, Joan Willimot, and Ellen Greene, witches in Leicestershire (London, 1619/20)

Two Sermons, lately preached at Langar in the Valley of Belvoir. By C. Odingsells (London, 1620)

Webster, J., *The Displaying of Supposed Witchcraft* (London, 1677)

Weyer, J., *De praestigiis daemonum Witches, Devils, and Doctors in the Renaissance.* Ed. and trans. Mora, G., Kohl, B., and Shea, J. (New York, 1991)

Witchcrafts, Strange and Wonderfull: Discovering the Damnable Practices of Seven Witches Against the Lives of Certaine Noble Personages ... Witch-Craft (London, 1621 and 1635)

Witches Apprehended, Examined and Executed, for notable Villanies by them

*committed both by Land and Water. With a strange and most true triall to know
whether a woman be a Witch or not* (London, 1613)

[W.W.], *A true and just Recorde, of the Information, Examination and Confession
of all the Witches, taken at S. Oses in the countie of Essex* (London, 1582)

Secondary Sources

Akrigg, G.P.V., *Jacobean Pageant or The Court of King James I* (London, 1962)

Almond, P.C., *The Witches of Warboys: An Extraordinary Story of Sorcery, Sadism
and Satanic Possession* (London, 2008)

Anderson, A., and Gordon, R., 'Witchcraft and the Status of Women – the
Case of England', in *British Journal of Sociology*, Vol. 29, No. 2 (June 1978),
pp.171–84

Anderson, B., and Zinsser, J., *A History of their Own: Women in Europe*, 2 vols.
(New York, 1988)

Andrews, W. (ed.), *Bygone Lincolnshire* (Hull, 1891)

Anglo, S. (ed.), *The Damned Art: Essays in the Literature of Witchcraft*
(London, 1977)

Ankarloo, B., Clark, S., and Monter, W., *Witchcraft and Magic in Europe: The
Period of the Witch Trials* (London, 2002)

*A Short-Title Catalogue of Books Printed in England, Scotland & Ireland . . .
1475–1640* 3 vols. (London, 1976–91)

Baroja, J.C., *The World of the Witches*, trans. Glendinning, N. (London, 1968)

Barry, J. (et. al.), *Witchcraft in early modern Europe: Studies in culture and belief*
(Cambridge, 1996)

Barstow, A.L., *Witchcraze: A New History of the European Witch Hunts* (London,
1994)

Barstow, A.L., 'Women, Sexuality, and Oppression: The European Witchcraft
Persecutions', in *World History Bulletin*, Vol. V, No. 2 (Spring/Summer
1988), pp.14–17

Bate, J., and Thornton, D., *Shakespeare: Staging the World* (London, 2012)

Bellaney, A., 'The Murder of John Lambe: Crowd Violence, Court Scandal
and Popular Politics in Early Seventeenth-Century England', *Past & Present*,
No. 200 (August 2008), pp.37–76

Bennett, W., *The Pendle Witches* (Lancashire, 1993)

Bever, E., 'Old Age and Witchcraft in Early Modern Europe', in Stearns,
P.N., *Old Age in Preindustrial Society* (London and New York, 1982), pp.150–90

Bostridge, I., *Witchcraft and its transformations, c. 1650–750* (Oxford, 1997)

Boyer, P., and Nissenbaum, S., *Salem Possessed: the social origins of witchcraft* (Cambridge, 1974)

Briggs, R., *Witches & Neighbours: The Social and Cultural Context of European Witchcraft* (London, 1996)

Burstein, S.R., 'Aspects of psychopathology of old age revealed in the witchcraft cases of the sixteenth and seventeenth centuries', *British Medical Bulletin*, Vol. 6 (Oxford, 1949)

Chambers, R. (ed.), *The Book of Days. A Miscellany of Popular Antiquities*, Vol. I (London & Edinburgh, 1869)

Charles, L., and Duffin, C. (eds.), *Women and Work in Pre-Industrial England* (London, 1985)

Chaworth-Musters, M.A., *A Cavalier Stronghold: A Romance of the Vale of Belvoir* (Kent, 1890)

Clark, A., *The Working Life of Women in the Seventeenth Century* (Abingdon, 2006)

Clark, S. (ed.), *Languages of Witchcraft: Narrative, Ideology and Meaning in Early Modern Culture* (London, 2001)

Clark, S., *The Elizabethan Pamphleteers: Popular Moralistic Pamphlets 1580–1640* (London, 1983)

Clark, S., *Thinking with Demons: The Idea of Witchcraft in Early Modern Europe* (Oxford, 1997)

Cockayne, G.E., *The Complete Peerage* (London, 1932)

Cockburn, J.S., *A History of the English Assizes, 1558–1714* (Cambridge, 1972)

Cockburn, J.S., *Crime in England 1500–1800* (London, 1977)

Cockburn, J.S., 'Early modern assize records as historical evidence', *Journal of the Society of Archivists*, Vol. V (1975), pp. 215–31

Cockburn, J.S., *Introduction to Calendar of Assize Records. Home Circuit Indictments. Elizabeth I and James I* (London, 1985)

Corbin, P., and Sedge, D. (eds.), *Three Jacobean Witchcraft Plays: Sophonisba; The Witch; The Witch of Edmonton* (Manchester, 1986)

Dare, M.P., *The Church of St Mary the Virgin Bottesford, Leics. and its Monuments* (Gloucester, 1972)

De Windt, A.R., 'Witchcraft and conflicting visions of the ideal village community', *Journal of British Studies*, Vol. XXXIV, No. 4 (Chicago, October 1995), pp.427–63

Douglas, M., *Witchcraft confessions and accusations* (London, 1970)

Durston, G., *Witchcraft and Witch Trials: A History of English Witchcraft and its Legal Perspectives, 1542 to 1736* (Chichester, 2000)

Ehrenreich, B., and English, D., *Witches, Midwives and Nurses: a history of women healers* (London, 1974)

Elbourne, J., *Bewitching the Mind: English witchcraft pamphlets, 1561–1736* (Colo Vale, New South Wales, 2003)

Elbourne, J., *The True Story of the Witches of Belvoir Castle* (Colo Vale, New South Wales, 2008)

Eller, I., *The History of Belvoir Castle* (London, 1841)

Elliott, H., and Stocker, D., *Lincoln Castle* (Lincoln, 1984)

Ewen, C.L., *Robert Ratcliffe, 5th Earl of Sussex: The Witchcraft Allegations in his Family* (London, 1938)

Ewen, C.L., *Witchcraft and Demonianism: A Concise Account derived from Sworn Depositions and Confessions obtained in the Courts of England and Wales* (London, 1993)

Ewen, C.L., *Witchcraft in the Star Chamber* (1938)

Ewen, C.L., *Witch Hunting and Witch Trials. The Indictments for Witchcraft from the records of 1373 Assizes held for the Home Circuit, AD 1559–1736* (1929)

Farrington, K., *Supernatural* (London, 1997)

Fraser, A., *The Weaker Vessel: Women's lot in seventeenth-century England* (London, 1999)

Gardiner, T., *Broomstick over Essex and East Anglia: an introduction to witchcraft in the eastern counties during the seventeenth century* (Hornchurch, 1981)

Gaskill, M., *Crime and Mentalities in Early Modern England* (Cambridge, 2000)

Gaskill, M., 'The devil in the shape of a man: witchcraft, conflict and belief in Jacobean England', *Historical Research*, Vol. 71 (1998), pp.142–71

Gaskill, M., *Witchfinders: A Seventeenth-Century English Tragedy* (London, 2006)

Geis, G., and Bunn, I., *A trial of witches: a seventeenth-century witchcraft prosecution* (London, 1997)

Gibson, M., *Early Modern Witches: Witchcraft Cases in Contemporary Writing* (London, 2000)

Gibson, M., *Reading Witchcraft: Stories of early English witches* (London and New York, 1999)

Gibson, M. (ed.), *Witchcraft and Society in England and America, 1550–1750* (New York, 2003)

Ginzburg, C., 'The Witches' Sabbat: Popular Cult or Inquisitorial Stereotype?', in Kaplan, S.L. (ed.), *Understanding Popular Culture: Europe from the Middle Ages to the Nineteenth Century* (Berlin, 1984)

Guazzo, Francesco-Maria, *Compendium Maleficarum* (1626), trans. Ashwin, E.A. (London, 1988)

Guiley, R.E., *The Encyclopedia of Witches, Witchcraft and Wicca* (New York & London, 2008)

Harris, A., *Night's Black Angels: Witchcraft and Magic in seventeenth-century English drama* (Manchester, 1980)

Harris, R. (et al.), *The Art of Survival: gender and history in Europe, 1450–2000* (Oxford, 2006)

Hart, R., *Witchcraft* (London, 1971)

Henderson, K.U., and McManus, B.F., *Half Humankind: Contexts and Texts of the Controversy about Women in England, 1540–1640* (Chicago, 1985)

Henningsen, G., 'The Greatest Witch-Trial of all: Navarre, 1609–14', *History Today*, 30 (November 1980), pp.36–9

Hester, M., *Lewd Women and Wicked Witches: A study in the dynamics of male domination* (London & New York, 1992)

Hill, J.W.F., *Tudor and Stuart Lincoln* (Cambridge, 1956)

Hoak, D., 'Witch hunting and Women in the Art of the Renaissance', *History Today* (February 1981), pp.22–6

Hodgett, G.A.J., *Tudor Lincolnshire*, Vol. VI of Thirsk, J. (ed.), *History of Lincolnshire* (Lincoln, 1975)

Hole, C., *Witchcraft in England* (London, 1947)

Holmes, C., 'Popular culture? Witches, magistrates and divines in early modern England', in Kaplan, S.L. (ed.), *Understanding Popular Culture: Europe from the Middle Ages to the Nineteenth Century* (Berlin, 1984), pp.85–111

Holmes, C., *Seventeenth Century Lincolnshire* (Lincoln, 1980)

Holmes, C., 'Women, witnesses and witches', *Past and Present*, Vol. 140 (Oxford, 1993), pp.45–78

Honeybone, M., *The Book of Bottesford: Continuity and Change in a Leicestershire Village* (Buckingham, 1989)

Honeybone, M., *The Vale of Belvoir* (2001)

Honeybone, M., *Wicked Practise & Sorcerye: The Belvoir Witchcraft Case of 1619* (Buckingham, 2008)

Hope Robbins, R., *The Encyclopaedia of Witchcraft and Demonology* (New York, 1959)

Hoskins, W.G., *Essays in Leicestershire History* (Liverpool, 1950)

Hults, L.C., *The witch as muse: art, gender and power in early modern Europe* (Pennsylvania, 2005)

Hutton, R., *The Rise and Fall of Merry England: The Ritual Year 1400–1700* (Oxford, 1994)

Jackson, L., 'Witches, wives and mothers: witchcraft persecution and women's confessions in seventeenth-century England', *Women's History Review*, Vol. IV, No.1 (1995), pp.63–84

Kelly, H.A., 'English kings and the fear of sorcery', *Medieval Studies*, 39 (1977)

Kenyon, J.P., *Stuart England* (London, 1985)

Kermode, J., and Walker, G. (eds.), *Women, crime and the courts in early modern England* (London, 1994)

Kieckhefer, R., *Magic in the Middle Ages* (Cambridge, 2000)

Kittredge, G.L., 'English Witchcraft and James I', in *Studies in the History of Religions Presented to C. H. Toy* (New York, 1912)

Kittredge, G.L., *Witchcraft in Old and New England* (New York, 1929)

Kors, A.C., and Peters, E., *Witchcraft in Europe, 1100–1700: A Documentary History* (Philadelphia, 1972)

Larner, C., *Enemies of God: The Witch Hunt in Scotland* (London, 1981)

Larner, C., 'Witch Beliefs & Witch hunting in England and Scotland', *History Today* (February 1981)

Larner, C., *Witchcraft and Religion: The Politics of Popular Belief* (Oxford, 1984)

Leuschner, K. J., 'Creating the "known true story": sixteenth and seventeenth century murder and witchcraft pamphlets and plays' (University of California thesis, 1992)

Levack, B.P., *The Witchcraft Sourcebook* (New York & London, 2007)

Levack, B.P., *The witch hunt in early modern Europe* (London and New York, 1987)

Levack, B.P. (ed.), *Witchcraft in England* (London & New York, 1992)

Levack, B.P. (ed.), *Witch Hunting in Early Modern Europe: General Studies*, Vol. 3 (New York and London, 1992)

Lewis, H., *The Witch and the Priest* (London, 1956)

Lockyer, R., *Buckingham* (Harlow, 1981)

Lumby, J., *The Lancashire Witch-craze: Jennet Preston and the Lancashire Witches, 1612* (Preston, 1995)

MacCurdy, E. (ed.), *The Notebooks of Leonardo da Vinci* (London, 1938)

MacDonald, M., *Mystical Bedlam. Madness, Anxiety and Healing in Seventeenth Century England* (Cambridge, 1981)

McElwee, W., *The Wisest Fool in Christendom: The Reign of James I and VI* (London, 1958)

Macfarlane, A., *Marriage and Love in England 1300–1840* (Oxford, 1986)

Macfarlane, A., *Witchcraft in Tudor and Stuart England: A regional and comparative study* (London, 1970)

Mair, L.P., *Witchcraft* (London, 1969)

Maple, E., *The Dark World of Witches* (London, 1962)

Maxwell-Stuart, P.G., *Witchcraft: a history* (Stroud, 2000)

Maxwell-Stuart, P.G., *Witch hunters* (Stroud, 2003)

Mendelson, S.H., *The Mental World of Stuart Women* (Brighton, 1987)

Miller, W. E., 'Samuel Fleming, Elizabethan Clergyman', *The Library Chronicle*, Vol. XXV, No. 2 (Spring 1959)

Monter, E.W., *European Witchcraft* (New York, 1969)

Monter, E.W., 'French and Italian Witchcraft', *History Today*, 30 (November 1980), pp.31–5

Monter, E.W., *Ritual, Myth and Magic in Early Modern Europe* (Athens, Ohio, 1983)

Mosley, C. (ed.), *Burke's Peerage Baronetage & Knightage*, 107th edition, Vol. III (Stokesley, North Yorkshire, 2003)

Neill, W.N., 'The Professional Pricker and His Test for Witchcraft', *Scottish Historical Review*, Vol. XIX (Edinburgh, 1922), pp.205–13

Newall, V., *The Encyclopaedia of Witchcraft and Magic* (New York, 1974)

Newton, J., and Bath, J., *Witchcraft and the Act of 1604* (Leiden, 2008)

Nichols, J., *The History and Antiquities of the County of Leicester*, 4 vols. (London, 1795–1812); (republished Wakefield, 1971)

Nichols, J., *The Progresses, Processions, and Magnificent Festivities of King James the First*, 4 vols. (London, 1828)

Nicoll, A. (ed.), *Shakespeare in His Own Age*, Shakespeare Survey, 17 (Cambridge, 1964)

Normand, L., and Roberts, G. (eds.), *Witchcraft in Early Modern Scotland: James VI's Demonologie and the North Berwick Witches* (Exeter, 2000)

Oldridge, D. (ed.), *The Witchcraft Reader – Second Edition* (London and New York, 2008)

Page, W. (ed.), *The Victoria History of Leicester*, 5 vols. (London / Oxford, 1907–64)

Page, W. (ed.), *The Victoria History of Lincoln*, 2 vols. (London, 1906)

Palmer, R., *A Ballad History of England from 1588 to the Present Day* (London, 1979)

Parker, G., 'The European Witchcraze Revisited', *History Today*, 30 (November 1980), pp.23–4

Peel, E., and Southern, P., *The Trials of the Lancashire Witches: a study of seventeenth century witchcraft* (Newton Abbot, 1969)

Peters, S., *The Witchfinder and the Devil's Darlings* (Ipswich, 2003)

Notestein, W., *History of Witchcraft in England 1558–1718* (New York, 1968)

Poole, R. (ed.), *The Lancashire Witches: Histories and Stories* (Manchester and New York, 2002)

Prior, M. (ed.), *Women in English Society 1500–1800* (London and New York, 1985)

Purkiss, D., 'The Witch in History', *Aerial*, Vol. XXIX, No. III (Calgary, 1998)

Purkiss, D., 'Women's stories of witchcraft in early modern England: the house, the body, the child', *Gender and History*, Vol. VII, No. III (November 1995), pp.408–17

Reay, B. (ed.), *Popular Culture in Seventeenth-Century England* (London and Sydney, 1985)

Robbins, R.H., *Encyclopedia of Witchcraft and Demonology* (1959)

Roberts, R.S., 'The Personnel and Practice of Medicine in Tudor and Stuart England', *Medical History*, Vol. VI (1962) and Vol. VIII (1964)

Roper, L., *Oedipus and the Devil: Witchcraft, sexuality and religion in early modern Europe* (London and New York, 1994)

Roper, L., 'Witchcraft and the Western Imagination', *Transactions of the Royal Historical Society*, Vol. XVI (2006), pp.117–42

Rosen, B. (ed.), *Witchcraft in England, 1558–1618* (Massachusetts, 1991)

Rowlands, A., 'Telling Witchcraft Stories: New Perspectives on Witchcraft and Witches in the Early Modern Period', in *Gender & History*, Vol. X (1998), pp.294–302

Russell, J.B., *A History of Witchcraft: Sorcerers, Heretics and Pagans* (London, 1980)

Sanders, A., *A Deed without a Name: the Witch in Society and History* (Berg, Oxford and Washington, 1995)

Scarre, G., and Callow, J., *Witchcraft and Magic in Sixteenth- and Seventeenth-Century Europe* (Basingstoke, 2001)

Scott, W., *Letters on Demonology and Witchcraft* (Ware, 2001)

Sharpe, J.A., *Crime in Early Modern England 1550–1750* (London and New York, 1999)

Sharpe, J.A., *Early Modern England: A Social History 1550–1760* (London, 1997)

Sharpe, J.A., *Instruments of Darkness: Witchcraft in England 1550–1750* (London, 1996)

Sharpe, J.A., *The Bewitching of Anne Gunter: a horrible and true story of football, witchcraft, murder and the King of England* (London, 1999)

Sharpe, J.A., 'Witchcraft and women in seventeenth-century England: some northern evidence', *Continuity and Change*, Vol. VI (1991), pp.179–99

Sharpe, J.A., *Witchcraft in Early Modern England* (Edinburgh, 2001)

Sharpe, J.A., *Witchcraft in Seventeenth-Century Yorkshire: Accusations and Counter Measures* (York, 1992)

Shipman, E.A., *The Church of St Mary the Virgin, Bottesford* (1982)

Smith, A.G. (ed.), *The Reign of James VI and I* (London, 1973)

Somerset, A., *Unnatural Murder: Poison at the Court of James I* (London, 1997)

Stewart, A., *The Cradle King: A Life of James VI & I* (London, 2003)

Stone, L., *The Crisis of the Aristocracy 1558–1641* (Oxford, 1965)

Stone, L., *The Family, Sex and Marriage in England 1500–1800* (London, 1977)

Stubbs, C.E., *Abraham Fleming: writer, cleric and preacher in Elizabethan and Jacobean London* (unpublished PhD thesis, Royal Holloway, University of London, April 2011)

Summers, M., *The Discovery of Witches: a study of Master Matthew Hopkins, commonly call'd Witch finder generall* (London, 1928)

Summers, M., *The Geography of Witchcraft* (London, 1978)

Summers, M., *The History of Witchcraft and Demonology* (London, 1969)

Swain, J.T., 'The Lancashire witch trials of 1612 and 1634 and the economics of witchcraft', *Northern History*, 30 (1994)

Swales, J.K. and McLachlan, H.V., 'Witchcraft and the Status of Women: A Comment', *British Journal of Sociology*, Vol. 30, No. 3 (September 1979), pp.349–58

Thomas, K., *Religion and the Decline of Magic* (London, 1991)

Thompson, R., *Women in Stuart England and America* (London, 1974)

Thurston, R., *The Witch Hunts: A history of the witch persecutions in Europe and North America* (Harlow, 2007)

Tillyard, E.M., *The Elizabethan World Picture* (London, 1998)

Trevor-Roper, H.R., *The European Witch-craze of the Sixteenth and Seventeenth Centuries* (Harmondsworth, 1969)

Tyson, D., *The Demonology of King James* (Minnesota, 2011)

Unsworth, C.R., 'Witchcraft beliefs and criminal procedure in early modern England', in Watkins, T.G. (ed.), *Legal Records and Historical Reality: Proceedings of the Eighth British Legal History Conference, Cardiff, 1987* (London, 1989)

Valletta, F., *Witchcraft, Magic and Superstition in England, 1640–70* (Aldershot, c.2000)

Venn, J., and Venn, J.A., *Alumni Cantabrigiensis*, Vols.1–3 (Cambridge University Press, 1922–4)

Wade, S., *Hanged at Lincoln* (Stroud, 2009)

Walker, B., *The Crone: Woman of Age, Wisdom, and Power* (New York, 1985)

Walker, G., 'Witchcraft and history', in *Women's History*, Vol. VII (1998)

Watkins, S.C., 'Spinsters', *Journal of Family History*, Vol. IX (London, 1984)

Wiesner, M.E., *Women and gender in early modern Europe* (Cambridge, 2008)

Williamson, H.R., *George Villiers, First Duke of Buckingham: Study for a Biography* (London, 1940)

Willis, D., *Malevolent Nurture: Witch hunting and Maternal Power in Early Modern England* (Ithaca, New York, and London, 1995)

Wills, G., *Witches and Jesuits: Shakespeare's Macbeth* (Oxford, 1995)

Wright, P. and J., *Witches in and around Suffolk* (Stowmarket, 2010)

Wright, T., *Narratives of Sorcery and Magic, From the Most Authentic Sources*, 2 vols. (London, 1851)

Wrightson, K., *English Society 1580–1680* (London, 1982)

Acknowledgements

It is my parents who, as ever, deserve the greatest thanks. Their continuing support has given me the time and space I needed to write this book, and I cannot thank them enough. I am also deeply grateful for the love and encouragement of the rest of my family, notably my daughter Eleanor and my sister Jayne, brother-in-law Rick, and nieces Olivia and Neve.

I have been fortunate to have been supported once more by the excellent team at Jonathan Cape, in particular my editor, Alex Bowler, whose inspired suggestions transformed the structure of the book, and Clare Bullock for her attention to detail. Geraldine Beare has once again produced an excellent index. I would also like to express my heartfelt thanks to my publicist, Hannah Ross, who has supported me so brilliantly for this and all of my previous books, and whom I shall miss very much when she moves on to her new role. My agent, Julian Alexander, has as ever been there to encourage, inspire and cajole in equal measure and at exactly the right moments. I am grateful, too, to his assistant, Ben Clark, and to Emma Gillett and Peta Nightingale for their help with publicity.

I am greatly indebted to Michael and Diana Honeybone for sharing their extensive knowledge and research on the Belvoir witches with me, and for very kindly giving me a tour of the places connected with them in Bottesford. I would also like to express my sincere thanks to Jennie Fowler, a talented young historian, for giving up so much of her time to help with the research. Her tenacity in tracking down articles in obscure journals is second to none. The fact that I met Jennie in the first place is thanks to Maureen and Frank Wright, who invited me to take part in their programme of history talks at Westbourne in West Sussex.

Alison Weir has, as ever, proved an inspiration, not least by bringing to my attention Hilda Lewis's excellent novel, *The Witch and the Priest*. Thanks are also due to Nicola Tallis, who generously shared her research notes with me, and to the Reverend Jeffrey Bell of All Saints Church in Tilford, Surrey and Kathleen Carroll for providing information on the Pendle Witches. I am grateful to Clare Stubbs, whose thesis on Abraham Fleming provided some invaluable material, as well as to Fiona Torrens-Spence for her insights into Katherine Manners. Julian Humphrys, David Souden, Kate Pugh and Len Clark all introduced me to some excellent books on the subject. I am also grateful to Anne Lawson for her help with Belvoir Castle, and for inviting me to give a talk in nearby Oakham to raise funds for Water Aid.

My research has taken me to a range of fascinating historic sites, archives and libraries. I am particularly indebted to the staff of the British Library, Bishop Grosseteste University Library in Lincoln, and Westminster Abbey. I am also very grateful to Helen Bates and Susan Payne for sharing their invaluable research on Lincoln Castle, and to Carol Bennett of Lincoln Cathedral for her help and enthusiasm. I would like to thank the staff of Historic Royal Palaces for the support that they have once more given me, and for enabling me to work in such awe-inspiring places. I also spent a very enjoyable two days with Mark Fielder and the Quickfire Media crew filming a documentary about witchcraft at Lincoln Castle and St Mary's Church in Bottesford.

It is no small irony, given the subject matter of this book, that among the many people who have cheered me along the way, the most vocal has been the Reverend Stephen Kuhrt, vicar of Christ Church, New Malden. As well as displaying a keen interest in the progress of my research, he also provided some invaluable advice on the references to witchcraft found in the Bible. Honor Gay has, as ever, proved unfailingly enthusiastic and insightful, and I have been buoyed up many times by her faith in me as a writer. A host of other friends have provided encouragement and practical support, notably Susannah Alexander, Marijke Andries, Tom Ashworth, Marilyn Canale-Jarman, Maura and Howard Davies, Lucinda and Stuart Eggleton, Rosie Fifield, Nicola Gough, Sophie Grant, Ros Green, Louise Groves, Sarah Holden, Tina Ingram, Judi and Alun Jones, Anna Larkin, Harriet Morgan, Carol and Rex Scoones, Ian Smith, Gaby Stubbs and Jo Tresidder.

Thank you.

Index